This is the first book to focus on the role of education in relation to music and gender. Invoking a concept of musical patriarchy and a theory of the social construction of musical meaning, Lucy Green shows how women's musical practices and gendered musical meanings have been reproduced, hand in hand, through history.

Covering a wide range of music, including classical, jazz and popular styles, Dr Green uses ethnographic methods to convey the everyday interactions and experiences of girls, boys, and their teachers. She views the contemporary school music classroom as a microcosm of the wider society, and reveals the participation of music education in the continued production and reproduction of gendered musical practices and meanings.

MUSIC, GENDER, EDUCATION

MUSIC, GENDER,
EDUCATION

LUCY GREEN

University of London, Institute of Education

CAMBRIDGE
UNIVERSITY PRESS

Published by the Press Syndicate of the University of Cambridge
The Pitt Building, Trumpington Street, Cambridge CB2 1RP
40 West 20th Street, New York, NY 10011-4211, USA
10 Stamford Road, Oakleigh, Melbourne 3166, Australia

First published 1997

Printed in the United Kingdom at the University Press, Cambridge

A catalogue record for this book is available from the British Library

Library of Congress cataloguing in publication data

Green, Lucy.
Music, gender. education / Lucy Green.
p. cm.
Includes bibliographical references and index.
ISBN 0 521 55517 5 (hardback). – ISBN 0 521 55522 1 (pbk.)
1. Feminism and music.   2. Women musicians.   3. Music and society.
4. Music – Instruction and study.   I. Title.
ML82.G74   1997
780'.82–dc20   96-24711 CIP

ISBN 0 521 55517 5 hardback
ISBN 0 521 55522 1 paperback

SE

For my children,
Sophie and Marcus

Contents

Acknowledgements

I would like to thank Charles Ford for reading and making detailed comments on a very early draft, and then repeating the exercise on extensive samples of a later draft. His criticisms, and our innumerable discussions, have added dimensions that would undoubtedly otherwise be missing. Keith Swanwick responded to a complete draft, as well as having kept me on my toes by raising questions in various exchanges of memos: all of this has been both challenging and supportive. Roberta Lamb encouraged me at an early stage, kept me posted with relevant news from Canada and then commented in detail on a complete draft, lending her scholarship, commitment and insight throughout. I would also like to thank the two anonymous readers for the Press, whose careful, perceptive criticisms, as well as encouragement, were stimulating.

I am deeply grateful to the many friends, colleagues and students who contributed ideas, raised questions or expressed enthusiasm during conference papers, lectures or seminars relating to this work. A number of people have also been generous in offering academic and editorial advice or assistance, responding to articles drawn from the work, or sending me copies of their own writings as well as information and other materials. I am especially grateful to my old friends Jenny Hand and Stephanie Cant for sharing their ideas at the very beginning, and to my colleagues Keith Swanwick, Charles Plummeridge and John Winter, without whose sustained support this book would certainly never have been finished.

A number of teachers and pupils took part in the study, giving generously of their time, and in many cases showing an enthusiasm and interest which far exceeded my expectations. I warmly appreciated this vital input, and would particularly like to acknowledge the part played by those who made me welcome in their schools.

It is customary to leave until last any mention of those people who have given support at home or in a personal capacity, without whose love and commitment few books would surely ever be written. In this particular case I come full circle: Charlie Ford, first and last. Without him this book would not have been possible.

CHAPTER I

Introduction

Rose-cheekt Lawra, come,
Sing thou smoothly with thy beawties
Silent musick, either other
        Sweetely gracing.

Lovely formes do flowe
From concent devinely framed;
Heav'n is musick, and thy beawties
        Birth is heavenly.

These dull notes we sing
Discords needs for helps to grace them;
Only beawty purely loving
        Knowes no discord:

But still mooves delight,
Like cleare springs renu'd by flowing,
Ever perfect, ever in them-
        selves eternall.

Thomas Campion, *Observations in the Art of English
Poesie* (1602)

Campion draws a likeness between music and woman, describing each
with highest regard as a mysterious, unattainable perfection. The beauty
of Lawra, and the beauty of the music which she smoothly sings, 'sweet-
ely gracing' each other, are intertwined. The 'lovely formes' are the
forms of Lawra's bodily beauty as they 'flowe' from her 'concent' to thus
display herself; and they are also the ephemeral forms of the music as it
flows in time. 'Heav'n is musick', and the birth, the revealing, of Lawra's
beauty is heavenly. A cloud appears: the dull notes. These are sung by
men: 'we', who are not heavenly music and are not heavenly woman.
Like the men who sing them, these mortal notes rely on dissonance for

I

their fleeting survival. Only purely loving beauty, the music sung by Lawra, untouched by man's condemnation to history, knows no discord. Here the meaning of the words forces the third verse on to the beginning of the last, replicating movement, the movement of delight which it is expressing. Beauty is now the stream of water that for ever flows from the clear springs; the stream of life that flows from immortal woman's womb; the stream of time in which music articulates its forms. Music and woman are linked: perfect, eternal, they flow; never still, they move away in their mysteriousness.

But there is a sinister edge to this seductive vision. In forging such a link between music and woman, the poem at the same time consigns them to a dangerous and marginalised existence on the outskirts of Man's world-sense. Both perfections carry with them the shadow of their opposite, a *volte face* with which woman and music are definitively marked: of licentiousness, error, decadence and temptation. Lawra comes tantalisingly close to Salome as she consents to reveal her beauty in the performance of song, just as music has since Plato inspired a history of dispute about its ability, on one hand, to raise mind and spirit above the earthly level and, on the other, to incite promiscuity and decadence. Not only does the poem trace this vicious circle of conspiring opposites, but it also implies a political relationship which is the pivotal centre of the circle. Just as history has ceaselessly repressed the musical achievements of women, so the music which Lawra sings is 'silent'. The silence of Lawra's music represents not a mere silence, but the active silencing by history, the regulation, the circumscription, the prohibition of women's musical practices.

Poetry does not express any eternal or universal human condition: on the contrary, the significance of art changes over history and differs between cultures. But there is a kernel in Campion's poem, a representation which may change over history, which may differ between cultures, but whose changes and differences are so slow, so minute, as to be almost imperceptible. The poem's portrayal of the intertwining of music and femininity, its suggestion of their mutual link with pure beauty and dangerous desire, and the contradictory adulation and repression of women's musical practices which it implies are images that straddle the centuries, containing as much relevance for the present as for Campion's time; and such images have held sway in many other cultures too. The power and extent of this symbolic liaison between music and femininity cannot result only from contingencies pertaining to this or that social or historical context. It must be possible to find something fundamental, somewhere, not in music or in femininity, but in the interaction between them as they are constructed through practice and through symbolic experience, which can shed light on that kernel depicted in their relationship. The driving motive behind this book, if it can be pinpointed at all, was the exploration of that possibility. My aims are to trace the two-faced representation of the link between music and woman as it has been perpetuated through history; to seek its embeddedness in musical meaning and its implications for women's musical practice; to contextualise it within a broader conceptual framework encompassing gendered musical meaning, practice and experience; and, most centrally, to reveal the participation of music education in the continued production and reproduction of gendered musical meanings and practices, through the everyday musical interactions and experiences of girls and boys in contemporary schools.

MUSICAL MEANING: A THEORETICAL UNDERPINNING

Ideology and discourse with relation to music

In an earlier book (1988) I made use of a concept of ideology, as a collective mental force which both springs from and perpetuates pre-existing relationships of economic and cultural dominance or subservience between social classes. One of the most salient characteristics of ideology is its tendency to maintain and reproduce existing relationships, by appealing to notions of 'common sense' as proof of its own legitimacy. Despite this, ideology is not a monolithic system of self-legitimation wielded by a ruling class which has the economic supremacy to define reality for everyone else; nor is ideology some sort of 'falsity', the exposition of which is supposed to reveal 'truth'. Ideology is, rather, a fragmented, contested field, under whose sway we all attempt, in one way or another, to make sense of our worlds, our relationships with each other, and ourselves. With reference to music, ideology operates to legitimate the superior value placed on concepts such as universality, autonomy, individuality or originality: properties which are held to be natural and spontaneous sources of eternal value that are unavoidably encapsulated by particular musical styles or pieces and that are absent from others.

In this book I wish to employ the related concept of discourse. This concept can be used in a flexible way, retaining the notion that ideas are systematised at a societal level, whilst cutting across notions of class. Thus the economic and cultural supremacy of a dominant social class splinters into a recognition of various struggles involving not just class, but ethnicity, gender and other social groupings.[1] There is then, within the over-arching ideological field, a multiplicity of discourses that come into play in various strategic relationships. At the same time as acknowledging this multiplicity, the concept of discourse accords a central position to individual agency. This includes a recognition that the formation of personal identity occurs both as a contribution to the collective identity of social groupings and as a result of the individual's subject-position with reference to the various discourses available to him or her. Discourse is a helpful concept in attempting to unveil the notion that what we take to be the 'truth' is not an eternal and unchangeable fact, but a construction brought about in the dialectical interplay between the historical processes of a society's reproduction and the individual's formation of identity. But at the same time as the flexibility of the concept enables us to recognise plurality and individuality, it would be idealistic to suppose that we can forget altogether about questions of social power. Clearly certain social groupings, whether they are classes, races, gender-groupings, nation-states or multi-national companies, do wield a great deal of power over other social groupings. It is necessary to recognise that a particular discourse may serve the interests of powerful groups, or may be dominant within a broad social context.[2]

The capacity of discourse to produce 'truths' is well illustrated in an example by Edward Said:

> If one reads a book claiming that lions are fierce and then encounters a fierce lion . . . the chances are that one will be encouraged to read more books by that same author, and believe them. But if, in addition, the lion book instructs one how to deal with a fierce lion, and the instructions work perfectly, then not only will the author be greatly believed, he will also be impelled to try his hand at other kinds of written performance. There is a rather complex dialectic of reinforcement by which the experiences of readers in reality are determined by what they have read, and this in turn influences writers to take up subjects defined in advance by readers' experiences. A book on how to handle a fierce lion might then cause a series of books to be produced on such subjects as the fierceness of lions, the origins of fierceness, and so forth. Similarly as the focus of

---

[1] I will use the word 'grouping' as both a verb and a noun. 'Grouping' (or to group) is something that we do collectively; 'a grouping' (or a group) is something to which we belong. Grouping cuts across class, ethnicity, gender, religion, sub-culture, and can be formed by various amalgams of these at different intersections. Nonetheless, these five groupings, amongst others, are identifiable as such and tend to be prominent in contemporary society.

[2] For seminal examples and discussions of discourse theory see Foucault (1981), Said (1978). The sociology of knowledge has also influenced my understanding of discourse. See e.g. Berger and Luckmann (1967); and Hekman (1986) for a helpful secondary text.

the text centres more narrowly on the subject – no longer lions but their fierceness – we might expect that the ways by which it is recommended that a lion's fierceness be handled will actually *increase* its fierceness, force it to be fierce since that is what it is, and that is what in essence we know or can *only* know about it . . .

Most important, such texts can *create* not only knowledge but also the very reality they appear to describe. In time such knowledge and reality produce a tradition, or what Michel Foucault calls a discourse, whose material presence or weight, not the originality of a given author, is really responsible for the texts produced out of it. (Said 1978, pp. 93f)

This excerpt refers specifically to books, but clearly, discourse can arise through other literally textual media such as newspapers or magazines; it can encompass other channels such as spoken commentaries on broadcasting networks or within educational institutions; and at a more informal level, it is set in motion through the interactions of people in particular social contexts. There are multiple discourses on music, constructed and perpetuated through diverse channels, including for example, music criticism and journalism, music academia and education, music professionalism, music marketing or musical sub-cultures. Some of the discourses on music are dominant, representing the interests of powerful groups within the wider social framework, or being unquestioningly accepted as 'common sense' by the majority of the social collectivity; others are subservient, or articulate alternative perspectives. I will employ the concept of discourse with relation to music, in order to illuminate many of the arguments throughout this book. In particular, this concept will help to illustrate the social construction of 'truths', not only about music but also about gender.

Musical meaning

It is helpful to keep the concept of a *discourse on music*, separate from the concept of *musical meaning*. In Green (1988) I made use of a theoretical distinction between two aspects of musical meaning, which will again form the basic building blocks for my discussion here.[3]

The first aspect operates in terms of the interrelationships of musical *materials* or, to put it simply, in terms of the sounds of music. In order for a

---

[3] The discussion of musical meaning in Green (1988) is a good deal more detailed and extensive than in the present text. It is indebted to the inspiring work of Leonard B. Meyer (esp. 1956), amongst other theorists, although my position differs from Meyer's in laying a more central emphasis on music's social context. For helpful recent discussions of musical meaning with reference to social context see Middleton (1990), Moore (1993), Walser (1993), Martin (1995), Brackett (1995).

musical experience to occur, musical materials must be organised in such a way as to have relationships, and these relationships must be perceived in the mind of the listener. For example, the musical materials might give rise to the listener's sense of whole and part, opening and close, repetition, similarity, difference or any other pertinent functional relationships. These relationships will normally accrue within any particular piece of music, but they will also arise from the listener's previous experience of a number of pieces of music that together make up a style, sub-style or genre. The organisation of the musical materials acts to construct what I will call 'inherent musical meanings'. These are 'inherent', in the sense that they are encapsulated within the musical materials; and they are 'meanings', in the sense that they are perceived to have relationships.

To put this another way: inherent meaning arises when, for example, one 'bit' of musical material leads us to expect another 'bit', or one bit reminds us of another bit, or one bit contrasts with another bit: then we can say that one bit refers to another bit, or one bit has significance in terms of another bit, or in loose terms, one bit *means* another bit. Inherent meanings are neither natural, nor essential nor ahistorical: on the contrary, they are artificial, historical and learnt. Listeners' responses to them and understanding of them are dependent on the listeners' competence and subject-position in relation to the style of the music. A piece of music whose materials are highly meaningful or very rewarding to one individual might be relatively meaningless or lacking in interest to another. There are thus multiple possible inherent meanings arising from any one piece of music. In sum, the *materials* of music physically inhere; the *inherent meanings* of music arise from the conventional interrelationships of musical materials, in so far as these interrelationships are perceived as such in the mind of a listener.

Whilst this aspect of musical meaning is necessary for musical experience, it is only ever partial, and can in reality never occur on its own. We have become accustomed to the idea that the social or cultural images of performers make an important contribution to their commercial survival. It would be surprising, for example, to see a record cover of Schubert songs depicting the soprano Kiri Te Kanawa in bondage with purple hair; and if we see Madonna in a respectable suit we interpret this as postmodern dressing. But the manipulation of performers' images is not a mere marketing strategy, for clothes, hairstyles or posturing on the sleeves of recordings are all details of a broader aspect of any music: its mediation as a cultural artefact within a social and historical context. Not only the context in which the music is produced and distributed but also the context of its reception affects our understanding of it. These contexts are not merely extra-musical appendages, but they also, to varying degrees, form a part of the music's meaning during the listening experience. Without some understanding of the fact that music is a social construction, we would ultimately be unable to recognise any particular collection of sounds as music at all. When we listen to music, we cannot separate our experience of its inherent meanings entirely from a greater or lesser awareness of the social context that accompanies its production, distribution or reception. I will therefore suggest a second category of musical meaning, qualitatively distinct from the first, which I will call 'delineated meaning'. By this expression I wish to convey the idea that music metaphorically sketches, or delineates, a plethora of contextualising, symbolic factors.

It is not possible to hear music without some delineation or other. We do not always have to be conscious of delineation, but it is always going on in our minds, as an integral element of our listening experience. In everyday life, it comes to us in various unnoticeable ways. For example, a piece of music might cause us to think about what the players were wearing, about who listens to this music, about what we were doing last time we heard it, if we have ever heard it before. In a live concert, we might in some way identify with, or recoil from, the sub-cultural values which we believe the audience hold in common. Some of these thoughts and beliefs will be so closely connected to the music, and so readily accepted by all members of the society, that we can say the music has come to mean, or delineate, them at a conventional level. Other delineations result totally from individual identity. As with inherent meaning, listeners construct the delineated meanings of music according to their subject-position in relation to the music's style.

Central to the conception of music as including both inherent and delineated meaning is the insistence on the irrevocably dialectical interface between the two types of meaning, such that neither can exist without the other insisting on its own presence. This is not to imply that both types of meaning always co-exist to the same degree, or that we are always *conscious* of both, or even either, of them. On the contrary, it is the very ability of each kind of meaning to become obscured that has caused a great deal of discussion and disagreement about music. The point of distinguishing between the two types of meaning is that, although they cannot exist without each other, each operates very differently in the way that it impinges on musical experience and in the way that it is 'put into discourse'.

The relationship between discourse and musical meaning

In the dominant discourse surrounding classical music, the delineations of the music tend to recede, leaving many listeners and devotees with the idea that classical music has none: that it is universal and autonomous in its expression of some ahistorical or essential human condition which mysteriously resides in its formal structures alone. Such an under-standing of music has been implicit, although rarely articulated explic-itly, in much criticism and academic writing.[4] It is also part of many commonsense attitudes towards classical music. For example, a student who found it difficult to accept the argument that classical music always has delineations brought to me the case of a string quartet rehearsing a Haydn movement. 'The players communicate through the inherent meanings', he said. 'They have no need of, or recourse to, delineations, which are anyway of no consequence to the music itself. Therefore we can say that in this case, the music has no delineations.' My response is that there *are* delineations, but that they can indeed be forgotten and even ignored by instrumentalists in an interaction like this – possibly the kind of interaction which is most highly valued by all those who have experience of playing music. Rehearsing in a group, when communica-tion takes place through the music itself, when words have hardly any function, when the substance of what is happening is what you 'say' through the music: there are few joys greater than this. But if we are trying to understand what is happening here in terms of musical meaning, we have to admit that the music is deeply immersed in several contexts, values, or what I put under the umbrella term delineations. The players assume them, and it is only on the basis of this assumption that their intra-musical communication through inherent meanings can take place.

For example, they all know that this music exists in the socially, histori-cally constructed category known as classical music; that it is art-music which demands careful attention; that the audience for whom they are rehearsing, if any, will sit still and quietly during the performance; that this audience will consist of people drawn from certain areas of society; that what they are doing is highly valued on the cultural market; that there are accepted ways of playing in an ensemble; that the opening of this or that particular quartet is widely taken to represent a lark or a

---

[4] The critique of the concept of autonomy is now widespread. See the references in note 3 above, and Wolff (1981), Kerman (1985), Leppert and McClary (1987).

sunrise; and that there are a host of other contextualising factors which surround the music. During a rehearsal of a string quartet these factors may appear to be of little immediate importance. But that cannot mean that they have gone away completely. The appearance of autonomy from social contexts is, in fact, possibly itself the very most prominent and prevalent aspect of the delineation of classical music! In an educational setting when we are not playing, but learning *about* music; in a political situation, when we are voicing a forbidden National Anthem; or in a religious context, when we are singing a traditional hymn: in such situations, delineated factors take on a greater explicit or implicit significance. The fact that the discourse surrounding some music overlooks or even denies them is a comment on the discourse, not on the music.

Contrastingly, the discourse surrounding a great deal of popular music tends to forefront the music's delineations at the expense of its inherent meanings. My student, who professed a strong dislike of popular music, had found this idea very easy to accept. Clothes and hairstyles, a particular way of walking, the overall 'look' of the musician, the label attached to the sub-style of the music, the musicians' or fans' affiliation to a sub-cultural value system, for example, are all delineated by various kinds of popular music, and have been taken by many critics and listeners to be the central things that the music has to offer. Unlike the discourse on classical music, which tends to ignore or even deny such contingencies, that on popular music goes to some lengths to emphasise them, and in the case of journalism rarely discusses anything else. The appearance then arises that the inherent meanings of the music are mysterious, unattainable, unable to be put into discourse at all. The music appears to be consumed by its delineations, and the content of these delineations appears to be an essential property of the musical notes themselves. This appearance is contrasted with the appearance of classical music's autonomy. It is, rather, a type of what I will call musical fetishism, which means a concentration on the music's cultural exchange value (or delineations) at the expense of its material makeup (or inherent meanings).[5]

In the above examples, I have used the words 'classical' and 'popular', on the assumption that they transmit a readily taken-for-granted meaning. To a large extent this is indisputable: even a child can make a conventionally 'correct' identification of whether certain pieces fall into

---

[5] The concept of musical fetishism is more fully explored in Green (1988, Chapter 7). Also see Moore (1993), Tagg (1994) for critiques of this problem in writing about popular music (which does not include *all* pop journalism!).

one or other of those two categories. However, there are many grey areas, in which categorisation is a more vexed issue; and there are many musical examples which may require further distinctions between sub-styles or the addition of other styles altogether such as jazz or folk music. By using the terms 'classical' and 'popular', as well as other similar terms, I am not in fact assuming the musical content of the categories; on the contrary, it is precisely the *mediation* of the music within the cultural exchange market to which I am referring. Handel's *Messiah*, for example, may be mediated as an autonomous, classical piece valued only for its inherent meanings, or as a popular piece whose delineations are of overriding significance, or as a mixture of the two. Furthermore, different listeners will interpret the mediation of a piece of music in different ways. In the present era, the boundaries of the stylistic categories of classical and popular music are in some ways being eroded, as the marketing strategies of different sub-styles adopt images and values borrowed from each other. Nonetheless, the distinction in value attached to inherent or delineated meanings, and their tendency to be broadly aligned with 'classical' and 'popular' music respectively, remain pertinent.

Delineations are in some respects separate from the listening experience, circulating instead in the discourse on music. In a way that is parallel to Said's lion example, cited earlier, the discourse on music does not merely describe and reiterate musical delineations. It goes further than that, to include, overlap with and even produce delineations. Indeed, musical delineations are the stuff of the discourse on music. But as such, they do not simply remain beyond the purview of the listening experience. On the contrary, and this is a crucial point, delineations that circulate in the discourse on music act back to influence our perception of inherent meanings during the listening experience itself. To put this another way, we are led to construct our expectations, our listening-stance, the level of concentration or seriousness which we bring to the listening experience, according to how we position ourselves with respect to the delineations circulating in the discourse on the music. This subject-positioning, in its turn, contributes to the ways in which we actually perceive the inherent meanings.

In sum, inherent meanings arise through the learnt syntactic processes of musical materials; delineated meanings consist of connotations or associations which derive from the position and use of music in a social context. The two types of meaning are dialectically interrelated and, although experientially inseparable, each type of meaning operates very differently, each acting in various ways upon the other, to affect our musical experience and the construction of our discourses on music. An understanding of both inherent and delineated meaning as distinct but necessarily present to some degree in all musical experience helps to unravel the discourses on music, and to expose ideas about music that masquerade as 'truths' when they are better understood as hidden expressions of value. I will go on to argue that it is through the mutual interaction of the different aspects of musical meaning with each other and with musical practice that we learn, amongst other things, our gendered relationships with music. These relationships are discursive formulations, intrinsically related to the historical, social organisation of musical production and reception and, fundamentally, to musical experience itself.

WOMEN'S MUSICAL PRACTICE: SOME FUNDAMENTAL ISSUES

Any commentary on the practices of people selected according to their sex necessitates some definition of what sex is assumed to mean. This may seem fairly obvious at first, but it quickly becomes problematic. The discourse on sex begs the question of where biological determinants end and historical constructions begin. Whereas some things clearly appear to be biologically determined, such as reproductive organs, others, such as capacity for empathy, do not. In the case of musical practice, it may seem simple enough to count the number of biological women in a symphony orchestra or a rock group; but it can never seem so very easy to state what, if any, other aspects of their womanhood are of any relevance to the fact that they are musicians, or the fact that they are being counted. It may be that the discourse on women musicians produces certain characteristics about which it is difficult to separate out the biological from the historical: for example their 'touch' on their instruments, or their attitudes towards group performance. Going further still, discourse constructs certain biologically determined men as having 'feminine' characteristics and, conversely, certain biologically determined women as having 'masculine' characteristics. The distinguishing lines between woman and femininity, man and masculinity are blurred, and yet distinction is invoked, implicitly if not explicitly, as soon as we begin to speak of women musicians, or men musicians. This problem is not something that I seek to resolve, least of all in an introductory chapter: on the contrary, it is one of the cutting edges of my discussion and one of the prime objects of my attention throughout the book. In what follows, I will adopt the now customary practice of using the word 'sex' with reference to the biological characteristics of women or men, and 'gender' with reference to historical constructions of femininity or masculinity. When I write of women or of women musicians, their biologically determined characteristics are merely the bottom line of the definition which I am invoking: the rest is always in question.[6]

My concern is centrally with gender as distinct from sexuality, although clearly issues of sexuality must frequently impinge on the area of discussion. Within the general term 'sexuality' I wish to include both heterosexuality and homosexuality, with the multiplicity of their possible psychological and practical manifestations. Recent writings on homosexuality and music have increased my awareness that in the world of music, alongside the regulation of heterosexuality as normal and unquestionable, there is another world which subverts that normality.[7] Homosexuals, or people with homoerotic inclinations, live, work and experience music alongside heterosexuals; but their musical relationships are imbued with different nuances, alternative layers of fascination, ambiguity or difficulty. I write as a heterosexual, but one who is concerned at least to attempt not to assume the state of heterosexuality in everyone else, or to assume that hetero- and homosexuality are entirely separate or opposed.

A pitfall of any generalising account of the category of women, especially with reference to a very wide historical and geographical purview, is that it tends to totalise, thus ignoring, obscuring and misrepresenting the diversities amongst women in and between different classes, races, religions and all other social and historical groupings. Women are clearly by no means a homogeneous group, and generalisation from one subgroup to another may be impertinent or misleading. We must therefore be cautious of the problems of totalisation; but at the same time this need not entail altogether abandoning a broad perspective. What such a perspective can allow, and this is what I aim for, is to explore that possibility which I raised earlier, of whether there is a kernel that runs through the history of women in music, which may be fundamental to discursive constructions of music or of women, or of both. In that sense, the recognition and exposition of some commonalities in women's

---

[6] For a seminal discussion of the sex/gender distinction, see Gatens (1983); for a helpful exploration of its significance from a sociological point of view, Barrett (1988a); and for a radical treatment, Butler (1990).

[7] For discussions of homosexuality and music, see Brett, Thomas and Wood (1994), Wood (1993), M. Morris (1993), Brett (1993), Bradby (1993a), Gill (1994), Castle (1993).

musical practices and their reception is valid. One limit that I have set myself is a concentration on relatively mainstream or well-known musical practices with reference to the broadly defined styles of classical, jazz and popular music in the West. My focus is on post-Renaissance Europe and post-eighteenth-century North America up to the present time. This is not to imply that people in other continents and eras have not also participated in many of the practices which I discuss. 'The West' is a loose, umbrella term referring more to a set of practices than to a geographical part of the world. Ethnomusicological enquiry concerning women in many parts of the world exposes significant differences in women's musical practices, further underlining the need for exercising continuous caution in making universalising claims. At the same time, it also points to some commonalities in women's musical practices across a wide range of cultures including non-Western and non-mainstream Western contexts. Whilst it is a specialised field that falls outside my purview, I will occasionally refer to ethnomusicological scholarship on women in order to compare or contrast my arguments.[8]

A concept that will be central to my discussion is that of patriarchy. This indicates a social structure in which there are multiple relationships of power, including economic power, physical power and the discursive power to construct 'truths', but in which the overall balance of power is held by men rather than by women. Cutting across and contributing to the maintenance of the unequal balance of power between men and women is a further division. This is articulated as a difference between the public and the private spheres. The public sphere involves the world of paid work, amongst other things; and the private sphere involves that of domestic or unpaid work, amongst other things. Within patriarchy, men circulate in the public sphere more than women, and women operate as workers in the private sphere more than men. But women do infiltrate the public sphere, and when they do so, it tends to be in areas that retain many of the characteristics which mark the private sphere. Thus the unpaid, private-sphere roles of caring, nursing, cleaning, catering, housekeeping and bringing up children translate into the paid, public realms of caring, nursing, cleaning, catering, service, secretarial administration and teaching. The role of sexuality in domestic life can also be seen to transform into that of professional sexual services

---

[8] For very helpful sources on ethnomusicological work on women, see two collections: Koskoff (1987c), esp. Koskoff's introduction (1987a) and Robertson's contribution (1987), and Herndon and Ziegler (1990). Also see Robertson (1993), Koskoff (1991), (1993), Post (1994), Payne (1993), Weiss (1993), Tolbert (1994).

provided by women. The terms 'public' and 'private' are not, therefore, literal descriptions of the actual degree of publicity or privacy with which work is carried out, or of the architectural space in which work is performed, or of the status of the work as paid or unpaid; but they stand, anachronistically in some cases, for a type of work that is gendered.

Within patriarchy, men and women not only fulfil practical gender *roles* such as the type of work that they do, but alongside this, they construct and negotiate sets of gendered *characteristics*. In extreme polarised form, masculinity is defined as active and productive; as committed to the pursuit of knowledge, hence rational, inventive, experimental, scientific and technological; as bound up with the production of Art, hence creative. At the opposite pole, femininity is defined as passive and reproductive; as involved in the nurturing of others, hence caring; as occupied in the production of Craft, hence diligent. Whereas men's pursuit of knowledge is commensurate with masculine prowess of the *mind*, women's reproductive and nurturing functions (menstruation, gestation, lactation) derive from feminine obeisance to the *body*. Whereas masculinity's mental capacity is manifest in *reason*, femininity's subjection to the body is associated with susceptibility to *feeling*. Whereas masculinity produces *culture*, femininity is bound to *nature*. Whereas masculinity is *stoical*, femininity, in ways that I have already highlighted through Campion's poem, is *contrary*: desirable and dangerous, offering both the comfort of the wife or mother, and the temptation of the sexual object or whore. The social construction of masculinity and femininity does not necessarily imply that all men are wholly masculine, or that all women are entirely feminine. On the contrary, as I have already mentioned, the characteristics of masculinity and femininity are each available to be adopted to greater or lesser degrees by men or by women. But there is a tendency for these characteristics to be associated with men and women respectively. Furthermore this tendency is enhanced in so far as masculine characteristics are more commensurate with occupation of the public sphere, and feminine characteristics with occupation of the private sphere.

Not only must the terms 'public' and 'private' or 'masculinity' and 'femininity' retain fluidity and symbolic significance, but so must the more concrete terms with which they are linked, 'men' and 'women'. These terms cannot be taken simply to designate two sociologically distinct groups in a single power-relation. Not all men have the same *kinds* of power over all women, there being racial, class, religious and other variations. By the same token, women in one social grouping may have certain kinds of power over men in the same group; and they may have a great deal of power over men in a different group. It is the male ownership of the overall balance of power, the articulation of power through the public sphere and the commensurate construction of gender characteristics that combine in the creation of a patriarchal society. The concept of patriarchal power does not involve a one-dimensional assertion of power by men over women: both sexes contribute to the perpetuation of their practical and their symbolic positions within patriarchy, and this contribution involves a certain amount of consent or collusion, and a certain amount of dissent or resistance. In a nutshell, I understand patriarchy as a *relationship* in which men overall have more power than women, articulated through a separation that is both empirical and symbolic, of public from private life.[9]

Knowledge of the history of women's musical practices is aided by a concept which I will call 'musical patriarchy'. The division of musical work into a largely male public sphere and a largely female private sphere is a trait of Western music history and also of many musical cultures from all around the world.[10] As with the more general characterisation of patriarchy offered above, the division between the two musical spheres is by no means clear-cut or absolute. On the contrary, women in the West and elsewhere have been very active in the paid, public realm of musical work, where they have been tolerated and even, in some cases, encouraged. But, as with patriarchy in general, women's public musical work has largely drawn on the characteristics of women's private musical work. Furthermore, women have mainly participated in musical pursuits which in some way enable a symbolic expression of 'feminine' characteristics. If we were to view patriarchal power over women's musical practices as one-dimensionally repressive, we would thereby cut off the possibility of understanding how and why women have been allowed to be musically active at all. In fact, one of the points that I will hope to substantiate throughout this book is that it is a combination of tolerance and repression, collusion and resistance, that systematically furthers the very gendered divisions from which musical patriarchy springs.

[9] This tends towards a sociological, as distinct from a psychoanalytic, model of patriarchy. See Barrett (1988a), (1988b) for a helpful discussion and a classic sociological feminist perspective. For seminal anthropological work on definitions of masculinity and femininity see Ortner (1974). For further discussions of patriarchy, and of definitions of men, women, masculinity and femininity, see Butler (1990).

[10] See Post (1994, esp. pp. 35–8, 44–6) for a helpful account of ethnographic work in this field and also a clear discussion of the relevance and limitations of applying the public/private model to music; also see Citron (1993, pp. 100ff), Reich (1993, p. 125), Eaklor (1994, pp. 43–4), Green (1994a).

MUSICAL MEANING AND WOMEN'S MUSICAL PRACTICE

In Part I, focussing on the concept of femininity, I will argue that the gender of a musical practitioner plays a large, and often unacknowledged, part in the discourse on music and in musical meaning. Earlier on, I cited the imaginary examples of Kiri Te Kanawa singing Schubert with purple hair, and Madonna wearing a respectable suit, to indicate that the manipulation of their images contributes to the delineated meanings of the music they perform. In less visible, more complex ways than through clothes and hairstyles, something definitive about the femininity of the woman musician, I will argue, itself forms a part of her music's delineated meanings. When we listen to a woman sing or play, and when we listen to music which she has composed or improvised, we do not just listen to the inherent meanings of the music, but we are also aware of her discursive position in a nexus of gender and sexuality. From this position, her femininity becomes a part of the music's delineations. Clearly, by my definition of inherent musical meaning as a virtual category which is purely to do with musical materials, inherent meaning itself can have nothing to do with gender. But the gendered delineation of music does in fact not stop at delineation: it continues from its delineated position to become a part of the discourse on music, and from that position to affect listeners' responses to and perceptions of inherent meaning, and thus our very musical experiences themselves. When music delineates femininity through a female performer or composer, we are liable to also judge the handling of inherent meanings by that performer or composer, in terms of our idea of her femininity. In a relationship of circularity, gendered musical practice, musical meaning and musical experience are entwined.

The production and reproduction of musical meaning as gendered has been crucial in the administration of women's musical practices throughout history. I will refer to historical scholarship, using examples of the practices of particular women at specific points in history, in order to make concrete and bring to life my theory of musical discourse and gendered musical meaning. On one hand, I have selected examples which I believe are representative of their time and place. On the other hand, I have included examples which I understand to be exceptional, or peculiar to their cultural context. Part of my intention is to develop a picture of the overall discourse on women in music, including both what is normal and what represents ruptures in normality. Although my examples are primarily illustrative, I also hope that some of the information involved will prove helpful to those readers who are not familiar with the history of women in music. Without knowledge of this history, the full impact of the gendered meaning of music will, I believe, be diminished; and furthermore, the constant fissure which has separated women from awareness of our own musical history will continue to be reproduced as it has been for centuries. In the final chapter of Part I, I will attempt to draw together the ideas put forward up to that point, in order to articulate a working theory of gendered musical meaning and experience.

GENDERED MUSICAL MEANING IN CONTEMPORARY EDUCATION

Part II will enter the contemporary school music classroom, in order to explore the present-day operation of the gendered musical practices and meanings that have been discussed in Part I: how they surface, how they are made manifest, how they are produced and reproduced. The school is a vital arena for the production and reproduction of practice and meaning. It encapsulates a world of diversity within a microcosmic version of the wider social network: a multi-ethnic, multi-faith, multi-linguistic, multi-social-class community of pupils and teachers from different backgrounds, with different perspectives, operating within different discourses. To open the door of the music classroom is to enter a miniature sound-world containing the latest popular charts hits alongside Mozart symphonies, African drumming alongside Bulgarian folk music, children's compositions alongside those of professional composers, and a host of musical riches. The music classroom is a place in which the present-day operation of gendered musical practices and meanings surfaces, both in the raw common-sense and in the considered perspectives of girls, boys and of their teachers. Together, pupils and teachers in schools reveal the workings of our contemporary construction of the discourse on music and gender in which, without necessarily being aware of it, we reiterate the gendered practices and meanings that are bequeathed by our musical, historical legacy. Most importantly, the school music classroom can illuminate some of the processes involved in the construction of individual gendered identity through musical experience itself.[11]

---

[11] A résumé of some central arguments put forward in this book is provided in Green (1994b).

PART I

Musical meaning and women's musical practice

CHAPTER 2

Affirming femininity: women singing, women enabling

DISPLAY AS A PART OF MUSICAL PERFORMANCE

In this section I will suggest that musical performance which takes place in full view of an audience normally contains an element of display. But first, I will present an interpretation of the nature of display itself, quite apart from music.[1] It is helpful to understand display as involving something metaphorically akin to wearing a mask. In these terms, the displayer can be seen as both presenting and protecting himself or herself by virtue of the mask. The mask is then that which is displayed. But display is not so much a single act by a displayer as a relationship, an exchange which is mutually constructed by both the displayer and an onlooker. The mask cannot be imagined by the displayer as something known only to him- or herself; on the contrary, the displayer must be aware of an other, the onlooker, who is also conscious of the mask. The presence and watchfulness of this other are a necessary part in what is a mutual construction of the metaphorical mask. For each participant – displayer and onlooker – the scenario cannot exist without the other. But this is not a mere truism: it is the essence of the relationship, its focal point and raison d'être.

The mask has an effect of splitting the displayer in two. From the point of view of the onlooker, the displayer takes on a double form, as both 'other' and 'mask'; from the point of view of the displayer, the self is doubled into 'self' and 'mask'. The mask is the central locus of the exchange. The participant, whether in the role of displayer or onlooker, is in some ways involuntarily captured by the imaginary mask as it is intended by the other; but in other ways, since he or she participates in the active construction of the mask, so can s/he 'play with the mask'

[1] The following discussion derives from a reading of Lacan (1979, pp. 106ff); and is also influenced by Hegel (1977, Preface and pp. 111–19), Marx (1977) and more recent feminist theorists, especially Mulvey (1975).

conceptually. Therefore, although the mask is mutually constructed by both displayer and onlooker, it does not represent any principle of equality between them. On the contrary, display involves the enactment of a mutual power differential. On one hand, the displayer is in the active position, and has the power of the lure, of spectacularity, the possibility of playing with the mask from that point of view; whereas the onlooker is passively in danger of becoming seduced and ensnared by the mask. On the other hand, the displayer is passive, weakened by the necessity to be partially concealed, to present a mask rather like a protective shield on which s/he must rely for the continuation of the relationship; whereas the onlooker has the panoptical, disarming power of the gaze, the possibility of playing with the mask from that point of view.

I wish to make a distinction between what I will call 'institutionalised display' and 'informal display'. By the former, I mean a scenario in which display itself is recognised as an integral part of a performance. Such display will usually take place on a stage or in some space with an equivalent symbolic separation between an audience and the displayer(s). By informal display, on the other hand, I mean a type of display that takes place all around us: in the streets, in the home, in places of leisure and places of work, through the variously suggestive adoption of particular postures, manners, glances, vocal tones, vocal inflections, clothing or other embellishments and accoutrements. Clearly, the two types of display will never be totally separate and are not opposed. Institutionalised display, in particular, may involve many of the nuances of informal display. But institutionalised display is nonetheless distinguishable in so far as it takes place in dedicated surroundings or particular contexts. In what follows, I will concentrate on institutionalised display.

Between the displayer and the onlooker in a musical performance there is not only the mask, but also the music. During the course of Chapters 2 and 3, I will argue that in the display of musical performance mask and music become entwined. In order to help think through this, I want first to posit display as involving two poles, between which we can map the degree of intention to display on the part of the displayer; and I will relate this to musical performance. On one pole is the full intention to display, where display is the sole object of the performance: the striptease, for example. It is not only the naked body[2] as a thing in itself,

---

[2] What exactly is included in the word 'body' is a moot point. When I use the term, I mean it to include the face and hair; and incidentally, in the case of sexual display involving other accoutrements such as underwear or make-up whose fetishistic role in the display may be crucial, these are also included in my use of the words 'bodily display'.

but the intentional act of revealing, the step-by-step construction of the metaphorical mask, that creates the lure here. A fully intentional act of display like this could hardly involve musical performance: the case of a singing strip-tease artiste (male or female), and even more so one who simultaneously plays an instrument is, I gather, rare, and this is undoubtedly because the stripper would be doing something other than displaying the body, thus throwing doubt on his or her full intention to display, distracting the spectator, diluting the mask. In general, a fully intentional act of display does not involve musical performance, and conversely, musical performance rarely has display as its raison d'être. Therefore this polar extreme does not itself enter into my discussion, but rather provides a point against which to measure different types of musical performance.

It might at first glance seem that at the opposite pole to the scenario of the striptease is that of the 'peeping Tom'. But this latter scenario does not in fact involve any kind of display at all, since there is no intention on the part of the person who is spied upon: no mask. Rather, at the opposite pole to the striptease, there is a type of display which is unintentional: the fact of inadvertently or even unwillingly putting the body in a position to be gazed at, not for the sake of inviting the gaze, but as a result of some other activity which cannot but involve the body in being looked at. Certain types of musical performance provide prime examples of this polar opposite. At the most extreme is a type of performance which takes place in front of an audience; which is intended to focus exclusively on musical inherent meanings; which is presented as being 'for the sake of the music'; and which participates in a discourse that raises inherent meanings to an autonomous level above social contexts. Even though such performance eschews explicit consideration of everything but inherent meanings, it always also implicitly involves the audience gaze on the body. Unlike the stripper's, the body of the performing musician in this kind of context is a mere off-shoot of the whole scenario: and yet as I hope to illustrate, its effects are never avoided. Every performer will be aware of these effects, as will every spectator, though they might not be involved in alluring or being lured themselves.

Clearly, within the view I have so far put forward, all musical performance in front of an audience would fall somewhere between the two poles, from near fully intended to near unintended display. In the middle, at various points between these two polar extremes, is a partly intended display in which for example a musical performer does intend to display his or her body, and at the same time aims to perform music 'for its own (inherent) sake'. Many nuances and ambiguities are possible, such as a display which is intended to appear unintended, a display which is denied but which is hypocritically and covertly celebrated. Mixtures of intended and unintended display are common in the case of a variety of musical styles and performance practices, the precise position of any one particular performance being determined by a variety of detailed factors which will be explored in the course of Chapters 2 and 3.

So far, I have put my case entirely in terms of live performance in front of an audience. But I now wish to suggest that the elements of display symbolised by the musical performer do not only form an integral part of the relationship between performer and audience in a live situation: they also enter and become intrinsic to musical meaning itself. Just as the type of concert venue, the clothes or the social standing of the audience, for example, contribute to delineated musical meanings, so the intended or unintended display of the performer becomes a part of the delineated meanings of the music he or she performs. Display therefore continues to be a delineation of the music beyond the live setting, entering into the musical experience even when the music is recorded, when the performer is concealed, or when we listen to music with our eyes closed. Then, just as all the abstract delineations of the music are still implicit in our conception, so is the type of bodily display of the performer: a delineation like any other. Furthermore, this display not only acts as an extra-musical association; it goes beyond that, entering into the delineations involved in the listening experience itself. The precise characteristics of the delineation and its effects upon our listening experiences will vary according to the performance and reception contexts, the style of the music and the subject-position of the listener.

One crucial factor which history has injected into the relationship of institutionalised display is an asymmetry according to the sex of the displayer. A male displayer and a female displayer are not the same. The understanding of display suggested above can clearly in theory operate on any axis, involving male or female in either the role of the displayer or that of the onlooker. But human history has dictated that different types of institutionalised display involve quite different connotations and gender-roles. On one hand, highly ritualised, institutionalised display of an intimidatory nature tends to be performed by males. It occurs particularly in pre-industrial communities, and is not merely rare but risqué in the West and many other parts of the world today. When industrial man has occasion to hint at it, in so doing he to some extent retrieves an element of lost masculinity from the recesses of mythology. The unusualness of such display is dramatically brought home by the New Zealand All-Blacks rugby team in their ritual show of strength and aggression which takes place at the beginning of the match. Although such intimidatory display by males does, in rare circumstances such as this, occur in post-industrial society today, it has for a long time been virtually non-existent.

On the other hand, and in direct contrast, the institutionalised displaying act in the realm of sexuality has a high profile in Western society, not being limited to striptease joints, but encompassing a wide variety of performance rituals including musical performance. Sexual display may be enacted by a man or a woman, but in its more overt forms such as sex-shows, it overwhelmingly tends to be enacted by women. More significantly, in whatever form it occurs and regardless of the actual biological sex of the displayer, the symbolic resonances of overt sexual display connote 'femininity'.[3] In sum, the most common institutionalised type of display and the most normal deployment of gender-roles within the relationship of display in the West involve an explicitly or implicitly sexual display in which the displayer is coded as 'feminine' and the spectator as 'masculine'.

It follows that male and female musical performers cannot have a symmetrical relationship to their audience. Indeed, the male performer has been implicitly or explicitly affected by the historical determinants which, I have argued, have made display a predominantly feminine act. The characterisation of musical performance as a 'feminine pastime' has for centuries negatively affected the availability of vocal and instrumental music education for boys, compared to girls, especially in families that had no need to earn their living; and as we will see, this characterisation still forms a considerable portion of contemporary attitudes amongst boys and girls themselves in schools. Furthermore, many writers have noted a tendency for music itself to feminise, and they have located a corresponding fear on the part of musicians, musicologists and music lovers. In an ideological conflation of effeminacy with homosexuality, this fear has surfaced in the form of homophobic denials and the writing-out of any hint of homosexuality in musical historiography or criticism. The extent of the fortifications defending the hegemony of

---

[3] Robertson (1993) gives an interesting analysis of the fluid, ambivalent and androgynous sexualities that are available to Hawaiian people, and of ways in which these are enacted partly through musical practices. She suggests that there are also many other cultures without polarised sexual differentiation (p. 122). It is necessary not to override this or to overlook the presence of homosexuality in all cultures. My argument is that within the West, display is coded as 'feminine' as distinct from female, and that the position of spectator is a 'masculine', not necessarily a male, one.

male heterosexuality in musical patriarchy and the mechanisms which have kept at bay the threat of effeminacy and homosexuality in the world of music have been the topic of ground-breaking recent work.[4]

But the female musical performer has quite a different relationship to the feminising powers of musical display. Not for her is this the overt and contradictory problem that it can be for the Western male. The fact that girl and women musical performers are always to some extent close to being thrown into a world of feminine sexual display is not at odds with historically constructed definitions of their femininity. It is not a throwing out into something new, something contradictory, but a throwing back to where they have, discursively, originated. Indeed, this self-recurring cycle of reference from the female back to the feminine is one of the intrinsic and enduring symbolic elements of female musical performance which is so eloquently portrayed by Thomas Campion, in his poem reprinted in Chapter 1. To summarise my argument: whatever their intentions and whatever the performance situation, male and female musical performers are both thrown into a world of display. But for the male performer, this contradicts his discursive position as masculine; whereas for the female performer, it affirms her discursive position as feminine.[5]

---

[4] On accusations of, and reactions against effeminacy in music, see for example McClary (1991), Walser (1993), Citron (1993), Tick (1993) and Chapter 4, pp. 89, 98f below. On expositions of homophobia in the musicological establishment see the powerful arguments in Brett, Thomas and Wood (1994), especially the introductory chapter by Koestenbaum (1994b), and the examinations of musicology's efforts to protect the hegemony of heterosexuality with reference to the musicological icons of Handel, Schubert and Britten, by Thomas (1994), McClary (1994) and Brett (1994) respectively.

[5] Mulvey's (1975) seminal article, 'Visual pleasure and narrative cinema', argued that women in Hollywood films functioned as the passive objects of the male gaze. Also see further critical work on this in Mulvey (1989), Kaplan (1984), de Lauretis (1987), Silverman (1988). Although her analysis has influenced my thinking and contains some points in common with the position offered here, there are some qualitative differences between the significance of display by actresses and actors on film and that of display by musicians, either live or on film. In the filmed scenario involving acting, the distribution of power between displayer and spectator is less dialectical than in the scenario of live musical performance. In films the camera intervenes between the displayer and the onlooker. The woman portrayed as Mulvey describes her, languishing passively in the film, has no control over that camera, its angles, its choice of focus. But in live musical performance, it is the music which intervenes, becoming entwined with the mask. The displayer, whether it is a man or a woman, does have a significant control over the music: the displayer is in fact the immediate source of the music. Live musical performance therefore affords a special type of power to the performer which is denied to the passive object of the film camera: the power of control over the music. I will say more about this later in the chapter.

In the case of filmed musical performance or music videos, there is a mixture of the two perspectives offered here. The display of the performer on film or video is more or less affected according to how much the performance appears to be live or to be dubbed. Where the performance is clearly live, as on a film of a symphony orchestra or a video of a heavy metal band on

MUSICAL MEANING AND THE DISPLAY OF THE WOMAN SINGER

In Chapter 1 (pp. 13–15) I put forward a view of patriarchy as involving a separation of the public from the private sphere, and as coinciding with a practical and symbolic tendency for not only men and women but also masculinity and femininity to be associated with the public and private spheres respectively. Masculinity tends to be defined as active, rational, inventive, experimental, scientific, unified, as a catalyst to culture and an emblem of the controlling powers of mind; femininity tends to be defined as passive, reproductive, caring, emotional, contrary, as a part of nature, controlled by the body. Men and women do not just adhere to immovable conventions: they both collude and resist in the adoption of practical roles and of symbolic gender characteristics. However, when they do cross over into the different spheres or adopt unconventional gender characteristics, they tend to carry with them residues of more normative associations. I now wish to suggest that women's singing, whether or not it crosses into the public sphere, largely reproduces and affirms patriarchal definitions of femininity.

The concept of affirmation, as used in this context, contains a deliberate ambiguity. On one hand, if femininity itself is regarded only as oppressed, manipulated, or in other negative terms, then the 'affirmation of femininity' would always refer to an oppressive process, a manipulative tendency, and as such, it would be seen as an object of critique. On the other hand, if the furthering of oppression, manipulation or other negativities was the only implication of the concept of affirming femininity, this would suggest that femininity itself possesses no liberating potential, no positive attributes, no attraction, indeed, either for women or for men. But if that were so, we could never begin to think about why people should have gone to so much effort, historically, in their interactions and in their cultural products, to preserve and reproduce femininity. Far from having purely negative connotations, the concept of the affirmation of femininity also connotes positive aspects. In short, femininity (and masculinity also) has bad sides and good sides, both for those who adopt it and for those who contemplate it; therefore the concept of the affirmation of femininity, likewise, carries both negative and positive connotations.

stage, an element of musical power is retained, although it is diluted by the interjection of the camera. Where the performance is obviously dubbed, as on popular music videos in which band members are seen playing and singing in accoustics that are totally at odds with those of the sound-track, the power of the performers is accordingly reduced, and their passivity increased.

As with all musical performance, whether intentionally or unintentionally, the woman singer is on display and is therefore engaged in an activity which, I have argued, is already coded as 'feminine'. It is helpful to pinpoint four particular aspects of women's vocal display which make it particularly affirmative of femininity.[6] First, display involves the construction of a metaphorical mask, a shield which both protects and draws attention to the body. As I mentioned earlier, the fully intentional displayer is unlikely to do anything other than display, unlikely therefore to sing and even less likely to play an instrument. Although not completely absorbed in display, the singer is, however, close to complete absorption, because of the intricate connection, indeed the unity, of the displaying body itself with the instrumental source of the singing. The voice is the one musical instrument whose sound-production mechanisms have no intrinsic links with anything outside the body. Rather, the voice springs from the body, entirely and (until modern amplification, which I will discuss later) without any extraneous aid. The body is the instrument. The singing woman is, literally and metaphorically, in tune with her body. At the same time, she is prey to its vicissitudes, which are dangerously present in the ready susceptibility of the voice. This embodied quality of vocal display is one reason for latitude towards the woman singer: embodied, she is no threat. But, contrastingly, as I noted earlier, danger lurks behind any mask. The woman singer, in her self-possessedness and her ability to lure, is invested with a power that is unavailable to onlookers, which becomes a threat that can only increase any potential fear and, therefore, aggression. This is one source of antipathy towards women singers, articulated as the habitual fear of the onlooker that s/he may become ensnared in the mask. In this typically contrary position, safely embodied yet dangerously alluring, femininity is affirmed.

The second way in which I wish to suggest that singing affirms patriarchal definitions of femininity is to do with the absence of technology in singing. Within patriarchy, man is constructed as being in control of nature through the harnessing of technology, woman as a part of the nature that man controls. No extraneous object to be controlled by the singing woman interrupts her construction of the metaphorical mask of display, since the musical sound-source of her performance remains

---

[6] For alternative critical examinations of women's voices and their symbolic manifestations, see Wood (1994) and the collection edited by Dunn and Jones (1994). I will return to some issues raised by these later. For the symbolism involved in the displacement of the woman's vocal range into the body of the castrated male, see Dame (1994).

locked in the body. The sight and sound of the woman singing therefore affirms the correctness of the fact of what is absent: the unsuitability of any serious and lasting connection between woman and instrument, woman and technology. Although the woman singer's metaphorically masked body itself may be a threat, its lack of potentiality to act upon an other object in the world is a relief. Because the spheres of nature and the body are associated with femininity and divorced from masculinity, and because singing involves the intended or unintended display of the body with no interrupting technology, the scenario of a woman singing leaves this association firmly in place. In this way the woman singer can continue to appeal to nature, to be natural; and her real ability to manipulate technology is temporarily effaced.

Thirdly, along with this contrary but (commensurately) entirely feminine vision, the image of the paid female singer who puts body and voice on public display has inevitably been associated in practically all known societies with that of the sexual temptress or prostitute.[7] Although not engaged in a fully intentional act of display, the singing woman in a public arena is dangerously, and tantalisingly, close to doing so. For this reason she is a threat and, as such, is open to abuse.

Fourthly, this very association with public sexual availability is opposed to an alternative face of woman which has always been present as the corollary of availability: the image of the mother privately singing to her baby, a practice which is allowed in all known cultures, and which must be one of the few universal customs of humanity. The connection between the public woman singer and her sexual availability has been made for millennia, just as has that between the private singer of lullabies and her maternal care. Thus the age-old dichotomy of woman as whore/madonna is reproduced in her musical practice as a singer.[8]

These four characteristics of femininity – the self-possessed yet alluring concentration on the body, the association with nature, the appearance of sexual availability and the symbolisation of maternal preoccupation – are affirmed and reproduced in the act of display

[7] For a general discussion of the links between women musicians and sexual availability with reference to ethnomusicology, see Koskoff (1987c), as well as the other ethnomusicological sources cited in Chapter 1, note 8, p. 13 above. I have also been informed by Murphy (1993), Lamburn (1991) and Doubleday (1991); and I would like to thank Naseem Ahmed for doing some research into Islamic writings on my behalf, and submitting to a lengthy taped interview on the subject with special reference to Pakistan and the Pakistani diaspora. I am not saying that all female vocal performance is always associated with sexual availability, but that some of it inevitably is.

[8] Again see the ethnographic literature and the references in note 5 above; see also Koskoff (1987b), (1993) who gives interesting analyses of a related range of issues as they emerge with relation to Hasidic Jewish culture in New York.

invoked by women's singing. The contradictions which they involve, far from representing logically alternative or mutually exclusive positions, actually go together, to articulate a space in which femininity is constructed as contrary, desirable but dangerous, sexually available but maternally preoccupied. When we hear music sung by a woman, amongst a multitude of delineations arising from the music's production, distribution and reception contexts, there will be a gendered delineation: a delineation of her display, her femininity.

The voice has a peculiar characteristic in respect of gendered delineation. Unlike instrumental musical sounds, the voice in practically all cases betrays the sex of its perpetrator. Voice and sex are immediately connected. In those few cases where a listener consciously cannot tell whether the singer is a man, woman, boy or girl, this in itself becomes a matter of a certain interest.[9] Because of the apparently immediate connection between voice and sex, the sound of a voice always appears to participate in the construction not only of gendered delineations but also of somehow gendered inherent meanings. But in fact the participation in inherent meaning is no different from that of any other instrument. The sound of a singing voice, including the tessitura, the pronunciation of vowels and consonants, the technique of breathing, the use of the throat to affect tone-colour, the use of diaphragmatic support, the level of vocal flexibility and control over dynamics, rhythm, intonation, phrasing: all these factors that go to make up a vocal musical performance are judgeable or have meaning with reference to the norms and measures of excellence of the appropriate style of music, in so far as the listener is competent to make his or her judgement. As such the voice carries and participates in the construction of inherent meanings. The voice will also be judged or will take on meanings in accordance with the type of display which the song, its context and the listener are between them able to invoke, and it is with reference to such areas only that the voice transmits delineated meanings.[10]

The contradictions contained in the fourfold delineation of the woman singer, described above, have been translated into a continuing saga of controversy throughout the history of music, concerning

---

[9] See Dame (1994) on voice, gender and sexuality with reference to castrati, and Castle (1993) on the subversion of vocal identity.

[10] The cultural resonance of vocal quality has been the subject of a considerable amount of discussion, some of which has been sparked off by Barthes' celebrated essay 'The Grain of the Voice' (1977). Again see the references in note 6 above, plus: Middleton (1990, esp. pp. 261–6), Frith and McRobbie (1978, esp. pp. 384–5), Laing and Taylor (1979, esp. pp. 46–7), Frith (1985), Shepherd (1987, pp. 164ff), Moore (1993, pp. 41–7).

whether, how much, where and when women should or should not be allowed to sing. Women have at all times been more free to sing than to play, and considerably more free to sing than to compose, but not to the extent of being wholly licensed. On the contrary, the vicious circle of opposition that I highlighted in Campion's depiction of the singer Lawra in Chapter 1 expresses itself in the fact that, to differing degrees at various times in history, women have been allowed to sing and criticised for singing, admired and disdained. This history of allowance and refusal of the woman singer illustrates and informs our present-day constructions, in which we continue to reproduce affirmative feminine display-delineations.

Women singing in classical music

In ancient civilisation it seems that there was little or no prejudice against women musicians of all kinds.[11] However, this situation gradually changed, presaging a cycle which was to revolve throughout the remaining history of the woman singer: upsurges of antipathetic reaction at various times, giving way at others to greater leniency. During the fourth century women were discouraged and eventually prohibited from singing in church,[12] a fact which was to affect their vocal practices for quite a few hundred years to come. From that time nuns, who formed about 15 per cent of the cloistered community (Yardley 1986, p. 15), were allowed to sing in the chapel of the convent, even in mixed settings. At a time when male musicians were beginning to enjoy brilliant careers in church and court, the convent provided women with the only institutionalised career opportunity in music open to them, and it is typical that this centred around singing: the role of cantrix, which was equivalent to the monasteries' cantor.[13]

---

[11] On women and music in antiquity and beyond to the fifteenth century see Meyers (1993), Teeter (1993), Touliatos (1993), Gergis (1993), Michelini (1991), Bogin (1980), Yardley (1986), Coldwell (1986), Marshall (1993a), Edwards (1991). In discussing women's musical history I am indebted to a number of sources for the factual information on which I draw. Information on the history of women in music has expanded rapidly in recent years and is now readily accessible. Amongst several other helpful publications, I would recommend the following as a balanced selection of starting-points for any interested reader new to the field: Ammer (1980), Block and Neuls-Bates (1979), Bowers and Tick (1986), Brisco (1987), A. Cohen (1988), Dahl (1984), S. Fuller (1994a), Gaar (1993), Handy (1981), Jezic (1988), Kent (1983), LePage (1980), Marshall (1993b), Neuls-Bates (1982), L. O'Brien (1994), Pendle (1991b), Placksin (1985), Sadie and Samuel (1994), Steward and Garratt (1984), Zaimont et al. (1984), (1987), (1991).

[12] Bowers and Tick (1986, p. 4), Neuls-Bates (1982, p. xii).

[13] Yardley (1986), Kendrick (1993) Pendle (1991a).

Nuns may have been the only institutionalised quasi-professional musicians, but there were also bands of travelling musicians which included women singers, and there were singing slave girls working in courts in southern Spain (Coldwell 1986, p. 43). On the amateur side, noblewomen and wealthy women were highly cultured and domestically musically educated. Although they undertook household management as their main occupation, they learned music as an accomplishment, in which activity they enjoyed no greater conventional restrictions than did their male counterparts. Both noblewomen and noblemen performed simple vocal monodies, often accompanying themselves on a stringed instrument.[14] From the fifteenth through to the eighteenth century all over Europe, nuns continued their vocal pursuits, and noblewomen continued to sing in domestic settings as a leisure activity. Travelling bands of musicians began to represent less of a social force, but the on-going trend of dramatic players lent a place to women, who began to sing on stage for the first time during the sixteenth century.[15] Other women had vocal careers in music, mainly in courts, and increasingly in the opera house.[16]

The question of whether women and girls should be allowed to sing was the subject of widespread debate, which arose with particular concentration in the middle of the sixteenth century[17] and continued to be a source of controversy for some two or three hundred years. The Council of Trent placed restrictions on the vocal practices of nuns, including banning them from singing polyphonic music.[18] Following this, a series of regulations, particularly in Ferrara and Milan, offer an extraordinary history of seemingly frantic attempts on the part of clergy to prevent nuns from music-making outside the chapel, right into the eighteenth century, when in 1728 the force of continuing resistance to these rules by some nuns finally caused the Pope to intervene (Bowers 1986, pp. 139–45).

Amongst women outside the convents, one of the most notable breaks into professional singing since antiquity occurred in Italy in the 1580s, when the first group of women singers to be paid by a court was formed at Ferrara.[19] This development was greeted with a mixture of disdain

[14] Coldwell (1986), Brown (1986), Edwards (1991), Pendle (1991a).
[15] Newcomb (1986, pp. 102f), Pendle (1991a, pp. 38f).
[16] See Bowers (1986), Rosand (1986), Sadie (1986), Pendle (1991a), Jackson (1991), Ehrlich (1985).
[17] Neuls-Bates (1982), Bowers (1986), Rosand (1986), Newcomb (1986), Brown (1986), Jackson (1991), Austern (1989), (1994).
[18] Bowers (1986, pp. 141ff) dates this specific decree as 1563; also see Jackson (1991, p. 64, where the date is printed as 1553).
[19] Newcomb (1986, pp. 92, 95f), Pendle (1991a, pp. 39–44).

and admiration from different parties. In 1581 Duke Alfonso d'Este of Ferrara took the *concerto* to the court of Duke Guglielmo Gonzaga in Mantua. A witness wrote:

[Duke Alfonso,] having with great ceremony caused His Excellency [Duke Guglielmo] to hear the music of these ladies, was expecting to hear them praised to the skies. Speaking loudly enough to be heard both by the ladies and by the duchesses who were present [Duke Guglielmo] burst forth, 'Ladies are very impressive indeed – in fact, I would rather be an ass than a lady.' And with this he rose and made everyone else do so as well, thus putting an end to the singing. (Cited in Newcomb 1986, p. 92)

It is both despite and because of such antipathy in some quarters that the female singing group quickly became exceedingly popular in others. By 1600 every Italian court had one, and a woman could aim for a professional career as a singer, both in a vocal consort and as a soloist, commanding in some cases an extraordinarily high salary.[20] At the same time, women began to perform more widely on the operatic stage. Some of the women singers retained fairly respectable reputations, others did not. One of the most famous and notorious of them (who also achieved renown as a composer) performed in seventeenth-century Venice in a literary men's club with the backing of her father: Barbara Strozzi.[21] Like many women singers, she suffered public abuse and accusations of sexual licence. She may indeed have been a courtesan of some sort (Rosand 1986, p. 172); but what is telling is that, had she been a non-singing courtesan, of whom there must have been hundreds, she would presumably not have inspired a public debate about her 'virtue'. When music enters the mask of display, it complicates the meanings of the relationship.

From the sixteenth right through to the twentieth century, it is no exaggeration to say that singing has continued to represent by far the greatest musical performance opportunity available to women, in both the amateur, domestic sphere and the professional, public sphere. Although the history of the woman singer has continued to be marked by controversy, overall the heat of the debate has gradually diminished. Today in the classical fields of opera and song as well as choral music, the woman singer is an unremarkable phenomenon who is granted due recognition for her ability to manipulate and interpret the inherent meanings of the music she sings, and who is able to operate without any

[20] Bowers (1986, p. 123), Newcomb (1986, p. 101), Jackson (1991).
[21] See Rosand (1986); also Jackson (1991, pp. 51–4). See Ehrlich (1985) for notorious women singers in England at the time and later.

apparent restrictions or disapproval on grounds of her sex. However, it would be naive to view this situation as an unmitigated exception to the norms of patriarchy. It does not represent women's release from the mutually constructed power differential between women and men: rather, it re-enacts this differential symbolically in the delineations of the music.

Just as delineated meanings in the dominant discourse surrounding classical music have been denied in favour of raising supposedly autonomous inherent meanings to a transcendent and universal level over and above carnal and mortal life, so the discourse around classical music today involves a denial that bodily display is any part of the music's meaning at all. This situation has gone hand in hand with the development of a large cohort of women singers, who have carved out a position which occupies one of the furthest ends of the polar distinction that I drew earlier between different types of display. The inherent meanings of the music they sing, in accordance with the discourse surrounding the music, are at the forefront of their music's delineations. Any gendered delineations arising from their performance are hastily swept away in favour of their own and their music's commitment to inherent meanings. Classical music's delineated autonomy and its focus on inherent meaning mean that people are not supposed to go to classical concerts or operas in order to gaze at the body of the singer; indeed those listeners who subscribe to this classical discourse would probably deny it with a metaphorical wave of the hand if they found themselves gazing.

But even in cases where display might be unintended by the performer and unsought by the audience, and no matter how many screens and veils are placed in front of it, the display of the singing woman is inescapable. In the discourse of classical music, her display is at the least legitimated by a sheen of 'respectability' as in the adoption of 'dress codes'; it is very often highlighted by spotlights whilst the audience remains shrouded in darkness; and it can even go so far as to be risqué, particularly when an operatic character such as Carmen or Salomé provides a convenient justification. The symbolic resonance of the singing woman is inescapably gendered, and this gendered quality is affirmative of patriarchal definitions of femininity: femininity as embodied and alluring, in control of yet subject to the vicissitudes of the body, integral with nature, available and desirable yet preoccupied and maternal, unpredictable, contrary. It is precisely because singing reproduces 'femininity', I would suggest, that women singers have for so long been able to occupy so prominent a place in the cultural sphere. Allowing women to sing in the home, in the convent or in public has never been a simple latitude. On the contrary, singing symbolically articulates and reproduces some of the enduring definitions of femininity which legitimate the very need for controlling women's activities in the first place. In a nutshell, allowing women to sing proves 'femininity', and thus justifies the need to control them.

If women's freedom to sing cannot be taken to represent any thorough challenge to patriarchy, neither should it be denied some powers of resistance. As I have already indicated, display invokes a mutual power differential between the displayer and the onlooker. The displayer is not merely a passive object but can gain an element of active control which is invested in the power of the lure. The display of musical performance also affords a different kind of power, through the control and manipulation of the music itself. Abbate (1993) argues that the woman opera singer derives a certain authority, and slips into a 'male/active/subject' position (p. 254), through being aurally resonant: 'her musical speech drowns out everything in range, and we sit as passive objects, battered by that voice' (p. 254). The phenomenology of live performance makes it possible for a singer, more than any other musical performer, she argues, to 'wrest the composing voice away from the librettist and composer. . .' (p. 254). In its most excessive forms such a phenomenon can be metaphorically linked to the concept of display, as a 'display of virtuosity'.

The woman singer is also able to resist patriarchal constructions of femininity, and furthermore to articulate alternative constructions of femininity, in ways that are deeply plumbed by Wood's (1994) invocation of what she calls the 'Sapphonic voice'. This voice indicates more than 'overtones and resonances' of voice production and of the body, being rather a 'mode of articulation, a way of describing a space of lesbian possibility, for a range of erotic and emotional relationships among women who sing and women who listen' (p. 27). Wood pins the voice on particular nineteenth- and early twentieth-century opera singers who articulated this possibility in multiple symbolic and practical ways: through the challenge their voices represented to normal vocal characterisations such as soprano or contralto, female-sounding or male-sounding; through the character of their voices, which were 'powerful and problematic, defiant and defective' (p. 28); through the sexual ambiguity or the feminine strength portrayed by their most hailed operatic roles; through the shrouded and suggestive secrecy or the lesbianism and passion of their private lives.

I call this voice Sapphonic for its resonance in sonic space as lesbian difference and desire . . . Its refusal of categories and the transgressive risks it takes act seductively on a lesbian listener for whom the singer serves as messenger, her voice as vessel, of desire.

Castle (1993) also writes revealingly of lesbian desire articulated in relation to the mezzo-soprano diva; and Pope (1994) indicates through her interpretation of George Eliot's verse drama *Armgart* how Eliot celebrated both the real, economic power and the symbolic, musical power of the nineteenth-century diva. Equally fascinating recent writing by gay men reveals yet another area in which the woman singer wields power. In a mode of resistance and criticality towards the mainstream patriarchal discourse on opera, the gay response introduces the persona and voice of the diva in an act of 'worship' asserted against heterosexual or homophobic respectability.[22] This dual power of display – both bodily display and the display of vocal virtuosity – creates a symbolic fissure in the affirmation of patriarchal definitions of femininity that, even in supposedly autonomous classical music, are otherwise produced and reproduced through women's vocal performance.[23]

Women singing in jazz and popular music

Women's involvement with singing passes over into the realms of jazz, popular music and almost all other vocal forms that have developed in varying degrees of contradistinction to what has become known as classical music through the late nineteenth and the twentieth centuries. Here, on most levels, the delineations of display operate in much the same way as in classical music, and for the same reasons. Thus, with reference to the four areas that I outlined earlier, in a nutshell: first, the woman singer continues to appear masked and enclosed in her body; secondly, this helps to affirm her closeness to nature and her alienation from technology; thirdly, public singing calls into question her sexual life; fourthly, she is contrarily counterposed as an image of maternal perfection in the domestic setting. As in classical music, there are also some ways in which she escapes patriarchal definition.

One of these ways is discernible in the source of a vast proportion of

[22] See Koestenbaum (1994a), M. Morris (1993) for vivid examples of this. Also see Bradby (1993a), Mockus (1994) for accounts of different ways in which lesbians relate to the identity of pop performers.

[23] An engaging analysis is of attitudes that prevailed towards the singing woman at the turn of the century can be found in Raitt (1992), which shows how three portraits of women singers by John Singer Sargent convey messages about their sexuality within the terms of the era.

jazz and popular music, which lies in the conjunction of European and African musical styles wrought by the slaves of the southern USA. The anonymous 'voodoo queens' of New Orleans, some of whom amassed considerable influence and fortune, were probably the most important transmitters of slave music during the nineteenth century (Dahl 1984, pp. 6f). Their singing fed into the women's blues and tent show traditions and beyond, in the persons of – for example – Ma Rainey and Bessie Smith, later followed by Billie Holiday, Ella Fitzgerald and others. Black women also took an active role in domestic and church singing, eventually making gospel an area in which women have without question excelled.[24] The display-delineations of many of the women singers of this music seem to break out of patriarchal definitions of femininity's embodied yet threatening attractiveness. Contrasting with the affirmation of femininity enacted by women singers throughout history, the performance delineations of the blues women challenged the historically constructed submission of women to their bodies and to domesticity, highlighting instead their migrancy, their physical and their economic independence. The blues women mocked the virgin/whore dualism by standing altogether outside it: they were constructed as both sexually active *and* maternal, never counterposing sexual availability with the image of the perfect wife and mother; nor were they necessarily heterosexual.[25] Like their colleagues in classical music such as those located by Abbate, Wood and others mentioned above (pp. 35–6), they harnessed the power of the lure, of spectacularity, and the power of the voice to establish a control over their audience and to represent a position of feminine strength.

The moment of optimism which these singers helped to make possible was short-lived, as Southern Black people's visions of freedom and even integration faded into an urban nightmare. There are a host of complex political and economic reasons for this, among them reasons connected with a wider social framework of oppression that cuts across gender: race. In the blues woman's struggle for independence, dominant musical discourse finally forced her image to conform not only to patriarchal but also to hegemonic racial definitions: along with her display of strength came the inevitable corollary of atavism. The Black singer of both sexes has been eulogised as the essence of what makes humans human: close to nature, wounded, betrayed and abused, yet with a

---

[24] See Dahl (1984), Placksin (1985) for excellent standard histories of women in jazz.
[25] See Carby (1990), Antelyes (1994) for informative and critical appraisals of the social and musical significance and influence of Bessie Smith and other blues women.

'human spirit' that lifts above the carnal level, through which he or she issues forth a universal song. The Black woman in this role ends up in one of her most familiar symbolic positions, as Earth-Mother, goddess.[26]

There are some further significant differences between the way that display functions in classical singing and the way it functions in non-classical singing (with gradations, of course, between the two). One difference is articulated by women singers such as the performance artist Laurie Anderson, who make use of technology as part of the inherent meanings of their music (see McClary 1991). They threaten in some ways to break out of definitions of femininity, by challenging women's alienation from technology. This puts them in a similar position to instrumental performers, who will be discussed in the next chapter. On the other hand, women whose voices are altered or otherwise alienated from their bodies through technology wielded not by the women themselves but by producers are in a quite different position. I will return to this shortly. In general, the amplification or recording of the voice does not interfere with the appearance of naturalness and bodily containment of the singer.

Another more thoroughgoing difference between display in classical and in popular singing involves those aspects of the discourse on music that arise from the relationship between inherent and delineated meanings. In the discourse that surrounds classical music, inherent meanings are lionised as having overriding importance. Display is made to operate as an inadvertent by-product of performance, and display delineations, like all delineations, are minimised, ignored or even denied. This lack of acknowledgement of display is symptomatic of the discursive construction of autonomy that accompanies the mediation of classical music. The same thing actually occurs in those styles of relatively autonomous popular music which delineate a high level of commitment to inherent meanings, such as various types of progressive rock, and also in some jazz. Differences between classical and non-classical music begin to arise most clearly with those styles of popular music in which delineations are unashamedly at the forefront of the musical meanings. Just as many

---

[26] An example of how this discourse runs is provided by Wilfrid Mellers (1986), who, for all his love and admiration, or more likely because of it, could not help succumbing. The history of the relationship between race and popular music and jazz is very complicated, and I have had to put it outside the bounds of this study. For a discussion of race and gender with reference to Billie Holiday see Brackett (1995), pp. 40ff. For an exhilarating polemic on the political implications of constructions of race and music see Tagg (1989); for a different enquiry into the links in the social construction of race and gender in music, Treitler (1993); for scholarly examinations of African American music itself, its effects and its social contexts, Floyd (1995), Maultsby (1990), Jones (1963). White women also sang jazz, one of the earliest respected and most famous examples being Connee Boswell. See Ammer (1980), Dahl (1984), Hassinger (1987).

kinds of popular music have for a long time worn their delineations on their sleeves, just as much popular music performance practice tends to make a great deal of display and spectacularity, so many popular musicians intentionally capitalise on it, and the discourse on popular music readily testifies to its importance. Indeed, as I noted in Chapter 1, typically the discourse on popular music – as it is found in rock journalism in particular – addresses itself to everything but the inherent meanings of the music, the topics of the body and corporeality being very much in vogue at the present time. Here, the delineation of display is no mere off-shoot but frequently a central factor. With reference to women singing, the sorts of music that provide examples include that of girl groups and popular solo female vocalists.

In the discourse surrounding a particular style or a particular performance of music, when inherent meanings are of less prominent importance and delineations are more overt, then it is more commensurate for the singer to pay relatively more attention to displaying the body. Like all other musical and general cultural meanings (including, therefore, those circulating around classical music), attractiveness is not something owned by the singer. Rather it is built up around singers, through their engagement with other networks of meaning including fashion, and of course through the type of display which they enact. Attractiveness is to some extent discursively constructed, not possessed. The degree of attention paid to displaying the body can be understood in terms of the construction of 'attractiveness'. As such, 'attractiveness' becomes part of the delineated meanings of the music. What often occurs in the sort of situation where display is forefronted is that the mere fact of the delineated attractiveness of the female singer causes listeners to downplay her ability and commitment with respect to the execution of inherent meanings. The more she goes in for displaying her body, the less likely it is that she is a 'good' musician. Likewise, the overt forefronting of display leads listeners to assume that the inherent meanings of the music are of relatively little importance or value. Listeners then hear the inherent meanings in a way which is influenced by their understanding of the delineated display. I will now indicate some of the ways in which these assumptions are played out.

Dating back to the beginnings of commercial white popular music in the Victorian music hall and musical comedy, some women's massive fame was partly due to the fact that 'the commodity being marketed was as much female sexuality as musical talent' (Russell 1987, p. 8). Jazz and blues women singers too have only in rare cases, such as those famous

names I have cited above, been respected, like their classical counterparts, for their ability to manipulate inherent meanings. In most cases,
achieving respect for the control and interpretation of inherent meanings as a woman singer of any ethnic origin in jazz has been extremely
difficult, not only for general widespread and ill-defined chauvinist
reasons, but because of the display-delineations that accompany the fact
of a woman singer. In the main, even the more professionally successful
type of jazz women singers were most prominent as soloists (often called
'canaries'), dressed in party frocks, backed by male bands and receiving
low pay and even lower respect.[27] As an example of the sort of terms in
which they were understood:

Ask any ten bandleaders as to their pet headache . . . nine will answer 'girl vocalists' . . . Yes, girl vocalists are a nuisance. Too many of them are beautiful, and
can't sing. Those who have talent are usually gobbled up by the movies or
shrewd promoters who exploit them . . . [But] no matter what stand you take,
you can't deny that a beautiful girl in front of a mike looks pretty good to the
paying males. (*Swing* magazine, October 1938, cited in Dahl 1984, p. 124)

The mere familiarity of such talk, even despite or perhaps because of its
vitriol, is enough to support my argument: the more that sexual
attractiveness becomes part of the delineations, the less respect is paid to
the singer's ability to manipulate and understand inherent meanings.
The ability of the singer is judged, not in terms of her management or
interpretation of inherent meanings, but in terms of her delineated
display. Conversely, of course, the less 'attractive' the singer is deemed to
be, the more listeners can suppose that she is 'good'. Otherwise, why else
would she be standing there singing?

To be sure, it cannot always be the case that a woman is *unfairly* denigrated as a singer. Clearly there is relatively good and relatively bad
singing by both men and women. Listeners will make judgements about
this in terms of the music's style, in relation to their own knowledge of
performance practice within that style. But what happens when the
woman singer is judged to be musically incompetent, that is, unable to
manipulate inherent meanings, independently of any judgement that
she is indulging in overt sexual display? The signifying chain then simply
occurs in reverse, a process which is poignantly portrayed in a scene of
the film *Nashville* (Robert Altman, 1975). A rather weak and seriously
deluded young woman with dreams of being a country and western star
finally gets her chance to go on stage. But her singing is inadequate, and

---

[27] Dahl (1984, pp. 121, 122–3); also see Placksin (1985); and the discussion in Brackett (1995), pp. 40ff.

the jeers which soon begin to greet her make it apparent that her embarrassed and confused decision to change her act and take her clothes off instead was the right one from the audience's point of view. Not only do the display-delineations of women singers suggest that the singer is incompetent to the degree that her bodily display is forefronted; but the more incompetent she is taken to be, the more she must be forced to pay attention to displaying her body.

Girl vocal harmony groups have spanned the 1930s to the present, most notably the tradition that started in the 1950s with the Chantels, and led to the Ronnettes, the Supremes, the Three Degrees and beyond.[28] One response to the girls' implicit loss of respectability, on the part of record companies in the USA of the fifties and sixties, was to promote an appearance of super-respectability. The Chantels, for example, had tutors and a chaperone, whilst MoTown ran a complete 'charm school' for their girl groups (Grieg 1989, pp. 17, 121). But this is merely an affirmative response to the dualism of the madonna/whore: if the girl singer is not one of these, she must be the other. Moreover, the discourse surrounding girl groups furnishes particularly pertinent examples of my argument above: that overt display causes attacks to be made not only on the ability of the singer, but also on the inherent quality of the music itself. For example, Grieg (1989, p. 140) observes that the Three Degrees had a reputation for being one of the most 'sexy' girl groups in the seventies. This reputation was by the same token the cause of extensive ridicule by the (white, male) music press, including not only accusations that the women were incompetent as musicians, but also the rubbishing of the inherent meanings of their music. Delineations arising from the display of the singer actually enter into the listening experience and, most significantly, from there they affect our perception of and attitude towards inherent musical meaning. They thus colour our entire experience of the music as a whole. To put this in a nutshell, overt sexual delineations of display influence the way we hear the music's inherent meanings, causing us to dismiss or even recoil from them. A judgement that at first appears

[28] Grieg (1989) is an invaluable source which overturns many of the prejudices with which people approach girl groups, by showing them to be other than passive decorations called in by a male producer to realise his fantasies. Also see Betrock (1982) on girl groups. Gaar (1993), L. O'Brien (1994), Steward and Garratt (1984) also powerfully dispel any such illusions about women in rock. At the same time, all these writers illustrate again and again how the sexuality of women popular singers and other women popular musicians has been exploited by record companies, male instrumentalists, song-writers, producers and managers of groups. Other valuable sources focussing on the views of women popular performers themselves are K. O'Brien (1995), Evans (1994), Raphael (1995). For a critical analysis of constructions of masculinity and femininity around girl-group music see Bradby (1990).

to be about musical inherent meaning actually results from, and operates as a delineation around, the display of the singer.

In direct contradistinction to the discursive construction of autonomy, this is evidence of a type of musical fetishism which, as I suggested in Chapter 1, is a common characteristic that marks much of the discourse on popular music. In the discourse of musical autonomy, which tends to be posited around classical music, the unquestioned status of inherent meanings operates to deny the very existence of delineations. Thus, in the most highly autonomous music, the bodily display of the singer is supposedly dismissed from any judgement of the music (even though it may be covertly celebrated). But in the operation of fetishism, the music is judged according mainly to its delineations, and the inherent meanings are heard only as reflections of those delineations. Thus in highly fetishised music, the display delineations which the listener attributes to the singer actually become a major part of the listener's judgement on the music as a whole. The more sexually overt those delineations are, the less truck the listener will have with the inherent meanings of the music.

From the 1960s at various times a number of girl and women popular solo singers have risen to fame, and many more have had less auspicious careers. The association between female singers and loss of 'respectability' is still mythologised, as I was reminded by *The Guardian* (December 1993), which stated that disreputable entrants to the Miss World competition have periodically been ousted on the grounds of being film-actresses, the girlfriends of porn giants, or singers. Display-related delineation is very much part of musical meaning today in popular music of many sub-styles. Examples of how it operates can be found in countless well-known cases of singers who delineate a high level of 'attractiveness', and whose vocal abilities and music at the height of their record sales receive nothing but sneers from all but their millions of young girl fans – and even in the case of the more challenging Madonna, about whom there might not have been so many books and articles written if not for the fact that the sexual display of her music's delineations implicitly calls into question both her musicianship and the inherent quality of her music itself, a quality which is, typically, nearly always ignored by commentators.[29]

---

[29] See Bradby (1992) for an incisive critique of the way cultural theorists ignore the inherent meanings of Madonna's music or, in fact, ignore the music altogether, focussing on the visual accompaniment as if the music were entirely dispensable. Bradby shows how a close analysis of the lyrics in relation to the music can be very revealing in terms of an all-round understanding of the meaningful potential of the video. For a critique of academic writing on Madonna see esp. Kaplan (1993). For an appraisal of Madonna from the point of view of musicology see McClary (1991), and for a response to this (not from a musicological point of view) Born (1992).

As Bradby's analysis (1993b) shows, the continuing insinuation and reproduction of the affirmative feminine delineation of the singer is reproduced even in that relatively recent musical style which many have tried to claim transcends racial, cultural and class as well as gender differences: house. She describes a legal case over the sampling of a woman's voice, involving a producer group called Black Box who had a massive hit in Britain with the song 'Ride on Time'. 'The video that accompanied the song on television showed a tall, sexy model . . . Katherine . . . "performing" the passionate vocal line.' But the vocal itself had been sampled from a song by the American soul singer Loleatta Holloway.

People I spoke to at the time saw her as having been totally 'ripped off' by Black Box; and indignation centred around the cynicism of Black Box in 'fronting' her voice with the tall, slim, sexy model, Katherine, in the video, as if ashamed to show the 'real' singer's body (fatter, older looking, more 'maternal'). In effect, Loleatta Holloway had been doubly 'ripped off', since not only had her voice been stolen by others to make money, but her person had been usurped by Katherine Quinol's image. (Bradby 1993b, p. 170)

This exploitation was worsened by the music press, which printed excessive photos of Quinol, and an allegation by a producer that Holloway did not understand technology. (No doubt Quinol did not 'understand technology' either, but had no need to because she could concentrate on displaying her body instead!)

Despite the continuation of the age-old affirmation of femininity in this affair, Bradby also points to some new possibilities which she suggests it raises for women. Although the women's separate contributions were not credited on the sleeves of recordings, she came across a credit for a video clip shown on MTV which listed both the lead singer (a different one, Martha Walsh) and the 'body' (Quinol again). One aspect of this new practice that we should welcome, she argues, is that at least both women were credited for their separate contributions, which is better than having no credit at all. Furthermore, this dual crediting exposes the deception of juxtaposing the voice and the body of two women, questions the primacy of the visual, and acknowledges the interference of technology in the representation of women performers (pp. 171–2). Bradby also argues that although these videos betray the fact that the Black female body, 'as manifested in the "grain" of the voice, is still serving as a touchstone of authenticity' (p. 172), the voices of the older singers evoke strength, maturity and deep emotions, all qualities which can appear to empower the younger women who are miming.

Such images, she points out, by giving older women's strength to younger women's bodies, can in some ways challenge the divorce of motherhood and sexuality that marks white popular music.

There is another area which suggests that the original articulation of an alternative femininity that characterised the images of the women singers of the classic blues has not completely died out. Some of the associations and lyrics of dance music dating from the 1970s and 1980s, which are often sampled or re-issued today, can be interpreted as comparative implicit and explicit statements of feminine independence. Also girl rappers, or super-stars such as Tina Turner, in many ways present an image of outspoken femininity operating unhindered in the public sphere; whilst singer-songwriters such as Jane Siberry proffer challenges to patriarchal conceptions of heterosexual femininity.[30] The connotations of performances by such women can become a part of the delineations that accompany their music, joining with the power of the lure, and at best the power of the voice, to form channels that connect the symbolic power of women singers in classical music to that of women singers in blues, jazz and popular music today.

The gendered delineations of singing

It is not just women who become sexual objects as singers. The delineation of display operates with either sex playing either role, and also playing roles that counter biological sex, as I observed at the beginning of the chapter. Thus male singers can also become sexual objects. It is appropriate that commentators on gender and chroniclers of women in popular music do not obscure the huge number of 'boy groups' and male solo vocalists that have existed in gospel, jazz and popular music of all kinds. Many of the things that are said about the way girl groups and soloists have been disdained apply equally, if asymmetrically, to them. Nor, as with women's display, does this sort of thing only happen in popular music, although not insignificantly the example I am about to

---

[30] With regard to dance lyrics, for example, the female sexual assertiveness and pleasure expressed by the Pointer Sisters' (1989) 'Slow Hand' is comparable to the blues singer Ida Cox's 'One Hour Mama', cited by Carby (1990, pp. 247–8), or to the more aggressive sexuality of e.g. the rappers Oaktown 3 5 7's 'Juicy Gotcha Krazy' (cited in Berry 1994, p. 195). Song-lyrics are obviously out of my sphere of study: but I couldn't resist this small point. See Rose (1994) for a social analysis and a detailed discussion of rap and of women's position in it; or Berry (1994), for an informative shorter source on women in rap; Gaar (1993), K. O'Brien (1995) on Siberry, and for an analysis of one of her songs, 'Mimi On the Beach', D. Morris (1995). Also see Mockus (1994), Potter (1994) on k. d. lang. Amongst other things, the latter two briefly address the sound of lang's voice in ways that echo Elizabeth Wood's Sapphonics discussed earlier.

give is of a very popular sort of classical music: when the opera-singer Pavarotti performed to a quarter of a million in Hyde Park, London on the strength of his hit single of Puccini's 'Nessun dorma' during the World Cup in 1990, several female reporters writing in the tabloid press did their utmost to turn him into a sex teddy-bear. Male popular singers often have to contend with the general sexual overtones and, furthermore, the feminine ambience which, I have argued, surround the display of the singer. Some male singers seek ways to ride potential accusations of femininity. Many attempt to turn them to their advantage through harnessing the power of spectacularity on stage, whilst others respond by visibly asserting machismo in their publicised lives off stage: issues which are revealingly probed by Walser (1993) in his discussion of heavy metal musicians (not just singers). In Part II, I will return in more detail to the relationship between masculinity and singing, with reference to the very widespread labelling of singing as 'cissy' by girls and boys in schools today. For now, it is necessary only to observe that, to whatever extent they do have a problem, men have always taken up public singing roles at least as much as, and often more than, women.

In sum, singers cannot but help invoke some level of sexual display, which becomes a part of the delineated meaning of the music that they sing. But in the discourse surrounding highly autonomous classical music, such meaning is already denied, and the woman singer today working in that area is relatively free from definitions that accentuate her femininity rather than her musicianship. She can participate in the construction of the appearance of musical autonomy by being heard to be in control of the inherent meanings of the music she sings, whilst her gender can be almost forgotten. Nonetheless, the very fact that her role has been allowed through history to develop into the most common musical performance role occupied by women is bound up with the fact that the woman singer affirms and reproduces fundamental patriarchal definitions of femininity.

On the opposite pole, in highly fetishised kinds of popular music for example, delineation is not merely denied but often celebrated by the discourse on the music. In this sphere, it is commensurate for the woman singer to forefront the attention she pays to displaying her body, so that 'female sexual attractiveness' becomes a prominent part of the music's delineations. In such cases, the delineations of display can be so strong as to make it virtually impossible for listeners, especially those who are already critical of the music, to hear inherent meanings without being in some way negatively influenced by the delineations. Either the singer is

taken to be incompetent to handle inherent meanings, or the music itself
is regarded as inherently lacking in value, or both. The more sexually
'attractive' the woman singer is constructed to be, the less seriously she
and her music can be taken.

The woman singer who signifies a high degree of sexual attractiveness
categorically affirms and reproduces those same patriarchal definitions
of her femininity which the relatively subdued singer of 'autonomous'
music more covertly conjures up. Whatever the quality of her musicianship and ability to control inherent meanings, she is judged by her
display. Only in a few subtle ways such as I have indicated – in the spectacular power of the lure, the virtuoso display of the voice, and the
appeal of a femininity which is not re-harnessed into the safe, 'natural',
'domestic' recesses of patriarchal definitions – can women's voices be
heard to claim some unspeakable quality that suggests an alternative
femininity, a different way for women to be.

WOMEN ENABLING

In the closing section of this chapter I would like to explore another
nexus of musical practices in which women have taken part, which are
connected to the arguments I have made above in that, like singing, they
tend to affirm and reproduce patriarchal definitions of femininity. I have
classed them together as 'enabling roles', for convenience, but also to
indicate that they have in common the fact of enabling other people to
hear, to learn and to make music, including the passing down of music
from generation to generation. This is not to imply that men do not also
have enabling roles in musical production and reception. It is merely that
there is something in women's enabling roles that binds them together in
a way which is of relevance to the arguments in this chapter. As with
singing, I will argue that women's position in these roles enters through
various channels into musical meaning.

In the eighteenth and nineteenth centuries women ran the numerous
musical salons which provided venues both for amateurs and for
flamboyant virtuosi to perform popular, romantic works.[31] The distinct,
serious, classical concerts of the Academy in Britain, in which the
highest value was placed on what I have called inherent musical

---

[31] See Ehrlich (1985), Weber (1975) for social histories of musical production and reception practices
   in the eighteenth and nineteenth centuries. See Citron (1993, pp. 104ff), S. Fuller (1992), for social-
   historical discussions of women's roles in the salons and of women composers of 'salon music'.
   See Whitesitt (1991) on Women's Music Clubs in United States concert life.

meaning, were run by men. These concerts, in the oft-cited words of William Weber (1975, p. 126) imposed 'a lofty intellectual definition through which – thanks to the traditional conception that men were more serious than women – they excluded the other sex from leadership, even though women attended classical music concerts just as much as men'. Women are still relatively absent from professional and influential positions in the management of autonomous music. Not surprisingly, the areas in which they have made the most notable mark continue to be in the popular realm, where women band managers have existed since the 1960s, growing in number particularly fast after punk. There are also increasing numbers of women producers, sound-engineers and music journalists, and a growth of women-only record companies and distribution networks.[32]

During the sixteenth and seventeenth centuries in Italy and elsewhere, the main employers of musicians were the church, court, theatre, private house and town (Bowers 1986, p. 135). A few schools began to employ music teachers during the seventeenth century, and this became an increasing trend through the eighteenth century, but there were as yet no music colleges.[33] Bowers notes with respect to Italy that 'all institutions that hired musicians employed many more men than women musicians, and some employed no women at all' (1986, p. 135). It may come as a surprise then that by the late nineteenth century women outnumbered men as professional musicians: but this was because the vast majority of them were involved in private teaching, not performing (and even less composing). Altogether there were many more music teachers than performers, and of these, the vast majority were women.[34] Self-employed piano teachers were the largest category of musicians in England by 1900 (Ehrlich 1985, p. 70), and Ehrlich's meticulous account leaves us in little doubt that 'it is reasonable to assume that the great majority of female musicians enumerated in the census were wholly or primarily teachers, rather than performers, as classification up to 1861 and after 1911 indicates, and abundant other evidence confirms' (1985, p. 104). The growth

---

[32] For information on women in the contemporary classical recording industry see Jepsen (1991); also Zaimont et al. (1987, pp. 120–77), (1991, pp. 321–71). With reference to the popular sphere, Steward and Garratt (1984), Gaar (1993), L. O'Brien (1994). There have been and are women-run distribution and recording networks, including Olivia Records, Women's Independent Label Distribution Network (WILD) and Redwood Records in the United States (see Gaar 1993, Petersen 1987).

[33] See Ehrlich (1985) for the general context of music education in eighteenth- and nineteenth-century England; Rainbow (1989) for a thorough history of music education; Fletcher (1987) for some general information on the history of music education.

[34] See Ehrlich (1985, esp. pp. 52ff, 104–5), Ammer (1980).

of music teaching in the home and later in the school as 'one of the few respectable occupations open to women, outside domestic service' (Ehrlich 1985, p. 105) is still reflected in the fact that women have dominated music teaching in Britain, as in the USA and all other nations which provide systematic institutional and private music education, throughout the twentieth century.[35]

Women have also passed down music in professional roles other than strictly teaching. I have already mentioned the anonymous singers of New Orleans who were transmitters of slave music (Dahl 1984, p. 6) and who thus safeguarded the roots of what was to contribute to some of the vital elements in the popular music of the twentieth century. The tradition of singing from which many of the 1950s and 1960s girl groups drew their inspiration and skill was not always gospel learnt in the church or family, or popular song learnt on the streets, but often ancient Catholic settings of the psalms passed on by nuns (Grieg 1989, pp. 11, 75, 112). Thus a link is forged over the centuries, right back to the establishment of the Church, cutting across chasms not only of time but of musical styles as well, in which women have passed on music through singing to girls.

Similarly the mother, whose role in music education has been considerable,[36] can fulfil her maternal musical duties in ways that affirm patriarchal definitions of femininity. The passing on of music through maternal lines occurs poignantly in the already-mentioned universally blessed practice of the mother singing to her baby. The strength and beauty of this womanly custom strike me when I remember my own maternal grandmother singing a lovely hymn-like wordless lullaby to me when I was a child, the same song my mother always chose and to whom her mother must therefore have sung it; which I sang to my children and which, when my daughter's other grandmother was dying, was the song the little girl spontaneously chose with which to wish her farewell. It is not because of mere whim that I have reverted to personal anecdote in order to illustrate this practice: its history is of course, unwritten. Not

---

[35] The younger and less specialised the pupils, the more women have tended to dominate; and they have entered music teaching posts at higher education level only relatively recently. For example the first ever female professor of music in Britain was appointed in 1994 (Nicola LeFanu at the University of York). For information on women's music teaching positions in the United States see Weaver (1994); also Ammer (1980); for further information on various countries see Zaimont et al. (1984), (1987), (1991).

[36] On the role of the mother in classical music education and informal musical perpetuation, see Citron (1993), Polk (1991). Regarding popular music, see Sara Cohen (1991, Chapter 8), who observes that mothers in 1980s Liverpool were (still) the main organisers and passers-on of music in working-class families. (Their sons then later joined bands that excluded girls, as will be seen in Chapters 3 and 7.)

only is a musical tradition of lullabies and children's songs passed down orally by the women of the family, but it is also women who pass down tunes in all kinds of folk music and in many forms that have entered into the popular sphere.[37] This kind of cultural perpetuation, ironically perhaps, contains unspeakable characteristics that are reminiscent of what is most deeply associated with a dubious notion of authenticity, the very condition which male-dominated rock music has striven to achieve. Femininity and musical authenticity are both, as always, the more desirable for being elusive.

I wish to suggest that women's prominence in the musical salons of the nineteenth century, their roles as amateur and professional concert organisers and musical administrators in the twentieth century, and their positions as formal and informal music teachers, in convent, school and home, have acted, like singing, to reproduce femininity. This reproduction has occurred as, within the concept of patriarchy outlined in Chapter 1, women have taken up position as home-keepers, carers of children and custodians of cultural tradition. In this role the woman of the salon, the female music administrator, the music teacher and the mother can fulfil all the marks of femininity assigned to their sex, engaging in musical performance only where it has appropriately 'feminine' delineations, and the problem of sexual display in a performance that anyway takes place in only domestic and educational settings need trouble no one. In a similar way to singing, the roles of teaching and passing on certain kinds of music involve the entrance of the woman, the entrance of the fact of femininity, into the music's delineations. The fine quality of a mother's rendition of a lullaby, of a teacher's demonstration of a song to a class of children or of a group of women singing together privately is not liable to be noticed in inherently musical terms: not least because there is no audience, or if there is one, it is made up of children who have no channels of power through which to articulate their responses; but also because even if adult observers are present, the performance situation and the fact of femininity in the delineations of the music distract attention away from the singer's ability to control the inherent meanings and also from the cultural value of the music itself. In such situations, many fine women musicians throughout the centuries

---

[37] In many communities of the world, women also commonly sing at births, funerals and weddings. See Post (1994, pp. 39–40), Tolbert (1994) and many contributions to the ethnomusicological literature, Chapter 1, note 8, p. 13 above. The celebration of the domestic caring work and the link of women to life and death are also thematic of definitions of femininity in patriarchy, as discussed in Chapter 1, p. 14.

have plied their skills to an audience very limited in size, very young or very indifferent. An example that springs to mind is the mother of the internationally renowned reggae musician Bob Marley, whom I saw on television demonstrating how he used to sing when he was a boy. The astonishing example of her talent flashed across the screen for a moment and disappeared without comment.[38]

SUMMARY

In this chapter I have argued that the relative success of women singers throughout history represents no simple freedom, but, rather, reveals the proximity of singing to patriarchal definitions of femininity. I have attempted to identify some of the gendered connotations of singing, and to link them with an on-going development of a theory of gendered musical meaning. The bodily display of the singer, I have suggested, becomes part of delineated musical meaning, and from that position acts to affect the way listeners actually experience inherent musical meaning. The precise effects of this vary, depending on the historical era, the performance situation, the subject-position of the listener and, crucially, the style of the music involved. At one extreme, the delineated autonomy of much classical music has allowed the contemporary woman classical singer a position relatively free of gendered delineations, in which she has developed a high degree of recognition for her musicianship. At the other extreme, certain types of fetishised popular music have placed the display of the woman singer's body at the top of the delineated agenda, damaging the capacity of listeners to judge the skill of the singer, or to judge the inherent meanings of the music, independently of any idea of femininity. In the passing down of certain kinds of music by women

---

[38] 'Bob Marley and the Wailers', *Arena*, BBC2, 15 June 1986. I do not intend to idealise the relationship between Marley and his mother, but am merely describing what I saw on the programme. Marriage and child-rearing are themes which run throughout the musical history of women. There are a considerable number of cases in many countries from at least the sixteenth century onwards throughout the classical tradition, and from the beginnings of jazz and popular music, of women who gave up or appear to have given up their musical activities upon marriage. See Bowers and Tick (1986), Hand (1983), Ammer (1980), Pendle (1991), Ehrlich (1985), Grieg (1989), Dahl (1984), Steward and Garratt (1984), Gaar (1993) and many more. Interviewees in many sources (see e.g. Bayton (1990), Grieg (1989)) come back again and again to the stress invoked by trying to have children and hold a marriage together whilst being an amateur or a professional musician. Obviously one never comes across men complaining about this. Many women musicians throughout history have succeeded in music apparently with the backing of their husbands, or, especially in the case of girls in popular music, brothers or boyfriends (as well as mothers and sisters). See Polk (1991), Bayton (1990), Steward and Garratt (1984), S. Cohen (1991).

from generation to generation, a similarly affirmative relationship between femininity and song has again enabled the woman's abundant fulfilment of that role. The gendered musical meanings that surround women's vocal performance and women's roles as music teachers are not merely wrong. They are discursive constructions which help us to interpret the musical world around us, and they are actively created and re-created not only by listeners and commentators but by male and female musicians and music teachers, in our musical practices and through our musical experiences.

CHAPTER 3

From affirmation to interruption: women playing instruments

DISPLAY AS PART OF INSTRUMENTAL PERFORMANCE

The woman instrumentalist is on display, and she does to that extent participate in the same discourse as the woman singer. But in certain respects, her display takes on rather different connotations. The differences vary in degree according to the performance context, the instrument played, the subject-position of the listener and a variety of other factors. For example, in an early nineteenth-century domestic setting, from the perspective of most observers, a woman pianist would have given rise to display-delineations that were to all intents and purposes just as affirmative as those of a woman singer; whereas on a public stage of the same era, a female trumpeter sitting in the ranks of an otherwise entirely male orchestra would have incurred radically different display-delineations, and in fact was quite unheard of. Why is it that – like singing – some instruments have for centuries been welcomed by women, and have been seen as acceptable or even desirable feminine accomplishments, whereas – unlike singing – certain other instruments have at various times been shunned by women, frowned upon or even prohibited?

I will approach this question through suggesting some fundamental, qualitative differences between the kinds of display delineations that arise from women's singing practices and those that arise from women's instrumental practices. To begin with I will present the discussion through a comparison of extremes: between highly affirmative singing practices on one hand and prohibitive or very unusual instrumental practices on the other. Later I will go on to consider my arguments in the light of concrete historical examples, including instruments that have been common as well as those that have been unusual for women.

The extreme, qualitative differences between the display delineations of the woman singer and those of the woman instrumentalist can initially be broached through taking the four aspects of display that I located with regard to singing in the previous chapter, and comparing them. First, I suggested that because the musical sound-source of the woman singer is her body itself, her vocal display appears to remain locked within a self-referring cycle from body to femininity and back again. The body is affirmed and celebrated. Contrastingly, the female instrumentalist, although her body is nonetheless either intentionally or unintentionally on display mediates the whole scenario through a piece of technology. The instrument which she wields or controls interrupts the centrality of the appearance of her in-tuneness with her body. This interruption also challenges my second category, the natural appearance of the woman, away from any associations with technology. Just as patriarchally defined woman is in tune with her body, so she is in tune with nature. Man, on the other hand, is defined as out of touch with his body and divorced from nature. Indeed nature is seen as a force which man controls, and the development of that control takes place partly through the harnessing of nature in technology. The necessity to control an instrument on the part of the woman player detracts from the affirmation of the association between woman and nature, for the woman player is clearly capable of at least attempting to control an alienated man-made object. No longer a mere part of the nature that man controls, she steps out, into the world, into the position of controller.

The instrument also has an effect on my third category, that of sexual licence. As I noted in Chapter 2, the fully intentional displayer such as a striptease artiste does not sing and is even less likely to play an instrument. The interruptive power of the instrument seriously detracts from the fullness of the intention to display. This in turn then detracts from the cogency of the accusation of sexual licence, making the sex-life of the woman instrumentalist less suspect, and her display less susceptible to interpretation as a sexual invitation, than that of the singer. Therefore my fourth argument must also be coloured by the case of the instrumentalist. I suggested that the image of the singing woman can represent the corollary of sexual invitation, becoming an idealisation of maternal perfection. But if the woman instrumentalist cannot be seen as 'whore', then neither can she be seen through a *trompe l'œil* as at one moment the whore, the other the madonna: she is neither.

In sum, women instrumentalists can engender display delineations qualitatively different from those that arise from women singers. They tend to be less 'feminine' than women singers in that they appear less locked into the vicissitudes of their bodies, less alienated from technology, less sexually available, and less the personification of the contrary image of the madonna/whore. The erosion of these four categories in the act of instrumental performance by women threatens a disintegration of some of the fundamental characteristics of femininity as it is constructed and negotiated by men and women within the overall context of patriarchy. Unlike the singer, whose performance activities tend to affirm and even accentuate femininity, the woman instrumentalist can systematically call into question and interrupt those very reassuring signs of masked female sexuality upon which patriarchal definitions rely for their cogency. She is not then so much that object of desire which is both loved and feared as a slight irritation. The display she enacts, rather than that of a playful or alluring singing bird, is that of a more controlled and rational being who appears capable of using technology to take control over a situation. Whereas the display of singing reproduces femininity by locking the woman singer in an affirmation of the contrary definition of femininity as susceptible, natural, desirable and dangerous, women's instrumental performance threatens to break out of patriarchal definitions and offer a femininity which controls, a femininity which alienates itself in an object and impinges on the world.

As with the singer, the display of the female instrumental performer becomes a part of the delineations of the music which she performs. Performance-related gender delineation in fact arises whether it is a man or a woman performer. But the delineation operates differently when it is a male instrumentalist. Those very qualities of instrumental performance which for the female player are interruptive of her femininity are for the male player relatively affirmative of his masculinity. For male instrumentalists throughout history, the delineation of gender has been nearly always metaphorically transparent: it is there, but we do not see it, we see through it. If there were an equivalent word for the sense of hearing, it could be 'un-sounding'; implying that the delineation of gender is there, but that we do not hear it, we hear through it. There are exceptions to this. One example occurs when men or boys play in environments predominantly associated with females, such as many nineteenth-century salons or many twentieth-century school concerts.[1] Then, the normal masculine delineation is threatened by the overwhelming femininity of the performance context. This context combines with that element of display which is always latent in performance, and together these factors can proffer a suggestion that the male per-

---

[1] On the salon and on Women's Music Clubs again see Citron (1993), S. Fuller (1992), Whitesitt (1991), Weber (1975), Ehrlich (1985). On the school, see Part II below.

former is feminine or effeminate. Secondly, male performers may choose to disrupt the taken-for-grantedness of their masculinity, by sporting overtly 'feminine', sexual aspects of display, such as make-up, high-heeled shoes or revealing costumes, as part of their stage-show and marketing strategy. Today the delineations of glam rock, some heavy metal and certain mainstream popular music are often bound up with the sexual display of the male performers.[2] But unless they are in a female environment, or unless they have consciously chosen to display signs of femininity, the gender of the male instrumentalist and its incorporation into delineation normally remain unquestioned and invisible within the heterosexual hegemony of patriarchy. It is counted as the norm, which means not counted, not apparently delineated at all. I will refer to it as the masculine performance delineation.

For women instrumentalists, such invisibility is not so easy. The interruptive potential of femininity arising from women's instrumental performance makes the femininity of the woman player into a noticeable part of the music's delineations. In becoming noticeable, the feminine delineation unveils the normally transparent, taken-for-granted masculine performance delineation. As this masculine delineation begins to be apparent, it acts as a filter, or as a measure against which we perceive and judge the new delineation of femininity. At a remove from the listening experience itself, this delineation of femininity occurs for example in contemporary discourse, as part and parcel of marketing strategies, in which the sexuality of the woman player is more or less accentuated. But gender is not merely an extra-musical association. It goes further than that, entering into delineation during the listening experience itself; and from this position, it acts without our conscious intention, to influence the ways in which we also hear and judge inherent meanings.

For example, the following comment was made in the context of a recent school concert, during a conversation which confirmed how rare it is to see a girl playing the drums:

There was this young girl on stage, and this enormous drum kit. I couldn't believe that she was going to play it: but she walked across the stage and sat down behind it, and she did play it – and she played it well too!

Behind the speaker's words is an indication that the idea of the girl's femininity, as well as other qualities such as her youthfulness and small size perhaps, had fleetingly become a part of the music's delineations.

---

[2] See esp. Walser (1993) on this, with reference to heavy metal.

But not only that: for beyond the level of delineation, when he listened to the music, he was 'listening out' to discover whether she could play well – that is, whether she could satisfactorily control or interpret the inherent meanings. Not only for this listener, but for all of us to some extent, I would suggest, the gender of the female instrumental performer, amongst other factors, enters into delineated musical meaning as an interruption to patriarchal definitions of femininity; and from there, it acts to affect our perception of inherent meanings.

Women's instrumental performance is therefore potentially inter-ruptive in two ways: it can interrupt our common-sense patriarchal constructions of femininity through asserting new, abrasive display delineations; and it can interrupt our perception of musical inherent meanings by inserting these delineations into the filter of masculinity through which we normally listen. The presence of the delineations will affect our perception of inherent meanings, in such a way as to give the appearance that we countenance femininity, not merely in the knowl-edge that it is a woman playing, or the sight of a woman playing – that is, not merely in the music's delineations, but in the sound: in the inherent meanings, or in what we take to be the 'music itself'.[3]

For reasons indicated at the beginning of the chapter, the argument that women's instrumental performance is interruptive to patriarchal definitions of femininity must always be contextualised. The level of interruption varies at different times in history, as well as according to different performance practices, instruments, musical styles and, of course, the subject-position of the listener. Most importantly, instru-mental performance has never been so interruptive as to prevent women from playing instruments altogether: on the contrary, if it was, we could not explain how women have become instrumentalists at all, let alone how some of them have achieved widespread recognition. In some cir-cumstances the delineations arising from women's instrumental per-formance have been less interruptive than in others, and have even become relatively affirmative. In other contexts, the delineations have

---

[3] Like singing, the display-related delineations of instrumental performance survive beyond the live setting. But by contrast with singing, it is impossible to tell whether an instrumentalist is male or female without being told or being able to see them. But we will discover that this impossibility is no deterrent for the construction of a plethora of arguments that women play instruments in inherently different ways to men. As with all discourses, there is a trace of 'truth' in this. It cannot be only listeners and critics who take on and reproduce delineated meanings; musicians them-selves are no more able to escape them than anyone else. Therefore musicians can reproduce gen-dered delineated meanings in the ways that they approach and control inherent meanings. This is something that I wish to take up in Chapter 5 and in Part II.

been interruptive enough to operate as serious deterrents and even taboos. So as to explore different ways in which feminine performance delineations can be articulated, and in order to give a background to our present-day situation, it is again helpful to invoke some historical examples.

During any examination of the history of women's instrumental performance practice it must be borne in mind that any restrictions experienced by women can never have involved only one-dimensional assertions of authority by men over a protesting female mob. On the contrary, there has been collusion as well as resistance on the part of both men and women. In musical patriarchy, collusion involves women's consent to the terms of the restrictions placed upon their musical practices. Such consent surfaces in subtle and often unnoticeable ways, through willingness to conform, through reluctance to deviate, through embarrassment and, extremely, fear. As regards resistance, certain women throughout history have refused restrictions on their performance activities by breaking strictures and playing taboo instruments in public places. Often such resistance has been the harbinger of major social changes in women's instrumental practices. But often, as is characteristic of patriarchy, these same practices have also to some extent assimilated and perpetuated certain qualities drawn from women's roles in domestic music-making. Collusion and resistance are never clearly distinct, the one containing elements of the other to some extent.

THE SOLO INSTRUMENTALIST IN CLASSICAL MUSIC

In ancient civilisation women amateur and professional musicians played all kinds of instruments including plucked strings, woodwind and percussion.[4] However, as with singing, this relatively unrestricted freedom closed in during the centuries following the birth of Christ, when the number of professional women musicians, the opportunities for women instrumentalists to perform, and the array of instruments available to women gradually shrank. This process gained momentum during the Middle Ages, coming to a head in the fourteenth century.[5]

---

[4] See Meyers (1993), Teeter (1993), Touliatos (1993), Gergis (1993), Michelini (1991).
[5] There is evidence of professional women musicians in fourteenth-century France and Italy. A Paris record of 1321 includes the names of eight women in the register of the guild of minstrels (Coldwell 1986, p. 46, Edwards 1991, p. 17), and there are other documents showing payments to women musicians (Yardley 1986, Coldwell 1986, Brown 1986, Newcomb 1986, Edwards 1991). But in general, professional women musicians were in decline.

Part of the reason for this was undoubtedly, as Newcomb (1986) and
Edwards (1991) make clear, the increasing technical demands which
accompanied the advent of polyphony. Whilst the most prominent
effects of these demands were on composition, which I will discuss in
Chapter 4, the intertwining of composition with performance in those
days meant that performance practice was concomitantly affected.
Amateur men and all women except for the most privileged nuns were
unable to keep up with musical developments, as they did not have
access to the training which increasingly became a prerequisite for this
more complex procedure. This training took place in the cathedral
school, church or university, institutions from all of which women and
girls were banned. It was also available through the court, where women
were not paid as musicians for another two hundred years, and even
then, as the previous chapter showed, they were paid mainly as singers.[6]

Just as the voice represents the least interruption to patriarchal
constructions of femininity, so the biggest, loudest and most technologically advanced instruments represent the greatest interruption; and the
history of women's roles in musical patriarchy reveals the fact that
unwieldiness, high volume or technological complexity tend to
characterise those very instruments from which women were originally
and have been most vehemently discouraged or banned.[7] For example,
by the fifteenth century debate about whether women and girls should
play instruments at all was keen (Newcomb 1986). A social commentator
whose views are taken as a classic statement of the times summarised his
position thus:

And, to repeat in part and with few words what has been said thus far, I want this
lady to know something of letters, of music, of the visual arts, and to know how
to dance and be festive. (Castiglione, *Il cortegiano*, Book 3, Chap. 9, translated by
and cited in Newcomb 1986, p. 101)

However her involvement with music was to be limited, as elsewhere in
the same text he writes:

[6] The Venetian *ospedali* of the sixteenth to the eighteenth centuries (see Baldauf-Berdes 1993, and
pp. 55–6 below for further discussion), were the first exception to the rule that girls did not receive
institutionalised music education. Both the church and the university, and by the mid nineteenth
century also the military (Ehrlich 1985, pp. 96f) had musical training institutions which were
solely the province of boys or men. Apart from convents and the *ospedali*, only private or family
instruction was available to girls and women until schools began to incorporate music during the
nineteenth century. Schools for 'young ladies' began to include singing and piano lessons, but
boys' schools at first did not follow suit: music was frowned on for wealthy boys, who were discouraged from it, especially, as Ehrlich drily points out, if they were good at it (1985, p. 71).

[7] In 'unwieldiness' I include the distortion of the face, as in woodwind or brass, and 'ungainly' or
sexually suggestive posture, such as the cello. Neuls-Bates (1982, p. xiii) notes this.

Imagine yourself what an unsightly matter it were to see a woman play upon a tabour or drum, or blow in a flute or trumpet, or any like instrument; and this is because the boisterousness of them doth both cover and take away that sweet mildness which setteth so forth every deed that a woman doeth. (Castiglione 1928, p. 194, cited in Dahl 1984, p. 39)

There is one particularly obvious exception to my suggestion concerning the size, complexity and loudness of instruments: this is the case of keyboards. These instruments, which have always been played abundantly by women, are indeed usually large, technologically complex and in some cases loud. But, as is characteristic of musical patriarchy, women's access to them was initially restricted to the private sphere of the home, and later, the religious sphere of the church.[8] Furthermore, keyboard instruments are played in a demure, which is to say 'feminine', seated position. They have commonly been used by women, in order to accompany that prime, affirmative musical practice in which women have always engaged: singing. For that reason, and also because they are capable of providing autonomous renditions of any music from two-part inventions to symphonic arrangements, keyboards have been indispensable aids to entertainment in the home; and their capacity to provide melody, harmony or counterpoint with the greatest of readiness has made them invaluable resources for the tuition of children. As I argued in Chapter 2, involvement in all these practices – that is, singing, domestic musical entertainment and children's music education – has not only been common for women, but is also on a symbolic level affirmative of femininity. Another main category of instruments for women is that of plucked strings, which are of course usually small and relatively quiet, and which can also be played demurely. As with keyboards, women have played these instruments largely in domestic settings to accompany the voice. These affirmative practices on keyboard and plucked string instruments date back to the dawn of history, survive through the Middle Ages and the Renaissance, and play a major part in the image of the accomplished young lady in the eighteenth and nineteenth centuries. Incidentally keyboards and plucked strings continue to be women's

---

[8] I have already argued that occupation of the private sphere by women musicians is a defining characteristic of musical patriarchy (Chapter 1). For interesting discussions of women's roles as keyboard players see Loesser (1954), Leppert (1987). As regards the church, it has a symbolic position outside the public/private dichotomy, allowing women a performance space whose appeal to spirituality escapes some of the contradictions otherwise associated with women's practices outside domesticity. See Post (1994, p. 43), who notes that more work on the position of the church in this dichotomy is needed. Also, as Philip Tagg pointed out to me, church organists are usually screened off, which therefore reduces the display element.

prime instrumental outlet, even to the popular music of the 1960s and beyond.

In Europe from the sixteenth century, and in America from the late eighteenth and into the nineteenth centuries, amateur women instrumentalists became increasingly common (although they remained far fewer in number than singers), continuing to play keyboards and plucked strings mainly to instruct, entertain and accompany singing in the home. Gradually, these amateur, domestic musical roles were carried over into the professional, public realm, a transition which is characteristic of women's roles within patriarchy generally. I will discuss women orchestral players in the next section; for now, my discussion will focus on public-sphere, professional soloists. A few individuals became known as professional solo instrumentalists, especially as pianists during the late eighteenth century, and by the mid-nineteenth century some such women were able to command the highest respect. Clara Schumann (1819–96), perhaps the first woman to be accorded credit in contemporary musical discourse, was the acknowledged peer of the top male performers of the day. She premiered works by Chopin, Schumann and Brahms, and brought many of Beethoven's sonatas to public attention for the first time. She was the first concert pianist to play from memory and without supporting artists, her standards and programming acting to change the character of the solo piano recital (Reich 1986, 1989). Women soloists on other instruments, most notably the violin, appeared towards the end of the century, when conservatories including the Royal College of Music in London and the Boston Conservatory of Music began to encourage them.[9] How can such public-sphere successes be

[9] See Ehrlich (1985), Bernstein (1986), Tick (1986) on conservatoires in London and Boston respectively. Also see Eaklor (1994) on the development of music education in Boston's public schools, 1838–1911. The Royal Academy of Music (RAM) in London was established in 1822 and straight away took an equal number of men and women, becoming a haven for women performers (Bernstein 1986, Ehrlich 1985). But it was considered deficient compared to the Paris or Leipzig conservatoires (Ehrlich 1985, p. 83). By the 1880s and until at least the 1930s, very few professional musicians had attended the RAM. Over 90 per cent of professional musicians had learnt their craft through apprenticeship, family connections, private tuition or self-tuition (Ehrlich 1985, p. 99). So women were being allowed into the conservatoires, but the conservatoires were not leading to inclusion in the profession. The Royal College of Music (RCM) was established in 1882 and had standards that were consistently recognised as better. The women students were still by far mainly pianists and singers, but the RCM women violinists began to make their mark slowly (Ehrlich 1985, pp. 112, 157f), as did women string players at Julius Eichberg's school in Boston (also see Ammer 1980). After 1870 music colleges grew in number, and gradually began to affect supply, especially through their external elementary exams. By 1890 in Britain, Associated Board of the Royal Schools of Music (ABRSM) candidates comprised 80 per cent elementary pianists, and 90 per cent girls. Most students at the conservatoires were women, and most became teachers (Ehrlich 1985, pp. 119ff).

explained, within the terms suggested by my identification of the inter-ruptive delineation of femininity in instrumental performance?

It is necessary to acknowledge the overall context of a wider political situation that embraced upper- and middle-class women's resistance to their incarceration in the home, and expressed itself in many fields, of which music was only one. Clearly, as a few women became increasingly successful in openly resisting restrictions on their performance practices, the sight and sound of a professional woman instrumental soloist became more common, by dint of sheer force. The interruptive poten-tial of femininity in the act of performance must gradually lose its potency as the listener becomes more accustomed to the delineation. Listeners are more able to listen attentively to inherent meanings the less distracted they are by interruptive delineations. The force of normality which gradually became invested in the increasingly common instance of a woman player was therefore both a cause and an effect of its own growing acceptability. Secondly, as with singing, the level of autonomy which the music delineates, operates to diminish and mollify the degree of attention paid to bodily display by the discourse surrounding the music. The more that the inherent meanings of the music are held to be autonomous essences, and the more committed to inherent meaning the woman instrumentalist is heard to be, the easier it is for the discourse on the music to dismiss any gender delineation out of hand. It is no coin-cidence that Clara Schumann was one of the most serious performers of the most autonomous music of her day.

In sum, I would suggest that the increasing normality of the delinea-tions arising from the woman soloist, combined with her commitment to the autonomy of the inherent meanings of the music she played, provide two related reasons why those women who achieved excellence on their instruments to the level required of a professional classical soloist were tolerated, and why extraordinary women like Clara Schumann were not merely tolerated but celebrated at the pinnacle of their profession. But this does not mean to say that such women can be understood as free from the effects of interruptive feminine delineations arising from their performance. On the contrary, they had to rise above these delineations, to disprove them, to present an alternative to them, to achieve the highest level of what was agreed to be excellence, before they could be deemed even eligible to be judged on the same platform as their male counter-parts: to be judged as 'musicians' rather than 'women musicians'.

Classical music that is mediated as highly autonomous has always existed in conjunction with less autonomous, more popular sub-styles. In the nineteenth century such relatively popular music was performed largely in the female-controlled, essentially private realm of the salon. Among male instrumentalists it involved flamboyant virtuosi such as Franz Lizst; and among women it included a number of very successful professional performers such as Cécile Chaminade.[10] The role of such performers in the delineation of femininity is, I would like to suggest, slightly different from that of their colleagues in highly autonomous music. The performance of relatively popular music in the domestic realm carries certain delineations which make possible a retrieval of some of the patriarchal constructions of femininity that mark the affirmative connotations of women's singing. Where the music lacked any claims to high autonomy, this meant that feminine delineations could more readily enter into the listening experience. But the interruptive aspects of these delineations could be diluted to some extent by various factors. For one thing, where the music was virtuosic, this enabled an enactment of a musical display, the connotations of which are not far removed from the affirmation of femininity which, I have argued, is contained in the very notion of display itself. For another thing, the hiving off of the performing scenario into the private realms of the salon, often containing an entirely female audience, legitimated the display by taking the sting of sexual availability out of it. In place of that was a connotation of feminine 'innocence', based on the assumption of female heterosexuality, which further bolsters up the ramparts of patriarchy. Popular women instrumental soloists, I suggest, were thus increasingly able to enact something closer to an affirmation of femininity than were their colleagues in the more public, male-dominated circuits of autonomous music.

In the first three-quarters of the twentieth century a great deal of classical music has continued to delineate a high level of autonomy. This autonomy has preserved a space in which women solo instrumentalists have been able to pursue musical careers without being repeatedly judged according to interruptive delineations of patriarchally defined femininity. Amongst pianists for example, performers such as Wanda Landowska, Myra Hess and Annie Fischer have followed Clara Schumann in the pursuit of highly committed and greatly respected careers. However, as the production world of classical music has increas-

---

[10] Although salons often involved large numbers of audience members of both sexes, their connotations included notions of domesticity, social 'connections' and privacy. On salons see Citron (1993), S. Fuller (1992), Whitesitt (1991), Weber (1975), Ehrlich (1985); on Chaminade, Citron (1993); on Lizst and effeminacy, Walser (1993).

ingly found itself to be in a commercial, competitive market, so it has been forced to develop marketing strategies, which of course by implication reduce the music's appearance of autonomy. This erosion of autonomy is partly decipherable in the display-delineations of many contemporary solo women players, where delineated femininity is more forefronted. For example, there is currently one relatively mild type of display which I have seen in a large number of photographs on recordings, posters or advertising fliers. The woman classical soloist has her back turned to the camera and is often wearing a low-cut back neckline. In this pose she can present a modest sexuality, not the cleavage but the spine, the one bringing to mind the other; whilst at the same time, having her back turned, she is apparently (and tantalisingly), besides having her photo taken, 'doing something else' which stands for 'playing her instrument'. This pose therefore to some extent retrieves an affirmation of her femininity, and allows her instrumental activities to be blessed; whilst inversely the amount of autonomy of her music that is salvaged contradictorily assures us of the lack of display-delineations. Desire is flattered, and delineation is at least reduced.

Recently a few women classical instrumentalists have begun to market their display-delineations in a more overt way. The cover of one of Ofra Harnoy's recordings of the Vivaldi cello concertos elicited criticism when it came out. Harnoy is pictured languishing in an exquisite ball gown with one hand resting on her hip, and the other on the cello, which lies against her body.[11] As she said on television (I am paraphrasing), 'If a man was pictured with his arm slung over his cello, no one would say anything about it.' But Harnoy cannot be free of the appearance that she or her record company were at least implicated in a marketing strategy designed to sell records. The process is no different from the management of delineations by Madonna, and it has similar effects on the musical meaning. The fact that it is even possible for a classical instrumentalist (and Harnoy is by no means the only one) to be marketed in such a way is symptomatic of wider cultural changes in the economic and cultural position of classical music. Just as contemporary musical reception practices are part and parcel of a certain breaking down of boundaries between the discourses surrounding classical and popular

---

[11] The record is the Vivaldi Cello Concertos, Vol. 2, with the Toronto Chamber Orchestra, conducted by Paul Robinson (RCA Victor/BMG Music, 1989, RD 60155). I came across information about reaction to the cover, as well as some interviews with Harnoy, in a television programme broadcast in London, c. 1990–1. I apologise for the fact that, even with the much appreciated help of the National Film Archive and the BBC Archive, I have been unable to trace details of the programme.

music, so this overt appeal to the woman's body in the music's marketing delineations represents the adoption of a popular music discourse by classical music.

The danger is that such an adoption will cheapen the music. The purchaser of the Vivaldi cello concertos who wants a serious performance totally committed to inherent meaning will be put off the Harnoy recording because of the overt bodily display-delineations on the cover. It is not the image itself so much as the frisson between the delineations and the precious autonomy of the music that I would suggest initiated criticism of the cover, in a world where critics had only to walk into the popular music part of the store to see hundreds of far more explicitly sexual covers which it would not even have occurred to them to mention. These display-related delineations, whilst putting off the audience for autonomous classical music, will of course help to sell the record to a different, newer audience less persuaded by the discourse of classical music's autonomy.

At an even further extreme, a while ago I saw a poster advertising a recording of a Bach solo violin piece by Vanessa Mae.[12] She was photographed standing up to her naked thighs in water, with a suggested 'wet T-shirt' look, and playing a white electric violin whose colour matched her clothing. Stand in a pool of water and play an electric violin? This seems to me to be a rather dangerous activity! It must be the case that she was not in fact playing the violin, or perhaps it just wasn't switched on, whilst the photo was being taken. An image like this represents the complete translation of a classical music discourse into a popular music discourse; and it almost parallels the marketing of popular music through the use of sexy women *pretending* to play instruments, the delineations of which I will discuss later in the chapter.

Today the gendered delineations that arise from women's solo instrumental performance in the realm of classical music range from being subtle to being overt. But they are never so subtle as to be non-existent. Gendered delineations are intentionally or unintentionally present not only in the marketing of a woman's performance career, but in the very act of performance as a category of display. On one hand, feminine delineations act as an *interruptive* barrier which has been overcome only

---

[12] The record was a single entitled 'Toccata and Fugue in D Minor', and is now available on cassette single (EMI 881681 4) and also on a CD single called 'Red Hot' (EMI 1995, CDC 5 55089 2). There is a small picture of the cover (the same as the poster), and an article raising questions about Mae's image with reference to the pop/classical split, in *Billboard* (4 March 1995, p. 1 and p. 44); thanks to Dave Laing for searching this out for me and sending it.

by a small number of women recognised for their supreme musicianship. For these women, it has been the most committed pursuit of the most autonomous music that has enabled them to overcome the interruptive effects of feminine delineation arising from instrumental performance. They are perhaps able to represent a symbolic alternative to patriarchal constructions of femininity, a type of femininity that is different. On the other hand, a woman player can today retrieve an element of the *affirmation* of femininity in ways that remain largely within patriarchal definitions. Her presentation of her display in the delineations surrounding her music not only is relevant to her record sales or concert bookings, but also, like all delineations, becomes a part of delineation during the listening experience itself. The deep irony in this is that women have had to resist the interruptive effects of their femininity, by using their femininity in an affirmative way that places greater emphasis on bodily display; and that, once affirmed, femininity risks reducing the seriousness with which women's instrumental music-making is taken. A few women today seem to be able to achieve the highest respect as musicians, and at the same time to affirm their femininity. One example is Anne-Sophie Mutter, the violinist. Such women perhaps represent the strongest contemporary challenge to the contradiction that has for so long existed between femininity and instrumental performance. But like their predecessors they are, by definition, exceptional.

WOMEN ORCHESTRAL PLAYERS

The first significant developments for women instrumentalists revolved around solo performance. The field of orchestral or ensemble playing brings with it new implications. From the Middle Ages until the eighteenth century the only females who had relatively unrestricted licence to perform music publicly on a wide variety of instruments, in ensembles, were in the first place nuns and later on girls and women in the extraordinary Venetian *ospedali*. This is no coincidence: the hiving off of the image of a female playing an instrument, particularly some of the larger and more unwieldy orchestral instruments which of course become necessary in an all-female band, to groups of women who were self-proclaimedly celibate or groups of girls who were orphans under the care of the church acted, I would suggest, as a temporary solution to the interruptive potential of femininity that is delineated by female instrumental performance. In ways that are comparable with the domestic incarceration of women's musical practices, such confinement to the religious sphere made their instrumental ensembles, at least for a while, relatively safe.[13]

Records of praise by contemporary witnesses did not disguise the unusualness of the sight and sound of women and girls playing certain instruments at all, or playing in ensembles. Even in these holy surroundings (or perhaps because of them) we can also detect signs of the sexual allure of singing and the assumed mismatch of female control over instrumental technology. For example:

I shall go on to say how in this our city almost all the convents of nuns devote themselves to music, both with the sound of many kinds of musical instruments and with singing; and in some convents there are voices so fine they seem angelic, and like sirens they allure the nobility of Milan to come to hear them . . . one hears select voices that are concordant in harmony, and minglings of divine voices with instruments, so that they seem to be angelic choirs that please the ears of the listeners and are praised by connoisseurs. (Paolo Morigia, *La nobilità di Milano*, Milan: Pacifico Pontio, 1595, pp. 186–7; cited in Bowers 1986, p. 25)

The women and girls at the *ospedali* were said to

sing like angels, play the viola, flute, organ, oboe, cello, bassoon – in short, no instrument is large enough to frighten them . . . The performances are entirely their own, and each concert is composed of about forty young women. (Charles de Brosses in a letter, c. 1739–40; cited in Pugh 1992, p. 13)

As I have already mentioned in connection with singing, by the mid-eighteenth century music-making in convents had been reduced to the necessities required for worship, via a series of increasingly rigorous edicts. The *ospedali* underwent a slow decline, finally becoming bankrupt after nationalisation towards the end of the eighteenth century (Baldauf-Berdes 1993, passim and p. 246).

From the sixteenth through to the nineteenth century, women were not allowed to play in orchestras alongside men. Rank-and-file positions in all orchestras were male-only preserves from their inception, and in the case of top orchestras this situation prevailed until the 1910s, continuing in some cases into the 1930s and beyond. Women first appeared as members of male orchestras during the last part of the nineteenth century, and then only if they were playing the harp. This is a particularly rare orchestral instrument which, being plucked, quiet and requisite of a demure sitting position, allowed for relatively affirmative

---

[13] On the Venetian *ospedali* see the scholarly account by Baldauf-Berdes (1993), or for a shorter version (1994). On nuns' instrumental activities around this time, see Bowers (1986).

feminine delineations. Aside from that role, women appeared on the orchestral platform only in front of a male orchestra as professional soloists, mainly on the piano or violin (Tick 1986, Ehrlich 1985). The female rank-and-file player has been less *allowable* than the instrumental soloist. Why?

Part of the reason, particularly clear in the first decade of the twentieth century, was, as Tick (1986, p. 333) and Ehrlich (1985, pp. 156ff) show, to protect men's jobs. Until 1904 in the United States it had been legal for the Musicians' Union to exclude women from union-controlled orchestras. But when the union became affiliated with the American Federation of Labor it could no longer do so (Tick 1986, p. 332). In response to what was a new threat of women entering male orchestras, there was a clear resurrection of what Tick (1986, p. 332) describes as the nineteenth-century ideology of feminine frailty. In Britain, similar objections were raised against women instrumentalists, who were kept out of male orchestras at first by a process of 'silent discrimination' and later by explicit claims that they lowered wages as well as standards, that they were biologically inferior and that they were hysterical (Ehrlich 1985, pp. 188–9). As an example of the terms of the debate, a 1904 issue of *Musical Standard* carried interviews of various New York conductors:

Women cannot possibly play brass instruments and look pretty, and why should they spoil their looks?

Woman, lovely woman, is always to be admired, except when she is playing in an orchestra.

In a little while men will wake up to find that they are closely and successfully being pushed in one more sphere by the fairer sex . . . fewer and fewer positions [will be] ready and waiting for them. . . (*Musical Standard*, 2 April 1904, cited in Tick 1986, p. 333)

In Britain Henry Wood was the first high-standing conductor to break with tradition, when in 1913 he allowed six women string players into the Queen's Hall Orchestra in London. The numbers of such players did not significantly increase until the Second World War, during which women were allowed to flood the major orchestras, for the ghastly reason that the ranks were depleted of men who were away fighting, or dead. After the war, however, many of the women were ousted. Sir Thomas Beecham justifed this action, saying in 1946 that 'women in symphony orchestras constitute a disturbing element . . . If a lady player is not well-favoured the gentlemen of the orchestra do not wish to play near her. If she is, they can't.'[14] The conductor of the National Symphony Orchestra in the United States was moved to respond to that comment:

The women in the orchestras I have had the pleasure of conducting . . . all proved themselves to be not only fully equal to the men, but to be sometimes more imaginative and always especially cooperative.

Hence I think Sir Thomas's jibe . . . though funny is also slightly unfair, and, as far as American orchestras are concerned, quite untrue. If anything their ability and enthusiasm constitute an added stimulant for the male performer to do as well. And as they were a veritable godsend to most conductors during the war years, and I think to Sir Thomas as well, it doesn't seem quite 'cricket' (to use his vernacular) to drop them now. (Hans Kindler, cited in Neuls-Bates 1986, p. 364)

Although job-protection was clearly an important contributory factor in the antipathy to the woman orchestral player, I would suggest that there were also other more nebulous sides to it, connected with the inter-ruptive effects of female instrumentalists' display-delineations. The woman rank-and-file performer was, and still is, more interruptive of patriarchal constructions of femininity than the soloist. On one hand, unlike the control of inherent meanings by her soloist colleagues in highly autonomous music, the individual execution of inherent mean-ings by the orchestral player is to some extent subjugated to the more mechanical requirements of the ensemble, and to the direction of the conductor. Her power to step outside delineation altogether and into a supposedly purely autonomous realm is concomitantly reduced. On the other hand, unlike her soloist colleagues in the more popular sub-styles of classical music, she does not engage in a relatively feminine act of solo, virtuoso display, and therefore cannot so easily be presented as a 'sexy image' that compensates for the threat of the instrument. A woman player sitting in the ranks, particularly when she is in a minority, must behave like and indeed must be like 'one of the men'. Furthermore, within a team made up largely of men, actively engaged in skilled work involving precise motor-coordination and control over technology, the participation of a minority of women represents a displacement beyond the bounds of the female, domestic environment and, as such, an intru-sion.

In short, the possibilities for the woman player to affirm her femininity in an orchestra are negatively affected by her subjugation to the

---

[14] Cited in Neuls-Bates (1986, p. 364) and also, differently worded, in Dahl (1984, p. 48), amongst other places.

collectivity; her reduced opportunity for virtuoso display; her demonstration of precise motor-control as teamwork alongside men; her departure from the private sphere into a male stronghold. As a result of these factors, the interruptive potential of the instrument in the act of performance is for the woman orchestral player a more serious obstacle than it is for the woman soloist. Unlike those men who do not excel as soloists, women rank-and-file players make visible the normally transparent masculine delineation arising from instrumental performance, inevitably falling back into an interruptive, relatively 'unfeminine' type of display.

In Europe and the United States from around the 1870s to the 1930s, musical life reached a peak in terms of performance opportunities (although this did not mean high pay or job security for anyone), and women were more active than ever before. This activity, combined with the orchestral closed shop described above, went hand in hand with the development and rapid growth of a multitude of all-women orchestras. Women's brass bands had first appeared in the States in the 1850s, and following a visit of the Vienna Damen-Orchester to New York and Britain in 1871, ladies' orchestras as well as chamber ensembles sprang up all over Europe and North America.[15] This meant of course that women increasingly learnt to play instruments which had been taboo for them since the disbanding of the convent and *ospedali* ensembles, especially brass, woodwind and percussion. It also instigated the first professional women conductors. Although these orchestras presented opportunities to women players, they were mainly restricted to playing light music, rarely being taken seriously and, as Ehrlich puts it (1985, p. 159), often insulting the quite considerable abilities of many of their players.

This same period saw the instigation of literally hundreds of all-women popular bands which played mainly in pavilions, tea-shops and music-halls. Like their more classical counterparts, these bands were restricted in their performance opportunities, usually being presented in the form of a gimmick or an 'attraction'. The lack of any trace of autonomy in their music had implications for the display-delineations available

[15] See Neuls-Bates (1986), Ehrlich (1985), Tick (1986) on women's orchestras and bands, and on their reception. In 1895 a USA journal, *Musical Courier,* noted that women orchestral players might make a success as long as they played a light repertoire and did not go on tour (Tick 1986, p. 330). But women had already defied this: the Boston Fadette Orchestra in particular tackled a repertoire of large-scale pieces, as well as touring extensively. As with the lighter bands, the derision with which it was at first greeted was gradually replaced by praise. Then came the backlash that I've already described.

to their players. I have argued with reference to soloists that the performance of music within the terms of a relatively popular discourse allows a slight retrieval of affirmative femininity. By the 1920s, some of the popular all-women bands also attempted to trade on an affirmation of femininity. But in a collective performance situation, I would argue, it is more difficult to do so. Those rows of indistinguishable half-costumed women who make up the ranks in troupes such as the Follies Bergères may be able to engage in an act of overt sexual display, but the woman player in a band is far too busy playing her interruptive instrument, and perhaps watching the conductor, for there to be any suggestion of her having a real intention to display her body.

The mismatch between women's group instrumental performance on the one hand and feminine sexual display on the other is illustrated in Greta Kent's (1983) delightful autobiographical account, with its accompanying photographs of women players from among her own family and friends. The women wore revealing costumes for the time, mostly showing legs. But, as Kent says, they often looked more like principal boys than show-girls (p. 41) and indeed the costume gloss concealed a genuine musical professionalism that was as far away from sexual availability as could be. Kent relates a story about a band called the Biseras:

In one theatre in Germany, it was discovered that, through some error in the contract, the troupe was expected to 'entertain' gentlemen after the last performance. The suggestion was absurd and angry scenes followed. Management made the excuse that the girls were not qualified musicians and legal action was taken. Back to London came the eight Biseras to attend the hearing, with Aunt Hilda sitting all day with her cornet 'at the ready' in the event of having to show her skill. (Kent 1983, p. 43)

A perfect demonstration of the contradiction that arises between the idea of a woman instrumentalist in a band and that of a prostitute: if the lady is genuinely one of these, the chances are she is not the other. How else could the excuse be made that the women were taken for prostitutes on the grounds that they lacked musical qualifications?

Another example of the loss of the possibility of affirmative feminine display for the woman rank-and-file player is provided by the famous Hollywood comedy *Some Like It Hot* (Billy Wilder 1959). If a woman player in one of the all-female bands was missing, and if no female replacement could be found for her, it was customary for her to be deputised by a man dressed as a woman (Tick 1986, p. 329). This practice was retrieved to considerable effect by the film, in which the two male stars disguise themselves as women instrumentalists in an all-female light band, in order to escape hitmen. The band's 'canary' is of course Marilyn Monroe, who could hardly have been portrayed as a player in the ranks! The real lady players are not thematised as women at all: on the contrary they are, symbolically, sufficiently like men for the two impostors not to be identified.

I want to suggest that antipathy to the woman orchestral and band instrumentalist has occurred not purely because men have sought to protect their jobs or because listeners and critics have set out to damn women's achievements for the sake of it. Rather, the delineations of women playing instruments in the ranks or in ensemble have been disruptive of patriarchally constructed characteristics of femininity; and this disruption in turn has had an effect on listeners' understanding of the cultural value of the music. The interruptive feminine delineation of collective instrumental performance is not a mere extra-musical association, but operates beyond the level of delineation, to affect listeners' perceptions of inherent meanings. This occurs not only in the case of listeners who are already antipathetic to the idea of the woman player, but also in the case of those who defend her. For example, even supporters of women players such as Wood and Kindler cited above, not to overlook that champion of women's rights Ethel Smyth, nonetheless expected women to distinguish themselves from men not only in their approach and behaviour but also in their playing: that is, in their control of inherent meaning.[16] Hence the expression 'feminine touch'. The nineteenth- and early twentieth-century exclusion of women from top classical orchestras (the discourse surrounding whose repertoire was under the sway of the discourse of classical musical autonomy) and the relegation of women to less autonomous female orchestras and light bands are therefore understandable not only as attempts to control women for economic or general cultural reasons but as a resultant part of musical meaning itself. When critics, selectors or fixers listened to orchestral or band music played by women, I would suggest that they heard the inherent meanings through the delineation of femininity, and that they judged the inherent meanings partly in terms of their conception of femininity.

As with the professional soloist of previous generations, women orchestral players have gradually come to be more accepted. By the 1940s, the golden age of all-women bands had waned, and orchestras

---

[16] Smyth wrote copious essays defending women players (1919), (1921), (1928), (1933). Also see several citations from contemporary debates in Ehrlich (1985, esp. pp. 157–8), Tick (1986), Neuls-Bates (1986).

were beginning to be increasingly mixed-sex, a process which has gained momentum as the twentieth century has worn on. I would again suggest that this growing acceptability has been brought about partly by the sheer force of women's resistance. The interruptive effects that feminine delineations have on listeners' experience of inherent meanings gradually reduce as listeners become accustomed to the delineations. The less distracted we are by interruptive delineations, the more familiar we can become with musical inherent meanings; and the more familiar we are with inherent meanings, the more personally rewarding our musical experience becomes. However, despite these far-reaching changes, orchestras have always included far fewer women than men, and this is still the case today overall. At the time of going to press, for example, the Musicians' Union in Britain comprised 6,674 women and 33,190 men.[17] In the 1930s in the United States, committees representing women, and later black musicians of both sexes, had begun to ask for auditions to be held behind screens so as to eliminate prejudice in selection procedures. But systematic, widespread adoption of this apparently perfectly simple and innocuous practice has never occurred, which can only be taken as further evidence that the performer must needs be seen before it can be deemed safe to judge the performance: the display-delineation thus, as ever, features in the judgement, and is vigorously denied.[18]

For women instrumentalists to enter the classical repertoire as professionals, we have seen that one of two circumstances has tended to pertain: either the women had to have achieved the standard required of a soloist, from which exalted position only has it been possible for the music's autonomy to obscure and deny the very existence of delineations of any sort, including gender; or they have had to make use of solo display as an affirmative part of the feminine delineations arising from the performance of their music, which then becomes concomitantly less

---

[17] Thanks to the MU for supplying these figures. Also see Zaimont et al. (1984), (1987), (1991), Samuel (1995), South (1991), J. Halstead (1995) for information on contemporary women orchestral players.

[18] According to Neuls-Bates (1986, p. 363) screened auditions were not adopted in the United States until the 1960s, and according to Ammer (1980, pp. 208–9) it was possible even then to detect the sex of the person auditioning, the screens serving to reduce nepotism and racism rather than sexism: yet another cue for the study of the intrinsic relationships between sex and race in music. Some Black musicians levelled charges of discrimination, but charges were dismissed because it was claimed artistic judgement is too difficult to prove (Ammer 1980, p. 209). In Britain, screens were introduced sporadically in the sixties, but died out during the seventies. I am grateful to Tony Lucas of the Musicians' Union for verifying this information. In Britain and elsewhere there are active feminist members of musicians' unions. See Fudger (1975), Hambleton (1975), Ammer (1980), South (1991), Zaimont et al. (1984), (1987), (1991).

autonomous. For orchestral and other ensemble players, both these options are less readily available. The interruptive effects of femininity in collective instrumental performance contexts are more prominent; and women in these areas have been segregated and denigrated in far greater measure.

WOMEN INSTRUMENTALISTS IN JAZZ AND POPULAR MUSIC

Since the inception of jazz, women in the USA, and soon afterwards in other parts of the world, have played jazz instruments. There are many parallels with their position in classical music. First, there is the question of access to training. Dahl (1984 pp. ixf and passim) reminds us how heavily jazz has relied on its sub-cultural community for training, especially with reference to improvisation, which has until very recently been available nowhere but among the musicians themselves. The overwhelmingly male make-up of these musicians, and the venues and the working conditions of jazz have all militated against women's access to training: an echo of their lack of access to music education in the fourteenth century. Secondly, jazz women's most common instrument has been the piano, although there have been representations on all the other relevant instruments as well. Thirdly, jazz has been accompanied by a male fear of economic competition: especially in its early stages, women were kept out of male bands. Those few women who did secure places were viewed with suspicion. Fourthly, soon after the development of the all-women classical and light orchestras mentioned in the previous section, all-women jazz bands began to form. As with their more classical counterparts, these ensembles were taken as novelty gimmicks.[19]

Once again, I would suggest that this exclusion and denigration of women jazz instrumentalists was a result not only of economic circumstances and conventional assumptions, but also of musical meaning and experience themselves. The concept of femininity arising from the woman instrumentalist's display enters into the musical experience, causing people to 'listen out' for femininity in the woman player's handling of inherent musical meanings.

When I was in my teens, I went with some friends to hear Woody Herman's band, and there, in the trumpet section, was a woman. We looked at Billie Rogers as if she had three heads and marveled that she could even finish a chorus. (Nat Hentoff, in the year 1979, cited in Dahl 1984, p. 79)

---

[19] See Dahl (1984), Placksin (1985), Kent (1983), Ammer (1980).

The interruptive quality of feminine delineations acts as an underlying symbolic legitimation of attempts to exclude women. Opposition has been expressed in terms so similar to those of the discourse on classical music that there is no need to further analyse the content. By way of illustration:

Why is it that outside of a few sepia females the woman musician never was born capable of sending anyone further than the nearest exit? . . . You can forgive them for lacking guts in their playing but even women should be able to play with feeling and expression and *they never do it.* (An anonymous critic in *Down Beat*, 1938, cited in Dahl 1984, p. 52)

A woman jazz musician responded:

feeling, tone and phrasing is [*sic*] a quality which girls alone are more likely to possess because of the aesthetic nature of their sex. I noticed girls, because of their feminine tendency, cooperate to make the rhythm section a united unit dependent on each other, rather than the masculine tendency to lead on his own instrument. (Cited in Dahl 1984, p. 52)

As with the discourse on women's instrumental performance in classical music, a special case is here being made for femininity including on one side an appeal to the woman's lesser ability and on the other side an appeal to her greater ability. Whichever way it is, femininity is heard to somehow get inside the inherent meanings of the music played.

Like her classical colleagues, the woman jazz player has had to rise above the norm in her ability to manipulate the music's inherent meanings, before she could transcend the interruptive delineations of her feminine display. Women have verified this necessity in countless interviews, such as the level-headed testimony of the jazz instrumentalist Fostina Dixon:

There is still some active discouragement of you if you're a woman – not as much, but psychologically, there is still some . . . Guys can still try to belittle you, make it seem like you don't have it together. So being a minority, you have to be noticeably better or they're not going to accredit you. If you're an okay player, then you're 'all right for a girl'. So you have to be an exceptional all-round player. (Interviewed in 1981 by Dahl 1984, pp. 174–5)

Even though jazz women have vigorously resisted exclusion, many of the obstacles put in their way continue to be active today. Recent ethnographic work amongst jazz musicians in New York has shown how forceful the masculine ethos and the exclusion of women from the jazz community still are.[20] Many of the most successful jazz women are deeply involved in arrangement, improvisation and composition, for which reason I have reserved further reference to their work for the next chapter.

The exclusion of women from instrumental performance in the classical and jazz fields is more than matched by their position in post-fifties popular music. Here, the interruptive effects of their display have been particularly strident. A split opened up during the 1960s between popular and rock music. The former was made up of the largely fetishised music of 'teeny-bopping' 'pop fans', the discourse around which treated the music as though it had little else to offer but flippant, hedonistic and adolescent-oriented delineations. The latter was constructed as having more serious and politically aware delineations; and its inherent meanings were raised to a status of transcendent importance that could almost match the autonomy claimed by much classical music. The only girl and women performers in either popular or rock music were singers, and those rare exceptions who did play instruments did so in the way women have done for centuries: plucking strings or playing keyboards to accompany themselves in song.[21]

I have argued that the higher the level of technology involved in women's instrumental performance, the more interruptive that performance is to patriarchal constructions of femininity. In the classical sphere, this has related mainly to the size and possible volume of instruments, as well as to the question of whether they can be played in a demure posture. In popular and rock music, the use of high-technology, electric, very loud instruments and their associated amplification equipment has become a norm of performance. Just as the keyboard has been an exception to the rule about size and volume in classical music, so have the electric keyboard and keyboard synthesiser in popular music. These instruments have been played quite commonly by women popular musicians, who have merely moved over to them from the piano: so much so, in fact, that keyboard synthesisers are sometimes associated with femininity, or effeminacy. For example, the male drummer of the thrash

---

[20] See T. Jackson (1993). I wish I could print every anecdote told me by postgraduate students over the last few years. On contemporary women in jazz see Dahl (1984), Placksin (1985); and for interviews with jazz women, Gourse (1995).

[21] The best-known example being Joan Baez. Others such as Joni Mitchell were also song-writers and are discussed under the category of composition in the next chapter. For all its 'progressiveness', rock music has been one of the most extreme examples of musical patriarchy ever. See esp. Steward and Garratt (1984), Petersen (1987), Grieg (1989), Gaar (1993), L. O'Brien (1994).

metal band Anthrax was asked 'Would you ever consider using key-boards as a major part of the song?' and replied 'That is gay ... This is a guitar band' (cited in Walser 1993, p. 130). (As well as the electric or syn-thesiser keyboard, women are able to use a bit of technology in the kitchen. I was about to give a workshop-lecture to a group of students whom I had not met before. I had previously asked those of them who played electric bass to bring in their instrument. I had a bass amplifier, but I could not find its mains lead. A male student who was due to play bass helped me look for the lead. As we rifled through the drawers of the cabinet where I keep small electrical accoutrements, to my amusement he volunteered 'It looks like the lead that goes into an electric kettle.') Although as we will see there are exceptions, the popular music instru-ments from which women have been most noticeably absent are the drums, electric bass and electric guitar.

Punk rock closed the split between rock and popular music to some extent, and opened opportunities for women and girls to take part as instrumentalists, even playing instruments which are still today largely male preserves. All-women punk and post-punk bands such as the Slits and the Raincoats grew up, presumably unwittingly, in the wake of their Victorian and Edwardian foremothers. However, there were two differ-ences between these bands and those of a century earlier. One was that the punk sub-culture publicly exploited, displayed and to some extent ridiculed the normally private sexual fetishism associated with the sado-masochistic mainstream world of wide-circulation pornography. The other was that punk mocked the obsession with technical instrumental skill which was perceived to have marked 1960s rock (and has also marked a great deal of other music for the preceeding several hundred years!). Because the delineations of punk rock included disdain for musical technicalities, the effect on inherent meanings was of course to simplify them massively. Both these factors helped to give women a new platform on which to perform as instrumentalists. How typical that this occurred in an arena where the very two related issues, of delineated sexuality and of the autonomous value of inherent meaning, were them-selves held up for questioning. Women's position was in any case never central to punk, which retained a host of masculine overtones in its aggression and its oedipal rejection of authority.[22]

Just as continuing resistance has lent women an ever-increasing repre-

---

[22] On punk see Laing (1985), Hebdige (1981), Frith (1983, pp. 155–64, 243–4, 266–8); and with specific reference to women's issues, Steward and Garratt (1984), Gaar (1993), L. O'Brien (1994). For a some-what fantastic polemic on misogyny in various categories of rock, see Reynolds and Press (1995).

sentation in classical music and jazz, so women popular and rock instrumentalists became increasingly common both in all-women and in mixed
bands during the 1980s. They even entered some traditional male bastions
on a fairly secure footing, the most surprising perhaps being as instrumentalists in heavy metal.[23] But their position was still precarious and they
remained a fairly small minority. Sara Cohen's (1991) account of the band
scene in mid-eighties Liverpool provides a vivid illustration of a particularly male-dominated arena. The few all-women bands that existed at that
time were recognised by the local Liverpool rock community only as gimmicks. Bands in the community hardly included any women instrumentalists at all, allowing women in only as singers whose explicit function was to
add glamour and sex. Even in their roles as the girlfriends of band
members, women were regarded as dangerous intruders who were liable
to split up the band. Just as Sir Thomas Beecham had said in 1946 that
'women in symphony orchestras constitute a disturbing element' (cited on
p. 67 above), so in 1985 one band member summed it up as 'The best way
to split up a band is to get girlfriends involved' (S. Cohen 1991, p. 210) and
another as 'Girlfriends are bad news for bands' (p. 219). Cohen reveals, in
graphic detail, the centrality of the male bonding involved in the act of
playing in a band, and the variety of exclusion procedures directed at
women on a day-to-day level. Further recent ethnographic work on practices and values amongst women in amateur or semi-professional popular
music groups is afforded by Bayton (1990, 1993a).

The woman's ability as an instrumentalist in popular music is open to
question, and crucially, I would argue, this question is related to the
delineation of femininity that arises from her bodily display. The interruptive effects of the instrument operate as with other musical styles, in
ways already described. For a woman to overcome these, she has had a
choice of two avenues. On one hand, as with her classical and jazz colleagues, she has had to rise above the norm and prove the highest level of
commitment and skill in her execution of the inherent meanings of the
most autonomous sub-styles of popular music before she can be free of
the interruptive effects of feminine delineation. She has had to present a
type of femininity that eschews display and concentrates instead on inher-

[23] For example the bass player Tina Weymouth in Talking Heads, the drummer Sheila E, or the
metal guitarist Lita Ford, amongst others. For some reason when writing about popular women
musicians, I feel under pressure to start making long lists of the most famous ones. I have not listed
many women in classical music and I am going to resist doing so regarding popular music. As
Bayton (1993b) reminds us, most accounts of popular music contain the names of only a few of
the most famous women, giving the impression that these were the only ones, and obscuring the
hundreds of others that have existed. I am wary of adding to this problem.

ent meaning. A few individuals have achieved this. On the other hand, a
type of display which restores a semblance of affirmative femininity is
available to the popular female instrumentalist. But the more affirmative
the display she enacts, the less seriously she is liable to be taken.

For example, in a ninety-minute television film on funk[24] the only
woman musician mentioned at all, and this only happened once, was a
singer (who sometimes accompanies herself on the piano). She was incidentally named in the context of a joke in which the British comedian
Lenny Henry assigned different roles as statesmen to various high-status
popular musicians: James Brown as President, Stevie Wonder as Minister
for Cultural Affairs and so on. The woman, who was 'Miss Aretha
Franklin', was assigned the role of First Lady (that is, the only one whose
position relied upon her sex and upon marriage). The only woman instrumentalist to be observed in the film at all was on a video of the United
States rock polymath sometimes known as Prince, not portrayed in a band
but alone in a room with him. She was playing the electric guitar.
Inevitably out of such a scenario a question arises, not only in the minds of
'dreadful male chauvinists', but out of the discursive air, out of the social
construction of musical meaning in which we all take part (and I confess
the question arose in my own mind): is she really playing the guitar?
Equally inevitably, when we attempt to answer the question (unless we
know who she is already), we take into account her display, or the significa-
tion of attractiveness which we take her to be enacting. If she is 'stun-
ningly beautiful' the chances are she is not playing the guitar. I mentioned
earlier (p. 64) the classical take-over of a popular discourse as exemplified
in a photograph of Vanessa Mae playing (or not playing) Bach on an electric violin in a pool of water. In popular music, the use of glamorous
women pretending to play instruments in order to add sexual allure has
been taken to the extremes of making the pretence absolutely explicit.[25]

---

[24] 'Funk', introduced by Lenny Henry; a London Weekend Television production of the *South Bank
Show* for Independent Television, 12 January 1992.

[25] For example, Steward and Garratt (1984, p. 132) observe that the British group Style Council used
two women miming instrumental performance on the weekly BBC music programme 'Top of the
Pops'. It was common for all performers on that programme to mime at that time, but in this case
the difference was that these were anonymous women who did not go on tour and were not pretending to play an instrument that they had themselves played on the original recording. A more
radical case of the same thing occurred in Robert Palmer's video for the single 'Addicted to Love',
in which top models were displayed openly pretending to play instruments (collected on *Addiction,
the Video*, Vision Video Ltd/Polygram 1992, Video 845383). In cases such as these, the delineation
of affirmative feminine display has gone so far along the way to calling into question the displaying woman's ability to play her instrument that the problem of playing it is altogether dis-
pensed with!

I have suggested that when the discourse surrounding a particular style of music lays great claims to autonomy, it can more readily deny or ignore feminine display-delineations. Alternatively, affirmative feminine display can be subtly enacted and at the same time hypocritically blessed by a discourse on music that retains some level of autonomy. When music is more popular still, affirmative feminine display can help in the construction of the music's popularity. Whilst some classical women instrumentalists have adopted marketing strategies which affirm femininity, popular women instrumentalists are in a position where it is difficult for them to avoid doing so. The more popular the music is marketed to be, and the more it trades on the fetishistic celebration of its delineations, the more affirmative feminine sexuality can contribute to this mediation. But the more affirmative the feminine display, the less likely it is that the woman will be given credit for her ability to play the instrument, and the less seriously her music is liable to be taken.

As with singing, not only women but men also have to deal with the display-related delineations of instrumental performance. I mentioned earlier that Walser describes some of the strategies employed by heavy metal musicians, the delineations of whose sexuality and display are very much at the forefront of the musical meaning, but who as serious musicians are committed to the execution of inherent meanings. This causes a conflict for them similar to that faced by women musicians.

Fans link visual signs of androgyny with an abdication of metal's usual virtuosic prowess. 'It seems like if you have the makeup you're thought of as less than a musician' complains Poison's guitarist C. C. Deville. (Walser 1993, p. 128)

Here, a high degree of delineated display of the body is associated with lack of commitment to the music's autonomy, or lack of ability to control inherent meanings. If you are wearing make-up or displaying yourself overtly this is what you bring upon yourself. If you are a man, you make an initial choice about the make-up and spandex. But if you are a woman, especially in the popular realm, you are displaying by default, or wearing at least metaphorical make-up: you are therefore almost unavoidably labelled as a lesser musician.

SUMMARY

Male instrumental performers, because of the symbolically masculine presence of the instrument in their performance, are in a less difficult position than male singers. Partly for that reason, history has dictated their normality, and they are relatively transparent: we do not have to listen to a man playing the drums; we can listen to the music played on the drums. Instrumental performance-related delineations are transparently masculine: we do not hear masculinity in the music; we assume it. We do not know it is there, until something occurs to shed light on it. Men's questionable position as instrumentalists does not surface unless in exceptional circumstances, such as when men perform in women's symbolically private realms, or when they visually question their masculinity. Women, on the other hand, are perceived not as 'instrumentalists' but as 'women instrumentalists', how much so depending not only on the instrument and the style of music that they are playing, but also on the degree of autonomy of the music, and the type of display being enacted. As with singing, a male player who forefronts bodily display risks his masculinity; a female one merely affirms her femininity. The difference between singing and playing is that with singing this affirmation of femininity has left the woman singer relatively unhindered by restrictions; in the case of instrumental playing the interruptive power of the instrument, and its dilution of the patriarchal construction of femininity, have caused relatively greater strictures on women's practice.

Throughout history, it has been virtually impossible for women instrumentalists to play in a public sphere without the delineation of their femininity being brought to bear on the inherent meanings of their playing. Instrumental performance by women interrupts patriarchal definitions of femininity to varying degrees. The most minimal interruption occurs with the soloist in classical, highly autonomous music. When the music is considered autonomous, and when the player displays great commitment to inherent meanings, her bodily display is accordingly reduced, and the delineation of gender is more readily denied. A relatively affirmative feminine delineation occurs when the music is fetishised, its delineations raised to a level of importance above the inherent meanings, and when the emphasis in performance is on virtuoso or bodily display. Here, the display element acts to retrieve and perpetuate some of the affirmative patriarchal definitions of femininity. The music being less autonomous, the gender delineations can be raised to a higher level. The greatest level of interruption to patriarchal definitions of femininity caused by women instrumental performers occurs perhaps with the rank-and-file woman player, both in mixed bands and all-women bands, and especially in music that does not require solo show or improvisation. She cannot so easily appeal to the autonomy of the inherent meanings of her playing as a form of compensation for the interruptive delineations of her instrumental control; nor can she retrieve a relatively affirmative feminine display.

With jazz and popular instrumental performance the interruptive effects of feminine display have again been overcome only by a handful of women who work in the most autonomous realms of jazz or rock, and who have reached a recognised level of excellence on their instruments. Like their classical forebears, these women have not simply escaped the effects of interruptive feminine delineation: they have had to rise above them. This avenue is, by definition, only available to exceptional women. For the majority, another avenue presents itself: that of harnessing a retrieval of affirmative bodily display as a self-conscious part of the delineations of the music which is performed. This kind of display is not antagonistic towards the wider commercial and cultural delineations of popular music and can even help to sell the music. But it can have a negative effect on the reception of the woman instrumentalist: the more overt and affirmative her bodily display, the more she signifies a lack of commitment to the music's inherent meanings, the less likely she is to be regarded as a serious musician, and the less seriously her music itself will be taken. There is a conjunction of sexual display and loss of musical value. Contemporary women popular performing musicians, singers as well as instrumentalists, have a great deal to overcome before the platform on which they perform is level with that of their male colleagues.

Threatening femininity: women composing/improvising

THE GENDERING OF COMPOSITION

The activity of musical composition is qualitatively different from that of performance, but this difference expresses itself to varying degrees. Some kinds of compositional activity, for example sitting in a silent room composing a piece of music in the imagination whilst consigning it to manuscript paper, are extremely different from performance. Others, such as spontaneously improvising a melody in front of an audience, are almost indistinguishable. In my use of the term 'composer' in this chapter, the constant quality of the composer's activity to which I will be referring is that of constructing music by choosing elements from a selection of pitches, durations, dynamics, timbres and textures. In general this will include improvisation as well as other non-notated activities such as the demonstration of a phrase to another instrumentalist, but at times I will make explicit reference to improvisation and other practices as distinct types of composition.

Different types of compositional practice affect not only inherent but also delineated musical meaning. For example, the production of classical music of the era of Haydn, Mozart and Beethoven used to involve both improvisation and notated composition. However, the delineations of this music today tend to override the improvisation, which has of course been lost to posterity, and to suggest that the music's inherent meanings rely entirely upon the score. The composer within such a style and viewed from such a perspective is constructed as working alone, possibly intermittently at an instrument, definitely on paper, away from any performance of the whole composition in real time, creating in the mind a complex and multi-faceted musical artefact which can only be conceived and subsequently communicated to others thanks to its notation. The archetypal expression of this notation-centric delineation in the discourse surrounding classical music occurs in the celebration of the composer's genius and of the music's transcendent greatness. A visual representation of it is to be found in portraits of great eighteenth- and nineteenth-century composers, frowning at sheets of manuscript with quill in hand. Such a delineation is misleading when viewed in the light of the working practices of many composers, such as Haydn at Eszterháza, for whom the score was often provisional.[1]

Unlike improvised pre-twentieth-century music, recordings as well as live performances involving improvisation in jazz, popular and folk music of many sub-styles are relatively accessible. These may include the almost total dissolution of composition into performance as in the free improvisation of modern jazz; or they may involve the interlinking of the two activities, as when a bandleader has instructed an instrumentalist to try out a new riff during rehearsal. The delineation of such practices in the discourse surrounding the music occurs in eulogies to the creative spontaneity of the composer/improviser, or the authenticity of the music. Visually, it is found in publicity photographs of jazz or rock musicians, who are unlikely to be portrayed poring over a score. In practice, again, such delineations tend to override the fact that much jazz and many kinds of popular music are composed using pen and paper (or computer-processed notation).[2]

Delineations like these are not only found in the discourse surrounding music. Some element of the compositional procedures that have gone into a piece of music is nearly always also a part of delineated meaning during the listening experience itself. In the case of a Mozart symphony, for example, a listener's awareness of an anecdote about Mozart composing whilst playing billiards; or in the case of an Indian raga, the listener's understanding that the sitar and tabla players are engaged in a complex improvisatory game of durations: factors such as these can become intrinsically woven into the listener's mental stance towards the music's inherent meanings as they unfold in time. The ways in which the delineations of different musical styles tend to play upon or

---

[1] For Haydn at Eszterháza see Landon and Jones (1988). A few performers today such as Robert Levin are reviving the practice of improvisation in Classical music.

[2] See e.g. Schuller (1968, Chap. 7, esp. pp. 327–8) for descriptions of Duke Ellington composing/improvising in rehearsal. When musicians who are predominantly identified with popular or rock music are on occasions photographed looking at a score, such as the late Frank Zappa, this portrayal functions as a sign that they also work, or have moved over into, the realms of classical music. See, for example, the booklet with *200 Motels* (United Artists Records, 1971, UDF 50003), or *As An Am* (Rhino Records International, 1991, ESMCD 956) which shows Zappa looking serious in front of a blown-up score. See Middleton (1990, pp. 103ff) for a helpful discussion of the significance and influence of notation on the study of popular and classical music respectively.

issue from the relationship between composition and performance, and the precise characteristics of composition that are salient during the listening experience vary according to the social and historical mediation of the music in connection with the subject-position of the listener.

It is helpful to distinguish two ways in which what can broadly be termed 'technical know-how' enters into composition. First, composition requires knowledge of the technology of voices, musical instruments and/or electronic sound-producing equipment. The more vocal, the less technologically informed the compositional process is; and the more instrumental, orchestral or electronic, the more technologically informed it is. In improvisation and other performance-related types of composition, whether of folk-song or contemporary mixed-media pieces, clearly the voice, instrument or other technology used itself comes directly into the compositional process. Secondly, a musical composition is itself in some senses a technical object, constructed in accordance with laws which are built up over a period of history through use and development of the musical style. Although these laws are thus historical, they also contain an element of necessity in the natural, physical properties of sound: for example the make-up of the harmonic series or the penetrating capacity of a flute tone at a particular tessitura over an orchestra.[3] This technical object, music, is not merely wielded but created by the composer. Technical know-how is therefore required before and during the compositional manipulation of musical inherent meanings, in various ways depending on the instrumentation or other forces used, the genre, the style of the music and the historical era of its production.

There is both a similarity and a fundamental difference of content between delineation relating to performance and that relating to composition. Both performance and composition give rise to a type of delineation concerning the activities and the personage of the musical producer. But whereas with performance it is a display of the performer's body which contributes to this delineation (as discussed in the preceding two chapters), with composition it is a *metaphorical display of the mind* of the composer which enters into delineation. Because composition requires knowledge and control of technology and of technique, quite distinct from the physical motor-control of performance, mind features prominently in all composition-related delineations. Whilst we

---

[3] Without recognising some autonomy in these elements we could not admit even the slightest objectivity to music, enough to distinguish it as something apart from ourselves. The objective status of music is discussed in greater depth in Green (1988, pp. 121f, 130f).

listen to music, it is not just the inherent meanings that occupy our attention, but also our idea of the composer's mental processes. Indeed, one of the elements of which we are aware, an element that we are prone to marvel at in our best musical experiences, is the mind behind the music.

As with all aspects of musical meaning, the strength of this delineation of mind varies in degree according to the music's style, its historical context and the subject-position of the listener. For example, the delineations surrounding composition with relation to classical music that is mediated as highly autonomous today afford to the mind the most privileged position, and hardly feature the body at all. It is, in such a discourse, Beethoven's ability to *conceive* the Ninth Symphony that is celebrated. Contrastingly, with reference to music that delineates less of a separation between composition and performance, the mind is delineated not as an isolated vessel but in conjunction with the body. Here, it is Charlie Parker's ability to translate his personality or his ideas into music through the manipulation of the saxophone that is applauded. Beethoven's body has little to do with the mainstream delineations of his symphony, delineations whose very existence is anyway denied by classical music discourse; Parker's embouchure, lungs, fingers have a lot to do with the delineations of his jazz, and are even celebrated as salient features of the total musical meaning.

Such an argument appears to invoke a mind–body split. However, I do not wish to claim the 'correctness' of such a split. On the contrary, it is precisely because this split is reproduced in the discourse on music and in delineated musical meaning that it is possible and necessary to invoke it. Further, such a split forms a definitive part of the very distinction between masculinity and femininity which is part and parcel of contemporary common sense. Rational man has been constructed as in control of his body, emotional woman as subject to its vicissitudes; technical man as in control of nature, sensuous woman as a part of it, to be controlled. Only in the dangerous throes of sexual desire and madness has man ever lost his reason and succumbed to the uncontrollable demands of his body and nature.[4] McClary (1991) argues that music's long association with the body and with subjectivity has caused music to be seen as a feminine realm (see pp. 79, 17–18, 151–2). This has in turn led to retaliation by men, who have attempted to control music objectively, to deny that it

---

[4] See the discussion of patriarchy in Chapter 1, pp. 13–15 above. Ford (1991) provides a detailed analysis of how this was worked out with relation to music in the philosophy of the Enlightenment. Also see Lidov (1987), who characterises performance and composition respectively as somatic and semiotic.

has any meaning (p. 79) and to present it as ideal, rational, objective, universal and transcendent, that is, as having 'masculine virtues' (pp. 17–18). It has also concomitantly led them to prohibit (p. 18) or exclude (p. 152) women from participation in music.[5]

The mind/body split that has plagued Western culture for centuries shows up most paradoxically in attitudes toward music: the most cerebral, nonmaterial of media is at the same time the medium most capable of engaging the body. This confusion over whether music belongs with mind or with body is intensified when the fundamental binary opposition of masculine/feminine is mapped onto it. To the very large extent that mind is defined as masculine and body as feminine in Western culture, music is always in danger of being perceived as a feminine (or effeminate) enterprise altogether. And one of the means of asserting masculine control over the medium is by denying the very possibility of participation by women. For how can an enterprise be feminine if actual women are excluded? (McClary 1991, pp. 151–2)

As already indicated, I agree that masculinity is associated with the mind and femininity with the body. I also agree that music is both cerebral and capable of engaging the body. But McClary is making too large a leap when she suggests that, because of this, music is in danger of being perceived as a feminine enterprise altogether. Surely, if it is both cerebral and to do with the body, then it has *both* masculine and feminine traits? Why is it then in danger of being perceived as altogether feminine? McClary loses the cerebral aspects of music, which are in the first place fundamental to her argument that there is confusion over whether music belongs with mind or with body. As a result of this loss, she is also in danger of overlooking some other reasons why, as she puts it, men have prevented women from participation in music. Even if we could accept that music has been perceived as altogether feminine, this is no reason why men should have asserted control over it. For why, if music has been understood as feminine, should men have wanted to claim it at all? Why would they not have just left it to women? It cannot be only because music and women are both associated with the body, or that both of them are feminine, that men have excluded women from music. The cerebral connotations of music, indeed the very tension itself between music's cerebral and its bodily traits, must also be considered to have played a part.

In order to illustrate this argument, I will return to the Campion poem that opens this book.

---

[5] Also see Citron (1993, p. 142), who makes a similar point. See Tick (1993), Smith (1994) for discussions of strategies to exclude women from music.

> Rose-cheekt Lawra, come,
> Sing thou smoothly with thy beawties
> Silent musick, either other
> > Sweetely gracing.
>
> Lovely formes do flowe
> From concent devinely framed;
> Heav'n is musick, and thy beawties
> > Birth is heavenly.
>
> These dull notes we sing
> Discords needs for helps to grace them;
> Only beawty purely loving
> > Knowes no discord:
>
> But still mooves delight,
> Like cleare springs renu'd by flowing,
> Ever perfect, ever in them-
> > selves eternall.
> > > *Observations in the Art of English Poesie* (1602)

It is not only that women and music are both associated with the body, but also, contrastingly, that both are *idealised* in a *meta*-physical way. Indeed some (but not all) of the very claims made for music's transcendent qualities, which McClary argues are 'masculine virtues' (above and 1991, pp. 17–18) asserted to control music, are for me the very characteristics that link it with femininity. The idealised construction of both woman and music grants them certain shared characteristics: fleetingly beautiful, ephemeral, desirable yet unattainable in their ineffability, contrived yet at the same time natural, they both possess a mysterious otherness, very unlike the stable, rational self-certainty of man in his opposition to nature. The idealised woman's ideal music, that of Lawra the singer, flows effortlessly from the mere fact of her femininity. As Lawra sings, 'like cleare springs renu'd by flowing', she does nothing that is at odds with her 'purely loving' function of bringing forth the species and reaching out to touch that 'eternall' upon which man can never lay his finger.

But as soon as history intervenes in this idealised relationship, the music which Lawra sings can no longer remain silent. Real music is artificial: 'dull notes' sung by men, who need discordant 'helps' to make their music work. It is this artificiality that implies mind, rationality, control, as distinct from and opposed to what is natural and what is of the body. I want to argue that this cerebral requirement of music, which is specifically a part of the delineations arising from composition, conflicts with patriarchal definitions of femininity as subjected to the vicissitudes of the body, and that this conflict is one of the reasons why women have been more radically absent from composition than from any other musical activity. As a performer, historical woman has been granted a certain control over music, a control which takes place most poignantly at the very moment of performance. In the ideal manifestation of this licence, Lawra reminds us, woman and music become entwined. As I have argued in Chapter 2, because the spheres of nature and the body have been associated with femininity and divorced from masculinity, and because singing involves the delineated display of the body with no interrupting technology, the scenario of a woman singing, which leaves this association in place, affirms femininity. With instrumental performance (Chapter 3), the necessity to control the instrument to some extent detracts from this association, depending on the situation, the musical style and the instrument played, producing a potential interruption to patriarchal definitions of femininity. As performers, women can to some extent or other engage in a display which may either affirm or problematise the body. But once women begin to compose, it is hardly any longer the body that features in the activity at all, for composition involves a metaphorical display of the power of mind. This cerebral power conflicts with patriarchal constructions of femininity to the extent that, when it is harnessed by women, it produces a threat to the sexual order.

In their unattainable, idealised otherness, music and woman are to be dominated, their qualities to remain ephemeral and therefore still fascinating, but not threatening, to the integrity of man. For him – the author of the poem, the listener who gazes at the singer, man the composer – for him the idea that one absolute otherness – woman – can turn around and control the other – music – is intolerable. Part of musical delineation includes the notion of the mind behind music, and part of the notion of mind is that it is masculine. The woman composer is by definition always already involved in challenging her possession of some of the defining characteristics of femininity itself. The fact of her metaphorical, delineated display of mind conflicts with her natural submission to her body. It is therefore music's cerebral properties, its delineation of a *masculine mind*, that have denied woman the untrammelled freedom to compose.[6]

---

[6] A consideration of racial otherness could be similarly applied to the White's hearing of Black music. Kilminster (1992) offers an interesting discussion, from a psychoanalytic perspective, of the view of both music and woman as the mysterious, unknowable Other to language. Also see Battersby (1989) for a discussion of the historical construction of woman as other, an area which has been widely discussed among feminists since de Beauvoir's *The Second Sex* (first pub. 1949).

As this chapter will go on to show, we have due historical cause to assume without question that the composer behind almost all the music we ever hear – and for many people this assumption will apply literally to all the music they *have* ever heard – is a man. On this basis, I will argue that music delineates not only a *masculine mind*, but also the notion of a *male composer*. This twofold delineation is the unquestioned norm, implicit or explicit, in our secondary knowledge about music and in the primary delineations of our listening experiences themselves. I will refer to it as the 'masculine delineation of music'. Sometimes the cerebral aspects of this delineation demand attention; at other times, its normative positioning of men in the role of composer is of central interest. Each side of the delineation is related to the other.

Certainly, the masculine delineation of music is subject to instability, vulnerability, jeopardy. Scholarly examinations of the construction of masculinity by musical historiography, or of the pointed misogyny of composers such as Charles Ives, testify to a fear on the part of some musicologists or musicians that the cerebral delineation of music may degenerate into effeminacy, or that the male stronghold of music may be infiltrated by women.[7] But this fear is not an indication that the masculine delineation of music is something entirely weak or dismissible: on the contrary, it merely furnishes us with extreme examples of how the delineation is defended and bolstered.

An awareness of the masculine delineation of music can help in understanding why it is that whereas women have been allowed to sing, and to some extent allowed to play, they have suffered the most extreme taboos, restrictions and limitations on their compositional activities throughout history. In what follows, I again wish to provide some historical examples in order to illustrate my arguments, and in order to find traces of the discursive constructions and musical meanings surrounding women and composition in the present day. Two points must be borne in mind. First, as I argued in Chapters 1 and 3 (pp. 14–15, 57), there has never been a one-dimensional assertion of power through which men have prohibited or excluded women from musical activities. On the contrary, women have always both resisted and colluded in the reproduction of their own relationships with music. Failure to recognise this dialectical

---

[7] On Ives' misogyny/homophobia and his appeals for masculinity in music, see Tick (1993). In Tick's view Ives' misogyny derived from a search for validity caused by anxiety about the effeminacy of music. Also see Smith (1994). For further critiques of characterisations of music as effeminate and dangerous, see Brett (1994, pp. 11–12), Thomas (1994, pp. 185ff), and McClary's (1994) telling account of the reception of her paper suggesting that Schubert may have had same-sex inclinations.

construction in women's composing history makes it look as though women's actual experience of the world and of music is immaterial, and as though only a transcendent political relationship has counted in a struggle to reach some pre-existing musical zenith. Secondly, the overall context of women's composing history includes both the fact that women have been prohibited, discouraged, ridiculed and written out of history and the fact that they have been praised and celebrated.

WOMEN COMPOSING: EARLY BEGINNINGS

As is the case with singers and instrumentalists, women composers are known to have existed in antiquity.[8] They later entered a period of decline, to begin their history anew in the convents of the Middle Ages. Although singing was the prime musical activity of nuns, later followed by instrumental playing, a few nuns studied music theory and composition. A tenth-century canoness, Hroswitha, had knowledge of Boethian music theory, and the twelfth-century abbess Herrad of Landsberg, who was an author and theologian, set poems to music. Hildegard of Bingen, b. 1098, is the first known major female composer, with seventy-seven completely notated plainchants and a number of substantial dramatic compositions to her name. Although she has for a long time been recognised as an outstanding scholar, musical circles have only recently begun to acknowledge her achievement as a composer. She is perhaps the only woman composer whose rediscovery is today challenging received opinion about the history of music, and this recognition may, it is thought by some scholars, necessitate revising the history of twelfth- and thirteenth-century music (Cogan 1991). There is also evidence that anonymous nuns in the larger convents may have been writing chant melodies during the twelfth and thirteenth centuries.[9]

I observed earlier (p. 58) that the advent of polyphony during the fourteenth century prevented all women except for the most privileged nuns from keeping up with technical developments, as they did not have access to the training needed for this more complex procedure. Although nuns in some of the larger convents are thought to have sung in polyphony, there is little evidence that they employed it in composition, and during the fourteenth century it became the art of male clerics. The

---

[8] See Teeter (1993), Touliatos (1993), Gergis (1993), Michelini (1991).

[9] On Hildegard and other nun composers around her time see Yardley (1986), Edwards (1991), Jezic (1988, pp. 11ff); and on her music, Cogan (1991) was very informative. Also see Marshall (1993a) on women's musical creativity in the late Middle Ages.

fact that women were excluded from the education necessary for innovative compositional work did not stop them entirely from composing. There is, rather, a slight caesura in their composing history, when they fell behind contemporary developments. Subsequently, during a rise of musical activity that occurred both inside and outside religious life during the second half of the sixteenth century, women began to adopt polyphonic procedures. But this initial caesura, although seemingly slight in itself, marks the tendency of women's composition to follow on behind that of men, in terms of recognised innovation or technical development, throughout most of the remaining history of music. We have seen that exceptional women vocal and instrumental performers have had access to the highest level of achievement of their art: in singing from at least the sixteenth century, and in instrumental performance from the eighteenth century and in a few cases earlier. Access to the education required to compose music in line with contemporary developments in the field, however, has been largely unavailable to women from the fourteenth century until the twentieth. It is in this context that we can begin to understand why it is that Hildegard was probably the last supposedly innovative woman composer for some eight hundred years, until Ruth Crawford Seeger (1900–53).[10]

Women first began to 'write down, sign, and publish their music during the final decades of the sixteenth century' (Pendle 1991a, p. 46) and amongst those who did so were nuns. Convents, particularly in Italy during this time, were increasingly incorporating music-making activities, as I noted in connection with performance in Chapters 2 and 3. Some novices had received intense music education at home. Through them, composition entered a few of the convents, where it gradually became established and remained for over a century. One of the earliest nun composers, Alleotti, was also, in 1593, the first woman to publish sacred polyphonic music.[11] During the seventeenth century nun composers continued to go from strength to strength, the most outstanding perhaps being Isabella Leonarda (1620–1704), who published over two hundred works, including in 1693 the earliest surviving instrumental works by a woman.[12] Amongst records of some very high praise

---

[10] On Seeger see Gaume (1986), Tick (1991).

[11] On Alleotti (c. 1570–1646) see Bowers (1986, pp. 129–30), Pendle (1991a, pp. 49–50). Vittoria and Raffaella Alleotti may have been sisters, or may have been one person who changed her name. Following this, in the period 1609–16, sacred pieces with basso continuo appeared from convents. See Bowers (1986), Kendrick (1993) for further information on music in seventeenth-century convents.

[12] Bowers (1986, p 137), Jackson (1991, pp. 64–5). Outside the convent, Marietta Prioli was the first woman to publish instrumental works, in 1665 (Bowers 1986, p. 119).

for the compositions of many nuns, the Paris encyclopedist and composer Sébastien de Brossard noted in the catalogue of his collection of
music: 'All the works of this illustrious and incomparable Isabella
Leonarda are so beautiful, so gracious, so brilliant and at the same time
so knowledgeable and so wise; that my great regret is in not having them
all' (cited in Bowers 1986, p. 141). Although nuns did thus make music
and even compose to great acclaim, their music-making did not continue
to escape restrictions much beyond the seventeenth century. As I noted
in the preceeding two chapters, their practices, especially those that
included polyphony, were checked by a series of increasingly frantic
injunctions, disobedience of which, at the worst, entailed excommunica-
tion. Gradually music in convents was forced down to the barest necessities required by worship, and in such an environment composition
eventually died out. Leonarda was one of the last nun composers to
excel.

Outside the convents, amongst amateurs, a small amount of evidence
suggests that by the fifteenth century aristocratic women were writing
secular monodic songs, and there is abundant evidence that by the
seventeenth century in Italy, France, England and Germany noblewomen composed as a leisure pursuit.[13] Apart from convents, there was
no institutionalised formal musical training available to women and girls
during this time, and those who did become professional composers
were educated in the home. Maddalena Casulana, active from the 1560s
to the 1580s, was the first woman to have her compositions published.
They first appeared in an anthology of 1566, alongside works by Rore
and Lassus; two books of madrigals followed between 1568 and 1570.
She achieved considerable renown, and there are records of high praise
for her music. Francesca Caccini (1589–1640) was also greatly acclaimed,
both as a singer and as a composer. She published her first book of songs,
for one and two voices, in 1618, and composed the first extant opera by a
woman, performed in 1625 (Cusick 1993a, pp. 282f). Barbara Strozzi,
active between 1644 and 1664, published an unprecedented eight books
of largely solo vocal music, and was the first woman to follow a performing and composing career outside of a court. In France, Elisabeth
Claude Jacquet de la Guerre (c. 1666–1729) received eulogies from the
highest places, published cantatas, harpsichord and violin sonatas, and
was the first woman to publish an opera.[14]

[13] Bowers (1986), Rosand (1986), Sadie (1986).
[14] On Casulana see Bowers (1986), Pendle (1991a); on Caccini see Cusick (1993a), (1993b), Bowers
    (1986), Jackson (1991); on Strozzi see Rosand (1986); on La Guerre, see Sadie (1986).

It would not be too much of a generalisation to say that, for both nuns and lay women up to the early eighteenth century the voice was by far the most central element of composition, and that a large proportion of women composers were primarily singers who performed their own works, often accompanying themselves on a stringed instrument. Women composed to great acclaim, but in limited genres only, mainly encompassing vocal, small-scale forms. Gradually, during the sixteenth and seventeenth centuries, they branched out into two-part and poly-phonic vocal music, then into small-scale instrumental music, only lat-terly and then rarely moving into opera.

There are many reasons for these limitations of women's composi-tional outlets. Some of the reasons lie in the continuing restrictions in educational and professional opportunities available to women at the time. Women were excluded from the post of *maestro di cappella*, which was the main position allowing a composer the opportunity to write large-scale instrumental or operatic works. They were also prevented from taking part in most musical activities within the church. The only large-scale works in which they could even perform were operas, and here they were involved only, inevitably, as singers. Although lack of opportunity does offer one helpful explanation of why women's compositional activities were circumscribed, I wish to consider this circumscription in more symbolic terms involving the masculine, cere-bral delineation of music and the insinuation of a conflicting notion of femininity into the meanings of music composed by women, as sug-gested in the previous section.

First, I argued that musical composition requires knowledge of the technology of voices, instruments or other sound-sources, and that this knowledge implies a masculine delineation of mind which conflicts with patriarchal constructions of femininity. I will now suggest that the more that technology is involved, the more masculine the delineation is, and conversely, the less that technology is involved, the less masculine the delineation is. In these terms we can understand why it was that the most technological, large-scale or orchestral music was prohibitive for women composers, whilst the least technologically demanding type of composi-tion, that for the solo voice, was the most common and accessible outlet for them. Secondly, I suggested that knowledge and control of composi-tional technique contribute to the masculine cerebral delineation, and conflict with femininity. Again, the more technique, the more masculine the delineation is, and conversely so. This is commensurate with the abundance of women composers in the field of solo vocal music, which in most cases obviates the need for the technicalities of polyphony. Thirdly, I have argued that singing is a highly affirmative musical practice for women. I now suggest that this is one reason why women were allowed to compose vocal music and, moreover, music which they often sang themselves. Not only is the voice itself affirmatively feminine, but the presence of the composer's own voice in the presentation of her composition, some of which might well have been improvised and would certainly be embellished, accented her body and allowed for a further reduction in the cerebral connotations that are carried by larger-scale instrumental music.

These three paradigms – the relative lack of 'masculine' technology, the comparative 'feminine' simplicity of technique and the inclusion of the 'feminine' connotations of the voice as the main compositional force – dilute the threat posed by the cerebral delineation of composition to the discursive construction of femininity, and even retrieve an element of patriarchally defined affirmative femininity. Together, these paradigms can, I believe, provide a way of understanding why it was that sixteenth- and seventeenth-century women were allowed and encouraged to compose, whilst at the same time being restricted to such an abundance of solo and small-scale vocal music. What interests me most of all in this is that it does seem to present some possibility of tracing that enduring kernel in the historical construction of music and femininity, which speaks to me so powerfully through Campion's verses: the performance of one's own solo vocal compositions, with or without self-accompaniment on a stringed or keyboard instrument, has remained one of the prime compositional outlets for women from the sixteenth-century members of the *concerti di donne* to the singer-songwriters of the 1960s, and up to the present day.

WOMEN COMPOSING IN THE EIGHTEENTH AND NINETEENTH CENTURIES

Productivity and opportunity

Increasing numbers of women took up composition in a semi-professional capacity during the eighteenth and nineteenth centuries. In the main they continued to produce solo vocal music, which crystallised in the nineteenth-century Lied and the popular parlour song. Some also produced instrumental chamber music. Most of their work was intended for consumption in the salons or other popular venues where, true to the woman's relatively affirmative role as singers and keyboard players within a domestic sphere, they continued to perform their work, both vocal and instrumental, themselves. Corona Schröter (1751–1802) and Juliane Reichardt (1752–83), both of whom wrote mainly solo vocal music, are two outstanding examples.[15] Gradually a few women began to produce large-scale instrumental, choral and operatic works.[16] A small number also began to compose instrumental chamber music in the compositional lineage of Beethoven, Robert Schumann, Brahms: a type of music that was more high-ranking and that has been constructed in this century as autonomous. The most well-known such composers had close family relations in elite musical circles, and include particularly Fanny Hensel (1805–47) and Clara Schumann (1819–96).[17] Despite their compositional activities, all these women were more active and renowned as performers than as composers. Hardly any of them considered themselves professional composers (Citron 1986, p. 232) or made names as composers, and their works were largely unpublished.

As the nineteenth century progressed, many women began to engage more insistently upon types of composition which were more masculine in their delineations: demanding more control over instrumental forces, more knowledge of musical technique and more separation of the role of composer from that of performer. Some of these women had to argue with publishers for the right to present even chamber music that made technical demands on the performer![18] A few others strongly resisted pressure from educational institutions, publishers and critics to relinquish the composition of large-scale forms or orchestral music. There are perhaps two outstanding examples. Luise Adolpha Le Beau (1850–1927) was the first woman to become a successful composer without having a professional performance career. Her works number over sixty-six, thirty-five of which were published. She had

---

[15] See Citron (1986), Reich (1991); also esp. S. Fuller (1992) on popular song-writers and other women composers in England; Weber (1975) on social class and gender divisions in concert-going practices.

[16] Among the most notable are Marianne von Martinez (1744–1812), who composed instrumental and choral works; Julie Candeille (1767–1834), who composed a concerto and operatic works; and Maria Theresa von Paradis (1759–1824), who composed operas and cantatas. See Citron (1986), Jackson (1991, pp. 82–8).

[17] See Citron (1993), (1986), Reich (1986). Also Reich (1993, pp. 140ff) where she discusses Hensel and C. Schumann as paradigms of the non-professional and the professional woman musician of the nineteenth century.

[18] S. Fuller (1992, p. 21). Two such women are Maude Valerie White (1855–1937) in Britain and H. H. A. Beach (1867–1944) in the USA. See S. Fuller (1992), Ammer (1980), Tick (1986), Neuls-Bates (1986), Jezic (1988).

performances all over Europe, and there are over three hundred surviving reviews (Olson 1986). Ethel Smyth (1858–1944), also not a performer, was greatly acclaimed during her lifetime, first for her large-scale Mass in D (1891), and then for the many operas which were performed in several venues in Germany, at the Royal Opera House in Britain and the Metropolitan Opera in New York.[19]

Although in the latter part of the nineteenth century there was an abundance of women singers, pianists and some string players in the performance classes of the conservatoires, women were virtually unknown in the composition class. Smyth wrote home about the sniggers which greeted her when, as the only woman ever to have done so, she walked into her first composition seminar at the Leipzig Conservatoire. Le Beau's private teacher made an exception to his rule of not teaching women when he took her on.[20] In Chapter 2 I observed that women teachers of the voice and certain instruments were plentiful: with composition, not so. Le Beau and her family believed that she was discriminated against professionally. One of the clearest – and in personal terms, as it turned out, most tragic – expressions of this is found in a diary entry:

The friendly old man who was, after all, a member of the Senate and was to decide along with the others about the conferring of the title 'Professor' . . . would have gladly used such a title for me. I could more than fulfill the stipulations regarding compositions to be submitted; they had not received such a work as *Hadumoth* in years! I could also submit Lieder and the prize-winning cello pieces. The question was only whether this title could be conferred on a woman at all, and especially in Berlin, which was fifty years behind the times, it could not even be considered. (Cited in Olson 1986, p. 288)

Criticism

As we saw in Chapter 3, many of the arguments about why women should not perform professionally in the nineteenth century were connected with protecting men's jobs.[21] There was no equivalent job market

---

[19] On Smyth, see Wood (1994), Bernstein (1986).

[20] See Reich (1993, pp. 135ff) on the availability of composition to women in conservatories. Smyth and Le Beau were among many who contributed to a debate about educational opportunity, publishing articles in defence of girls' and women's education. See Olson (1986). Restrictions on education also arose in similar ways regarding painting. Women were not allowed into life classes, the highest apogee of artistic endeavour, up until the 1870s, when the Pennsylvania Academy of Fine Arts was the first to relax the rule (Parker and Pollock 1981, p. 35 and fig. 22, p. 36).

[21] See esp. Tick (1986, p. 333), Ehrlich (1985, pp. 156 ff); and pp. 67–8 above.

in composition, Tick (1986) points out, and yet a debate about women's capacity for composition ignited and burned for some decades. Being of less practical consequence than that surrounding performance, this debate involved 'weighty intellectual concepts about creativity and biological determinism rather than social propriety and money. The debate was all the more fierce for its abstractions' (Tick 1986, p. 333). Attention centred on a 'paradox in nineteenth-century beliefs. If music was the art of the emotions, it logically followed that women, who were believed to be more emotional than men, should excel in its creation' (Tick 1986, p. 333). The fact that they had not was defended by women composers and their supporters as the social and historical result of lack of opportunity and education; and it was cited by their opponents as evidence of woman's innate inferiority, her emotionality being explained away as superficial or hysterical.[22] Women's lack of mental capacity, combined with a great number of other flaws, was the *coup de grâce* of those who opposed the idea of the woman composer.

Women's ability to compose was not only questioned theoretically but also assessed in contemporary reviews of women's works. The idea that music involved a combination of masculine and feminine traits was common in nineteenth-century musical pedagogy and criticism.[23] At the surface level, certain devices such as different types of cadence were (and often still are) customarily called 'masculine' or 'feminine'; and at a more background level, musical form was frequently depicted as follows. The first 'theme' of sonata form was deemed masculine, and the second feminine. The altered key of this latter being wayward, it needed to be brought home and tamed back into the tonic key by the return of the first theme at the recapitulation. Whole pieces of music were also liable

---

[22] In the USA George Upton denied women's ability to compose in *Woman in Music* (1880), which was consistently referred to by other writers. In England the Revd H. R. Haweis published *Music and Morals* (1877), which argued, like Upton, that women should encourage the great composers and should perform music, but not compose. Also see Brower (1894), who took the same view. Fanny Morris Smith (1901) and, much later, Sophie Drinker (1948) defended the woman composer in reply to Upton. Tick (1986) provides the most focussed contemporary discussion of the debate that I have come across, centred on the USA. Also see Neuls-Bates (1986), Citron (1993). See Ehrlich (1985) for some discussion of the debate in Great Britain, although he is mainly concerned with orchestral performance. There is a much-needed contextualisation of the class issues involved, in Hand (1983). See Rieger (1985) with reference to Germany. Tick (1993) discusses these issues with reference to Charles Ives' fabled misogyny. Also see Smith (1994) on modernism and the reaction to the feminisation of music.

[23] See especially Citron (1993) and McClary (1991), who include discussion of this practice as well as citations from influential music theorists and others (e.g. *re* A. B. Marx: Citron, p. 135, McClary, p. 13; *re* Vincent D'Indy: Citron, p. 136). This idea is not archaic and can still be found in text-books today. (Thanks to Christina Grossi for informing me that it is absolutely normal in contemporary Brazilian pedagogic texts.)

to be depicted as masculine or feminine, such as when Robert Schumann described Schubert's trio Op. 99 as 'passive, lyric and feminine', and his Op. 1 as 'active, masculine and dramatic'.[24] There was thus an existing discourse which involved the attribution of qualities of masculinity or femininity to music. Feminine devices, feminine structural functions or feminine whole pieces were understood to be delicate, sensitive, decorative, wayward or to possess other qualities typically associated with women themselves, whereas masculine music was contrastingly seen as strident, virile, bold and so on.

These assumptions are understandable as expressions of a particular aspect of nineteenth-century musical aesthetics which, although opinions within it varied, can be characterised by its tendency to gravitate around the attribution of programmatic or other extra-musical associations to music. It is helpful to understand the processes involved in this thinking in terms of inherent and delineated musical meaning. The masculine or feminine qualities which were attributed to the music are understandable as delineations, and the musical devices themselves to which the qualities were attributed, as inherent meanings. These two types of meaning are liable to be confused in such a way that the delineations take over the entire discourse surrounding the music, and come to appear as though they are part of the inherent meanings. This type of confusion of the two types of meaning – the mistaking of the one for the other as delineations are taken to be inherent – represents what I have called musical fetishism. Its workings are illustrated in the approach of nineteenth-century critics to music by women. When judging compositions by women, they employed this pre-existing pedagogic discourse invoking masculinity and femininity as a way of evaluating the women's work. In order to illustrate the fetishism involved in this, I will make distinctions between three different types of such criticism. In practice the three categories tended to dissolve into each other to varying extents: I have drawn them up merely as a didactic aid.

First, if reviewers, listeners or fellow musicians thought the woman's compositions were aesthetically or technically poor in some way, this failing was understood as 'feminine', and was often expressed by use of that more categorically negative derivative, 'effeminate'. This effeminacy was located in the music itself, without reference to any distinction such as that suggested between inherent and delineated meanings; and

---

[24] Cited in Tick (1986, p. 336) from Schumann (1964, p. 121). For a full discussion of the disourse on Schubert's 'effeminacy' see McClary (1994), and for particular references to sources see pp. 209, 213–14, 227.

its presence was explained by the fact that the composition was by a woman. One sad, early example of this is in the words of a woman describing her own work:

There is no greater joy than composing something oneself and then listening to it. There are some pretty passages in the Trio, and I believe it is also fairly successful as far as form goes. Naturally, it is still only woman's work, which always lacks force and occasionally invention.

A year later she wrote:

I received the printed copies of my Trio today, but after Robert's D Minor [Trio] I did not care for it. It sounded effeminate and sentimental. (Clara Schumann, cited in Reich 1986, p. 268; also in Citron 1993, p. 56; Kallberg 1992, pp. 116–17)

Another example is:

The symphony of Mrs. Beach is too long, too strenuously worked over and attempts too much . . . Almost every modern composer has left a trace in her score, which in its efforts to be Gaelic and masculine ends in being monotonous and spasmodic . . . There is no gainsaying her industry, her gift for melody . . . and her lack of logic. Contrapuntally she is not strong. Of grace and delicacy there are evidences in the Sicilana [*sic*], and there she is at her best, 'but yet a woman'. (*Musical Courier*, 23 February 1898, pp. 29–30, cited in Tick 1986, p. 344)

Secondly, if the music was considered at all valuable, then its value was attributed to feminine characteristics, which were dissimilar to those in the examples above only to the extent that they were seen in a positive rather than a negative light. In fact the citation above does provide an example: Beach is 'at her best' when she displays traces of 'grace and delicacy'. Similar words, such as 'the ornamentation is sensitive', 'the melodies are charming', were commonly employed. For example:

When [the composer] George Wakefield Chadwick first heard Mrs. Beach's symphony 'Gaelic', he is said to have exclaimed: 'Why was not I born a woman?' It was the delicacy of thought and finish in her musical expression that had struck him, an expression of true womanliness, absolute in its sincerity. (*Etude*, February 1904, cited in Tick 1986, p. 344)

It is already apparent in the quotation above that woman's supposed proximity to feeling was also cited as a positive contribution of her gender to composition. The attributed emotionality of women, it is worth noting, was assumed to derive from the womb, which since the eighteenth century was seen as the seat of hysteria and is still widely taken to be the cause of pre-menstrual tension: female emotionality thus legitimated the view of woman as subjugated to her body and unable to free her mind. The valorisation of emotion in music is understandable as a part of nineteenth-century idealised notions of music as the 'breath of the soul' (Hegel 1975, pp. 889ff), notions which survive well into the present especially through Suzanne Langer's (1955) understanding of music as 'the warp and weft of feeling'. Therefore when emotional woman could express herself in emotional music – so much the better. For example:

The melodic devices are not mere imitations of the chief beloved masters of the time, as is the case with almost all female compositions that are known to us, but, rather, they have come from her heart and thus have, some more, some less, their own special qualities. (*Allgemeine musikalische Zeitung* 29 (August 1827), cols. 542–4, *re Sechs deutsche Lieder* 1827 by Reichardt, cited in Citron 1986, p. 234).

Thirdly, there were cases in which women's music was acknowledged to be highly successful; but for obvious reasons this was understood as extraordinary, and was overtly held to be so in the reviews themselves. Such music by women was almost invariably praised mainly for its astonishing masculinity. Thus the most successful woman composer was one who could be deemed capable of composing like a man. Countless reviews testify to this assumption. I have gone to one of the most successful women composers to show how it operates with her, and taken the liberty of quoting at length from Olson's succinct account:

Certain characteristics of Le Beau's style, especially her control of form and her power, energy, and spirit, were consistently referred to by critics and reviewers as *männlich* (manly). August Bungert, for example, wrote concerning her Piano Variations, opus 3: '[The final variation] subsequently plunges passionately and boldly on and becomes so violent, that one has quite forgotten by the end that the composer is a woman; indeed, one could think that one were dealing with a capable man, who can truly strike earnestly and hard as here'. Her most striking 'masculine' characteristic was her capacity for musical conceptualization. As one critic put it, 'Her abilities include solidity in development, taste, and a feeling for beauty and pleasing sound, as well as earnest, we should like to say, masculine ways of thinking, in relation to the comprehension of the independent tasks of the art'. (Olson 1986, p. 297)

Critics saw Smyth, too, to be free of the qualities usually associated with women's work. Her opera *Der Wald* had made history as the first opera by a woman to be performed at the Metropolitan Opera in New York (and incidentally the last for at least another eighty years), and had received a ten-minute standing ovation. A reviewer for the *New York Times* wrote:

Miss Smyth is very serious, and the opera sounds the note of sincerity and res-
olute endeavor. She uses the vocal and orchestral resources with masculine
energy, and is not afraid of employing the most drastic means of modern
expression. (Cited in Bernstein 1986, p. 322; also in Wood 1994, p. 50).

The terms in which this astonishment at the woman's manly achievement was expressed were associated with delineations of virility such as
'passion', 'boldness', 'violence', 'resolution' and so on. Such delineations
derive from the gendered language, described above, that was already
available to critics of the era, only this time they were reversed in the
application of virility to music by women. This kind of delineation also
made an explicit link with what I have described as the cerebral connotation of composition, exemplified in the reference above to Le Beau's
'masculine ways of thinking'.

As Tick says, the critical language such as that employed in the examples above did not in itself confine the female composer. 'She, like
Schubert, could write either masculine or feminine music. However, the
language of Romantic music criticism degenerated into the language of
sexual aesthetics, in which the potentialities of the individual female
composer were defined through the application of sexual stereotypes'
(Tick 1986, p. 336). It is the word 'degenerated' that is crucial here. The
use of the labels 'masculine' or 'feminine' to describe music (or in my
terms the use of such labels as delineations) is in itself only expressive of
wider ideas about the characteristics of masculininity or femininity,
compared to whatever extra-musical associations presented themselves
with particular pieces of music. But the use of the labels to judge the
value which is supposedly inherent in a piece of music, and beyond that
the use of these gendered concepts as *causal explanations* of musical qualities according to the gender of the composer, represents a radical fetishisation of the music.[25]

During this chapter and the preceding two chapters, I have suggested
some ways in which the femininity of a performer or composer enters

---

[25] Such a procedure was also located by early feminist literary theorists, and put eloquently by Mary
Ellmann: 'With a kind of inverted fidelity, the discussion of women's books by men will arrive
punctually at the point of preoccupation, which is the fact of femininity. Books by women are
treated as though they themselves were women, and criticism embarks, at its happiest, upon an
intellectual measuring of busts and hips' (1968, p. 29). There are also several examples related to
fine art. Although women artists were recognised in the nineteenth century, they were treated
with the same mixture of curiosity and antipathy, combined with occasional praise, that greeted
women musicians. Their work, like that of women composers, was stereotyped into categories of
the 'feminine', marked by characteristics such as delicacy. Just as women composers were
marginalised into simple song-writing, women artists were marginalised into the crafts (Parker
and Pollock 1981, pp. 33ff).

delineated musical meaning. By my definition of inherent musical meaning as purely and logically to do with musical materials, inherent meaning itself can have nothing to do with gender. But I have argued that the gendered delineation of music does not stop at delineation: it continues from its delineated position to affect listeners' responses to and perceptions of inherent meaning. In the realm of performance, I argued in Chapters 2 and 3, for example, that if the delineation of a piece of music involves overt sexuality on the part of the female performer, listeners are disinclined to pay much attention to her manipulation of the music's inherent meanings. It is not only that there is a high degree of feminine display in the delineations of the music, but that those delineations then cause us to hear and interpret the inherent meanings in a certain way. In the case of composition also, when critics have been aware that the composer is a woman, they have tended to perceive the inherent meanings of her music in terms of delineated femininity. This is one reason why a great deal of music by women has been denigrated for its effeminacy; why much other music has been more favourably received as displaying positive feminine attributes such as delicacy or sensitivity; and why a small amount of music by women has been incredulously hailed as equal to music by a man. In these last cases the inherent meanings of music by women have broken through the fetishistic effects of feminine delineations: then, because critics could no longer attribute 'femininity' to the inherent meanings, they instead denied the femininity of the composer.

The fetishistic effects of feminine delineations are particularly easy to discern in cases when listeners change their opinions of music after having made an unexpected discovery that it was composed by a woman. There is an illuminating example of this nature provided by a Scandinavian music critic in the early part of this century.[26] He was in the habit of writing highly positive reviews about a particular composer, and it was only after a number of reviews had appeared that he discovered the composer was a woman. He carried on writing good reviews, but his language changed. His praise ceased to describe the music with words like 'strident', 'virile' and 'powerful', and began to include words like 'delicate' and 'sensitive'. What had happened was that his new knowledge that the composer was a woman, or, in the terms I am

---

[26] I have searched high and low for my source-reference on this. All I know is that I read it in a book on literary criticism, not music; I failed to make a note of it; mentioned it to a colleague who bears witness to the fact; and passed the book back into I cannot discover which library. It was only later that I recalled the story, as a particularly pertinent illustration of the points being made here.

suggesting, the new delineation of the femininity of the composer, affected the way that he also heard and articulated his opinions of the inherent meanings. One cannot help wondering whether, had he known the sex of the composer all along, he would have found any merit in the compositions to begin with. Another similar illustration, this time of the way that sexual delineations can affect listeners' hearing of inherent meanings, is provided by the contemporary criticism on Tchaikovsky. Reception of his music changed around the time that his homosexuality came to light, when critics introduced descriptive terms such as 'hysterical', 'effeminate' and 'structurally weak'.[27]

The delineation of mind in music by women composers breaks with the normal, implicit, connotations of femininity. The woman who displays her mind by virtue of being a composer threatens patriarchal definitions of femininity. This is why, on the one hand, femininity itself has been used to explain the attributed failure of a composition and, on the other hand, when the quality of inherent meanings of a composition itself could no longer be denied within the aesthetic terms of the era, the gender of its creator has had to be denied instead. Whereas the least successful woman composer could blame her failure upon her femininity, and the tolerably successful woman composer could attribute her success to her femininity, the most successful woman composer could bless her luck that she was not feminine. Whichever way around it was, effeminacy, femininity, womanhood were brought to bear as unavoidable influences upon the judgement.

Although a few women were given entry to a compositional brotherhood, even they were ironically denied access to that apogee of artistic achievement, genius: an isolated, solitary male ego who is able to wrestle with the forces of creativity which threaten his reason, and to overcome them in the production of a work of art that reaches a universal, autonomous realm beyond the strife of the human condition. In his artistic struggle, the genius actually comes dangerously close to losing his masculinity, which is based on his isolated individuality and rationality, and succumbing instead to a feminine creative passion. But at this very point, where the male becomes feminine, where the solitary becomes universal, and where the rational becomes creative, the woman is excluded. 'One thing that the history of the concept of "genius" reveals is that being a woman and being "feminine" are radically different

---

[27] I am quoting these terms from McClary (1994, p. 210), who is glossing work done by Malcolm Brown and presented at the 1990 meeting of the American Musicological Society.

things. It is *women* who have been excluded from culture; not the "feminine"' (Battersby 1989, p. 138).[28] Thus whereas the most well-received
women composers were, at the height of their achievement, recognised
as masculine, the most successful men composers alone attained the pinnacle of genius, where they could be praised for qualities normally seen
as feminine.

WOMEN COMPOSING/IMPROVISING IN THE TWENTIETH CENTURY

The classical field

The flurry of activity which produced so many women composers in the
late nineteenth century gave way to a period of relative decline in
numbers, but nevertheless spawned some remarkable composers. Lili
Boulanger won the Prix de Rome in 1913 and her sister Nadia became an
influential teacher of composition.[29] Ruth Crawford Seeger (1901–53),
perhaps the first recognised innovatory female composer after Hildegard,
was immersed in a circle of the most forward-thinking United States
musicians of the day. Many of her techniques foreshadowed developments that were later to become widely used, including total serial
control, note-clusters, cell-permutations, sound masses and layers,
dynamic counterpoint and other devices (Gaume 1986). In 1930 she
became the first woman to be awarded a Guggenheim fellowship for
European study in composition. In Britain composers such as Elizabeth
Maconchy (b. 1907), Elisabeth Lutyens (1906–83), Nicola LeFanu (b. 1947)
and Judith Weir (b. 1954), in the USA Scottish-born Thea Musgrave (b.
1928) and Nancy Van de Vate (b. 1930), in Russia, Sofia Gubaidulina (b.
1931) and many more in these countries and elsewhere have filled
concert-halls and recording studios with music encompassing all genres.[30]

   It has been increasingly the case during the twentieth century that
many of the most successful women composers in the classical field have
reported discrimination less vociferously than their foremothers. Seeger

---

[28] Battersby (1989) traces the development of the concept of genius as the 'bedrock of European
   culture' (p. 3) from earliest known times to the present, and provides some helpful arguments
   about its relevance for contemporary feminism. I will return to this in Chapter 9. Garnett (1995)
   provided some valuable insights on, amongst other things, the interface between genius, femininity, women and composition in the nineteenth century.
[29] See Citron (1991), Jezic (1988, pp. 139–46).
[30] For information on contemporary women composers, two very useful comprehensive sources are
   Zaimont et al. (1984), (1987), (1991) and Sadie and Samuel (1994). Also see LePage (1980). The
   question of 'women's music' will be explored in Chapter 5 below.

did not 'overtly question her place in a male-dominated society' according to Gaume (1986, p. 382); she assumed equality with the men she met
professionally, and she encountered a minimum of discrimination.
Some of the established women composers who took part in a questionnaire in 1980 also claimed to experience little discrimination, and others
are notorious for their disdain of feminism (whatever that may mean to
each individual).[31] Growing feminist interest and activism around questions of musical opportunity, combined with a wider social climate in
which women are increasingly gaining access to education and professional roles in many spheres, are without doubt responsible for at least
diminishing the normative masculine delineation of music in contemporary society. But despite these improvements, the assumption that the
composer is a man is still far from unreasonable.

As the useful survey by LeFanu (1987) shows, the proportion of women
composers in Britain then amounted to around 15 per cent and, more
tellingly perhaps, performances of their work to less than 5 per cent. In
May 1995, BBC Radio 3 (the main sponsored classical music station)
listed 11 women composers, and 840 men composers (J. Halstead 1995,
p. 346). In the 1990 BBC Promenade Concerts brochure, one woman
and 90 men composers were listed; in the 1995 brochure, 5 women and
106 men (Samuel 1995). There is no evidence to suggest that figures are
radically different in other countries, and similar ratios are reflected in
all sources that I have been able to consult. Not only minority status but a
sense of discrimination amongst many contemporary women composers is very strong indeed. The post-sixties rebirth of Women in Music
networks, which amongst several other activities organise competitions,
performances and broadcasts of music composed by women, in
Canada, Denmark, Britain, Spain, Japan, the Netherlands, Switzerland,
the United States, Germany and other countries (see Gottlieb 1991), also
testifies to the continuing existence of a need to bolster and defend the
woman composer.

Not only does part of all musical delineation still contain the normative assumption that there is a man behind the music; the cerebral
delineation of composition continues to carry overwhelmingly masculine connotations. The underlying presuppositions of music criticism

---

[31] For the questionnaire and its results see Barkin (1980), (1981), (1982). This involved a number of,
mostly North American, professional women composers who wrote freely about their experiences as composers, and their opinions on the significance of gender in the world of composition.
Although it makes interesting reading, the responses remain uninterpreted raw data. See J.
Halstead (1995, pp. 286ff) for a helpful discussion of the views of some contemporary women
composers, both pro- and anti-feminist.

stemming from the nineteenth century have survived without much compromise in the discourse on classical music today. Jill Halstead's (1995) work, involving case-studies of nine twentieth-century British women composers, allows a detection of three types of criticism, similar to the three categories which I drew up earlier. The first category involves the assumption that a woman's music can be heard to fail, for the reason that it is by a woman. A comparable attitude is expressed below, in the denigration of the woman for trying to compose at all. This newspaper article was entitled 'She composes in the kitchen':

To the milkman, the grocer, and the baker . . . Mrs Ruth Baker is just another customer. In the world of music she is Ruth Gipps, housewife composer . . . Her next big work is now being completed in the intervals between making the beds, cooking the breakfast and preparing lunch. (*Daily Mail*, 24 October 1946, cited in J. Halstead 1995, p. 150)

As Halstead says:

Ruth Gipps is described in rather mocking terms: the implication is that this woman, whose prime function is to be a housewife, is merely a part-time composer. Ruth Gipps was then aged twenty-five; she had already completed about fifty works including two symphonies; she had had her first composition published at the age of eight. At the Royal College of Music she had collected all the composition prizes, becoming one of Vaughan Williams' most promising students. This disturbingly flippant account allows the reader to suppose that Gipps is a rank amateur, and that her attempts at composition may well be less than competent. (J. Halstead 1995, p. 150)

As recently as 1989 it was still possible for a major British newspaper to publish an article which seriously argued that women were incapable of composing 'good' music.[32]

Secondly, the idea that women's music is good because it displays feminine characteristics of grace, delicacy or emotionality:

Tate's on the other hand is a more feminine talent. She began with light-fingered and light-hearted music . . . But she developed and went on to more deeply felt works . . . of which *Nocturne* . . . enshrines disturbing emotions of war, all the deeper because so quietly and quiveringly imagined . . . (Howes 1966, p. 293; cited in J. Halstead 1995, p. 247)

And:

Miss Gipps does not make the mistake of trying to beat male composers at their own game, but instead makes the most of the virtues of her own sex. There is a

---

[32] By Bryan Magee (1989) in *The Guardian*, cited in Cant (1990a, p. 1).

distinctly feminine grace and delicacy about all her work . . . (Editorial, *The Strad*, January 1947, cited in J. Halstead 1995, p. 247)

Thirdly, the notion that when a woman's work succeeds, this is to be explained in terms of its masculinity:

Maconchy made her mark with string quartets and shows a disposition towards an intellectual source of inspiration rather than sensibility or emotion. If this is regarded as a masculine trait it corresponds to a robust trait in her personality which enabled her, for instance, to represent English composers in Moscow as president of the Composers' Guild. (Howes 1966, p. 293; cited in J. Halstead 1995, p. 246)

Or:

The fact that no-one surveying the whole range and character of [Grace Williams'] music would be able to tell, without prior knowledge, that it was the work of a woman rather than a man is in part a measure of her success . . . (Boyd 1980, p. 10, cited in J. Halstead 1995, p. 242)

Both sides of the masculine delineation of music – the assumption of the male classical composer bequeathed to us by history, and the cerebral, masculine connotation of composition – are still in operation. I have argued that musical delineations are not closed unto themselves, but that they affect our perception of inherent meanings. In the face of the twofold masculine delineation of music, what happens when we do discover a woman's mind behind the music is that her femininity then enters the delineation as an unusual and noticeable fact, which conflicts with the delineation of mental capacity arising from composition. From that position, delineated femininity acts to alter our attitude towards the inherent meanings of the music. We are then liable to judge the woman composer's handling of inherent meanings in terms of our idea of her femininity. It is not that there is anything feminine about the inherent meanings, but that the idea of femininity filters our response to them. The fact that some critics have been able to hold on to their conviction that women cannot compose is not, then, the result of pure prejudice: it is something which they apparently learn from their experience of music itself. I would therefore suggest that it is something which is difficult for everyone, and this must include myself, to resist.

Jazz

Many of the women who have been employed as jazz pianists throughout this century were also composers and/or arrangers with male bands.

The ironic reason for this is that the middle-class tradition of educating girls in piano and theory, which applied to girls of several ethnic origins, equipped them with certain notational and theoretical skills which the early jazzmen in particular lacked but found helpful. Lil Hardin Armstrong and Mary Lou Williams provide pertinent examples.[33] In jazz, improvisation has more status than notated composition, spontaneity more than theoretical or technical know-how. Thus it should be no surprise that women were more acceptable in the role of composer or arranger than that of improviser; that women composers working with notation were in some cases acknowledged to be more skilled at this task than the men in the bands for whom they worked; or that women were commonly productive as composers in some of the notation-based relatives of jazz such as ragtime. Such licence and acknowledgement contain and perpetuate the age-old relegation of women to the less important, since supposedly less creative and authentic, aesthetic tasks. Like their foremothers in the fourteenth century, jazz women did not have access to the training required for the most innovatory developments. Nearly all of this training took place through improvisation, in venues where women were employed as waitresses and prostitutes, even as singers, but where they would have been 'true anomalies' (Dahl 1984, p. 12) as improvising instrumentalists. Even though a few women did perform in the improvising circuits, they played only accompanying roles, rarely taking an improvised solo.

The masculine cerebral delineation of music which I have described in relation to classical music has operated in almost exactly the same way in relation to jazz, certainly for the greater part of this century, only with application to the realm of improvisation rather than notated composition. In the citations below, the three categories of nineteenth- and twentieth-century classical music criticism located above (pp. 98–101) can again be detected. First, the assumption that femininity is a cause of musical failure:

Jazz is a male language and women just can't do it. (An anonymous male jazz pianist in 1973, cited in Dahl 1984, p. 3)

Why is it that outside of a few sepia females the woman musician never was born capable of sending anyone further than the nearest exit? . . . You can forgive them for lacking guts in their playing but even women should be able to

---

[33] For information on jazz women, see Dahl (1984), Placksin (1985), Gourse (1995), Hassinger (1987); also, to some extent, Kent (1983). There is a Women's Jazz Archive at the University of Wales, Swansea, Great Britain.

play with feeling and expression and *they never do it.* (An anonymous critic in *Down Beat,* 1938, cited in Dahl 1984, p. 52)

Secondly, the idea that feminine qualities such as delicacy or proximity to feeling can be expressed by a woman composer as positive attributes of her music: a woman jazz musician responded to the statement above thus:

feeling, tone and phrasing is [*sic*] a quality which girls alone are more likely to possess because of the aesthetic nature of their sex. I noticed girls, because of their feminine tendency, cooperate to make the rhythm section a united unit dependent on each other, rather than the masculine tendency to lead on his own instrument. (Cited in Dahl 1986, p. 52)

The reader may have noticed that the above two citations were also made with reference to performance in Chapter 3. Because of the close connection of performance and improvisation in jazz, they are just as legitimately read with reference to composition. Another example is:

The fact that she is a woman has no bearing on Miss Williams' stature as an artist, but on the other hand, should not lead us to ignore or deny that her music has a delightfully feminine ambiance. (Dan Morgenstern, liner notes to *Jazz Pioneers,* Prestige Records 7647, cited in Dahl 1986, p. 60)

Thirdly, the idea that successful women composers are not really women:

So fully has [Mary Lou Williams] made it that in discussing her work one almost forgets she's a woman. (Barry Ulanov, *Metronome,* July 1949, cited in Dahl 1986, p. 60)

These citations also remind us of the impossibility of listening to music by a woman without judging its inherent meanings in terms of our idea of her femininity.

As in classical music, there are today increasing numbers of women composing and improvising in jazz;[34] and in the realm of jazz criticism, the masculine delineation of music and its interrogation by feminine delineations are also beginning to recede. But in jazz, there is a particular force to this, precisely because of the closer ties which jazz 'composition' has to performance. The woman jazz improviser cannot be concealed, can never be part of an invisible construction of cerebral genius, cannot be taken for a man, because she not only composes but performs: not only uses her mind but displays her body. When her position in this nexus of feminine musical delineation fails to elicit the

---

[34] Barbara Thompson, Marilyn Crispell, Annie Whitehead are among the better-known names. For more information see the references in note 33 above.

age-old responses, a strong impression is made. For example, a 1994 advertising flyer for 'The Annie Whitehead Experience' contained the following words:

With Annie's writing trademark of deep harmonies and rich melodies and Kim Clarke's divine and hard driving funk grooves, this promises to be a classic union.

> 'Her fierce gritty trombone must be the most ubiquitous sound in British music right now.' (*City Limits*)
> 'Annie Whitehead, the woman who everyone turns to when they want a class trombone player.' (*Beats International*)
> 'Now is the hour to acknowledge a woman who is arguably the country's premier jazz and reggae session trombonist.' (New Musical Express)

(Jazz Moves Ltd, 98 Hazelville Road, London N19 3NA; and the London Arts Board)

Albeit in the context of a promotional flyer, this depiction of a female performing and composing musician breaks right out of the negatively valued, limiting feminine delineations which have dogged women musicians and women's music in so many countries for so many centuries. I will not try to predict where it will lead. It is at the moment a chink of light which suggests the possibility of a different realm: I wish to wedge the chink open and return to it in another context, in Chapter 9.

Popular music

Women composers have experienced strongly the negative effects of music's twofold masculine delineation when they have taken up compositional and improvisatory roles in popular and rock music. The best-known women composers in these areas have continued the tradition, begun in the sixteenth century, of writing popular songs. The New York Brill Building of the late 1950s to the mid-1960s housed perhaps the two most prolific and successful such women composers: Carole King and Ellie Greenwich. As with their foremothers, many women popular songwriters have performed their work themselves. Included among these are members of girl groups, although their work was frequently not credited (Grieg 1989), and a long list of well-known solo names, from Carole King's launch of her performing career, to Joni Mitchell, Dory Previn, Kate Bush, Annie Lennox, Randy Crawford, Joan Armatrading, k. d. lang, P. J. Harvey, and many more.[35] These women have perhaps

---

[35] See Gaar (1993), Steward and Garratt (1984), Grieg (1989), Evans (1994), L. O'Brien (1994), K. O'Brien (1995), Mellers (1986) on women composers in popular music.

enjoyed more public credibility and less critical prejudice than any other category of female composers since the singer-songwriters of Renaissance Italy.

There are two sides to this. On one hand, as I have already argued, the singer-songwriter is a relatively unthreatening role for women, and in many ways, it affirms traditional notions of femininity. The reconstitution of this age-old affirmative symbolisation in the realm of women's composition was epitomised in an advertisement on Virgin Radio in the spring of 1995. It was for a new album entitled *Girls and Guitars*, featuring twenty female singer-songwriters including many of those I have named above. Such a record labels the songs as 'women's work', turning the fact of femininity into a sales gimmick in ways that replicate the fetishisation and marginalisation of women's compositions which I have already described and which have gone on for a very long time. On the other hand, despite this pessimism, I believe that these women and their colleagues in all other fields of composition in the past and present, can and do represent an alternative side of femininity such as I have located with reference to women singers and instrumentalists: the force of their resistance in both practical and symbolic refutations of patriarchal definitions cannot be ignored. I will return to this in Chapter 9.

Increasing numbers of women are now involved in popular music composition and arranging beyond vocal composition, although of course most popular music *is* vocal and so there are relatively few other outlets anyway. But the heavily technical, technological, innovative, experimental, structurally larger-scale and progressive rock or rock-derived music of bands from Pink Floyd to Naked City are as male-associated in their compositional delineations as is any Beethoven symphony; and compositional or creative aspects of 'roots' popular music such as the blues still readily claim a wholly masculine delineation.[36] As Chapter 3 indicates, women are moving into the performance of such music, but it remains the case that few of them take leading compositional or improvisatory roles. Women are assumed to have no technical knowledge of these kinds of music, or even any knowledge at all. (I recently gave a lecture-workshop to a group of music graduates on a Post-Graduate Certificate in Education course. The focus of the workshop was on teaching music in schools, with special attention to inner-city classrooms of multi-ethnic, bilingual, musically illiterate pupils aged eleven to thir-

---

[36] See Reynolds and Press (1995) for a radical perspective on the assertion of machismo and the expression of misogyny in rock. Also, Hisama (1993) on rock's fetishisation of far Eastern women, focussing on Mellencamp, Bowie and Zorn.

teen. One of the activities which I introduced involved ways in which to get such pupils playing simple riffs and twelve-bar progressions in time with each other and with a drum kit, on electric keyboards. Before the break I indicated that those pupils who could manage to play the progression well with the left hand could begin – whilst waiting for the others to catch up with them – simple preparatory improvisation work with the other hand. I suggested that the easiest notes on which they could start were the same notes as those in the chord, with a flat third added. In my experience, this is a manageable technique to use with thirty inner-city kids of different abilities in one room, and the pupils find it achievable and stimulating. When we then broke for coffee, a male student came up ever so pleasantly and explained that the blues actually had a special scale. 'Oh!' I dissimulated with a mildly amused embarrassment that he should think I did not already know this. Encouraged by my exclamation, which he must have taken to be an indication of interest, he showed me the 'blues scale' on the piano.)

A high level of recording (or production) technique is involved in very recent popular music styles, and here again, the control over a musical style which has gradually claimed its own need of legitimate expertise is entirely male. The implications of this are forcibly demonstrated in Bradby's (1993b) analysis of rave, cited above in Chapter 2, in which she exposes the exploitation of one (maternal) woman's sampled voice on a video with a different (sexy) woman apparently doing the singing. The company involved, Black Box, were sued by the woman whose voice had been sampled, Loleatta Holloway. The issue that I want to note here is Bradby's comparison of this case with that of a different one, involving M/A/R/R/S. Whereas women were typically involved in the first case as performers singing and miming, men were involved in the second case as the producers and owners of musical ideas. Whereas the woman in the first case sought litigation over the men's sampling of her voice and its alienation from her body, the men in the second case sued other men over the sampling of their music and their rights in intellectual property. Bradby says:

The all-male nature of this case . . . reflects where men had positioned themselves in relation to ownership and authorship in popular music. In the case of Loleatta Holloway versus Black Box, the underlying issues . . . involved the position of women in relation to performance and the criteria we use to identify a body as that of 'the performer' . . . With M/A/R/R/S the issue was the sampling of men's ideas; with Black Box, it was the sampling of women's bodies. (Bradby 1993b, p. 172)

There is little that could better summarise the exclusion by default of women from the notion of composition, the ownership of compositional production by men, or the delineation of the masculine mind by music than this scenario; at the same time, it reveals how the very workings that started to exclude women from composition, or to claim composition as masculine, in the sacred polyphonic music of the fourteenth century are still operating in the contemporary era.

SUMMARY

I argued in Chapter 2 that the freedom of woman to sing does not represent her release from patriarchal definitions of femininity but, rather, reproduces and affirms those definitions. Unlike singing, I argued in Chapter 3, public instrumental performance by women to some extent interrupts patriarchal conceptions of femininity. In the current chapter, I have suggested that composition by women presents an even stronger challenge. The idea of a woman mentally manipulating or controlling music is incommensurable and unacceptable, because women cannot be understood to retain their dependent, bodily femininity at the same time as producing a cerebral and potentially autonomous work of genius. The effects of this threat are evidenced in the practices of women composers and the reception of their music throughout history. Women's access to the kind of music education required for contemporary compositional developments originally became restricted at a time when the first major technical developments in music for centuries were rearing their heads in the shape of polyphony. Compositional activity after polyphony becomes increasingly separate from that of performance, requiring more control over instrumental technology and musical technique. At its most extreme points, this kind of composition gives rise to a delineation of the genius of the transcendent male ego. In the hands of a woman, it threatens the natural bodily submission of her femininity by clearly demonstrating that she also has a mind. Highly prized improvisatory practices, likewise, are incommensurable with a woman musical creator because the patriarchal construction of her femininity conflicts with their delineations of creative, mental capacity.

The music of many women has been denigrated because of the conflict between the cerebral connotations of the act of composition and the bodily connotations of femininity. Women's music has also been recognised as displaying more affirmative feminine characteristics, but has thus been marginalised and limited. In both cases, the fetishisation of the feminine delineation has led critics, listeners and musicians alike to understand the music's inherent meanings through a filter of femininity. Only the most successful woman composer, whose music conforms to contemporary definitions of what music should be, has been judged on the basis of the inherent meanings of her music. She has then been recognised as an honorary man, her femininity, her real woman's achievement, remaining unsung. Music delineates masculinity, a male mind, a man behind the music; and this has become so normal and acceptable that we do not even notice its presence, until something happens to break it. The masculine meaning of music arises partly by virtue of the clash between the bodily connotations of femininity and the cerebral delineations of composition; it also arises by virtue of the minority status of women in – and even, in some types of music, their exclusion from – the role of composer. In a relationship of circularity, it is then used to justify that exclusion.

There is a difficult and central question which I have begged all the way through this chapter: that of aesthetic, specifically musical, value. If it is suggested that women composers or women's compositions have been unjustly devalued, then that must imply taking some alternative stance towards their value. This in turn indicates the application of some criteria by which to judge musical value. I would not defend the view that aesthetic value is totally relative, which is to say, that each listener's hearing of a piece of music is equally valid. At the same time, there is no single, final and correct way of listening to or judging any piece of music. It is a matter of maintaining a sensitive balance between socio-historical relativity in the construction of aesthetic value, and the subject-position of the receiver and the producer of the art. In order to ascertain whether there is any aesthetic value in a work, we must attempt to make our criteria explicit. Although this suggestion is currently wholly out of fashion, unless we seek *some* sort of criteria we cannot understand the art of either our own era or any other era as anything but a random expression of some mysterious human essence. In fact, unless we actually look at or listen to works of art or other cultural artefacts and attempt to judge them in some way, how can we know anything about them at all? In the case of music there is a need for a theory of musical meaning, which I have so far tried to address with relation to gender, which contextualises judgements about musical value in terms both of the music's style and of the cultural location of its production and reception, in relation to the plethora of musical meanings that persist in any social situation. On the other hand, there is also a need for comparative analytical work on men's and women's music. These are two of the subjects of discussion in the next chapter.

CHAPTER 5

Towards a model of gendered musical meaning and experience

So far I have been discussing musical meaning in terms of the gender of the performer or composer. Another area in which meanings about gender and sexuality can be very clearly constructed is that of song lyrics and opera libretti. The verbally articulated meanings of lyrics and libretti are not part of the virtual intra-musical or inherent meaning of music; rather, words are conspicuous vehicles for conveying musical delineations. A growing number of writers have discussed the gender and/or the sexual implications of the verbal content of song lyrics and opera libretti, quite apart from any musical analysis.[1] There are also several other approaches which are of a different nature in that they make very close connections between inherent meanings and the delineations of the words, sometimes coming near to dissolving the boundary between the two. A certain amount of work of this nature has been done with reference to popular song. Such work seeks to illuminate the mutual exchange between a song's verbally delineated meanings and their gestic or structural replication in inherent meanings.[2] In the field of classical music, most (but not all) of this kind of attention has been paid to opera, which provides a provocative object of criticism where relations between the sexes and the construction of masculinity and femininity are explored overtly through the libretto, with relation to more covert significance in musical structures. Although their analytical and philosophical methods are all different, these approaches have in

[1] See e.g. Clément (1988), S. Cook (1994), Carby (1990), Berry (1994), Grieg (1989). The literature on music video which addresses the narrative or images rather than the music is vast. See Stockbridge (1990), Kaplan (1987), (1993), Lewis (1990), (1992). There are also examples of alternative strategies in women's music which centre around lyrics/libretti, when opera composers have taken the opportunity to set feminist libretti, or when song-writers have set feminist lyrics in popular and rock music. E.g. *re* opera, LeFanu's *Blood Wedding* (1992); and on rock, see Petersen (1987, pp. 205–6), Gaar (1993).

[2] See esp. Bradby and Torode (1984), Bradby (1990), (1992). See Middleton (1990, esp. pp. 227–32) for a helpful discussion of the relationship between music and words with special reference to popular music.

common the ability to expose the power of vocal music to express *more* than the words to which it is set, laying bare some of the traditionally unexamined assumptions that the music of the operatic canon is universal and innocent of political significance.[3]

The music/word relationship provides a highly fruitful forum for demonstrating the musical articulation of gendered meanings, but I have put any detailed discussion of the relationship between words and music outside the bounds of this study. Such work implies, and sometimes explicitly addresses, a further, major question which does closely impinge on my area of discussion. This question is: can even absolute music be understood as a gendered discourse? In the first section of this chapter I will examine how this question has been approached in some of the major work in the field of feminist musicology, focussing mainly on the contribution of Susan McClary (1991) as well as that of Marcia Citron (1993).[4] In the second section of the chapter I will attempt to pull together various threads which have emerged during the book, in order to weave an overall theory of gendered musical meaning and to relate this theory to an interpretation of gendered musical experience.

CONTEMPORARY FEMINIST APPROACHES TO ABSOLUTE MUSIC

Some central issues

McClary's work on absolute music is grounded in the notion that music can 'influence and even constitute the ways listeners experience and define some of their own most intimate feelings' (p. 9). Because of this, music participates actively in 'the social organization of sexuality'. Thus, one of the principal tasks of feminist music criticism would be to examine the semiotics of desire, arousal, and sexual pleasure that

---

[3] For analyses of the interrelations between operatic music and words or plot, with special reference to gender/sexuality, see McClary (1991, Chapters 2, 3 and 4), (1992), Ford (1991), Brett (1993), Wood (1993), (1994), Abbate (1991), (1993), Citron (1993, pp. 70–5), Wheelock (1993), Cusick (1993b). Also, on sacred cantata (Bach's *Wachet auf*), see McClary (1987, pp. 41–55); on song, Hamessley (1994), Scott (1993) (both classical and popular in a very wide sense).

[4] Although many writers have contributed to the field, McClary's *Feminine Endings* was the first monograph (actually a collection of autonomous, linked papers) to break away from compensatory historiography and into feminist critique. Citron (1993) represents another important monograph. The area has developed rapidly, and as with any academic field, there is widespread critical debate between scholars, and a rich variety of approaches. Much of this is to be found in Solie (1993), Cook and Tsou (1994), Brett, Thomas and Wood (1994), Ford (1991), Marshall (1993b), Dunn and Jones (1994). Also see Lamb (1991b), (1993), (1994b), (1996); Koza (1994a), (1994b); Green (1994b) on feminist musicology in relation to music education.

circulate in the public sphere through music' (p. 9). Her project is to demonstrate ways in which music is concerned with 'the arousing and channeling of desire, with mapping patterns through the medium of sound that resemble those of sexuality' (p. 8). She works out her theory through two related concepts. One involves the identification of musical teleology; the other is the idea of a narrative which is played out in musical structures. These concepts are linked in that they are both deciphered through the location of intra-musical hierarchical relationships.

First, on teleology, McClary argues that in music from c. 1600 to 1900, tonality itself is the principal musical means for arousing and channelling desire, through instilling expectations, withholding their fulfilment (pp. 13–14) and promising a final catharsis. This occurs at the surface level from theme to theme, for example; at the middleground level from key area to key area; and at the background level of a whole movement. With the breakdown of tonality, these same principles of creating and finally satisfying desire are adopted in different musical styles from rock to post-tonal and neo-tonal music, through various other structural means. Here McClary is describing one post-tonal example, an early programmatic composition on 'Jack and the Beanstalk' by Janika Vandervelde:

A kind of pitch ceiling consolidates, against which melodic motives begin to push as though against a palpable obstacle. As frustration mounts, the urgency of the motivic salvos increases; they move in shorter and shorter time spans, until they succeed finally in bursting through the barrier with a spasm of ejaculatory release. This musical gesture appears prominently in many of our favorite repertories. It guarantees our identification with the music, for its buildup hooks us, motivating us to invest personally in sequences of seemingly abstract musical events; and we are rewarded for having thus invested in its patterns of yearning when they reach cathartic fulfillment, which mysteriously becomes our own experience of libidinal gratification. (1991, pp. 112–13)

With reference to further musical contexts in which the 'unembarrassed reassertion' (p. 113) of this gesture is to be found:

The gesture is only slightly more graphic and literal in pornographic films, in which key structural moments of tension and release likewise are conventionally embodied through what is called the 'money shot' – close-up footage of a discharging penis. (p. 113)

What are the assumptions behind these notions of tension and release? This question leads us to McClary's second related concept: that of narrative paradigms. Soviet narratologists and many theorists working in film and media studies[5] have argued that all fictional heroes have male characteristics, regardless of the text or image which depicts them, and that narrative always includes an obstacle, characterised as a female Other that must be controlled or otherwise subjugated. I have already mentioned in Chapter 4 (pp. 97–8) that it used to be customary in nineteenth-century pedagogic and critical practice to characterise the first theme of sonata form as 'masculine' and the second theme as 'feminine'.[6] McClary argues that this practice is translatable into the idea that in sonata form the first theme serves the narrative function of the male protagonist/hero, and the second theme serves that of the female Other, being constructed as a foil or obstacle which is overcome or contained for the sake of narrative closure by the return of the tonic key. After 1900, rather than taking the form of a second subject in a new key, the Other may be merely an alien terrain through which the piece passes before closure. In the case of popular music (see esp. pp. 159ff on this), which also usually avoids the narrative schema of Other keys, all that is needed to turn the music into this narrative is for a musical detail to be construed as Other; in this way, McClary argues, climax and resolution are achieved in many popular songs.

A comparable position is taken up by Citron (1993, pp. 133–4). Focussing on nineteenth-century concert music, she also invokes the contemporary pedagogic and critical references to themes as masculine and feminine, arguing that 'sonata form became a metaphor for the gendered struggle' (p. 134). Even though not all sonatas necessarily exhibited masculine and feminine themes, the very existence of these codes tells us 'a great deal about the representation of women and men in society, how ideologies affected how music itself was conceptualized and described, and how music had close ties with ideals and processes in society' (p. 137; also p. 141). Although she says she does not wish to enter into the topic fully, Citron acknowledges, with McClary, that sonata form could be considered to contain an element of musical Otherness which is infused in many readings with the label feminine, and which 'must be squelched so that the inexorable dominance of the tonic emerges as victor' (pp. 139–40).[7]

---

[5] For example McClary cites Propp (1968), Lotman (1979) and de Lauretis (1987). Also see Kaplan (1993) for critique.

[6] As well as Tick (1986) already discussed (Chapter 4, pp. 97–8 above), also see McClary (1991, pp. 13–17, 68–9) and Citron (1993, pp. 132–44) for further details about this.

[7] Treitler (1993) discusses medieval chants in terms of their contemporary masculine and feminine associations, viewed as emblematic social constructions of their era; a position which he distinguishes from that of McClary in terms of its attention to the unavoidability of the participation of the critic in the process of construction. Also see Kallberg (1992) on gender and ideology in the piano nocturne.

At various points, McClary identifies the operation of teleology and narrative by virtue of musical hierarchical relationships, which, she says, are themselves identified with the binary oppositions that underpin the foundations of Western thought (1991, pp. 123–4, 66, 135). This theoretical position allows for the concept of a musical semiotics of desire and narrative to be released from any necessary ties to specifically gendered discourses. For example, the Other need not always be interpreted strictly as female (p. 16): it can be anything that stands as an obstacle or threat to identity and that must therefore be purged or brought under submission for the sake of narrative closure. The hero and its obstacle in tonal narrative are functional roles which can be mapped onto other deeply embedded oppositions in Western thought: for example, reason and feeling, culture and nature, mind and body, masculininity and femininity. Music has multiple meanings, and the tensions of music can be read in many ways: they are taken as simply 'the way music goes' (p. 16). However, McClary suggests that the opposition of male and female is the most fundamental of all. It is through such conventions that 'gender and sexuality are most effectively – and most problematically – organised in music' (p. 17).

Later in the book she illustrates how such a position can be brought to bear with reference to a different piece by Janika Vandervelde. Having analysed the piece in some detail, tracing its gender symbolisation, she says that the connection between the piece and gender is not a necessary one. 'What has this piece to do with gender?' (p. 123).

It should be clear by now that *Genesis II* calls into question much more than simple male/female roles in society. Indeed, the piece addresses a very basic level of Western culture's metaphysical foundation, a level at which many of the essential binary oppositions underlying our value system are laid distressingly bare: culture/nature, progress/stability, individuality/community. As has been implied throughout this reading of *Genesis II*, one can read its tensions in terms of the various excessive qualities of modernity – the capitalist undermining of more mercantile economic processes, imperialist invasions of 'primitive' societies, scientific quests that replace ecologically grounded philosophies of nature with threats of nuclear destruction, the programs of urban renewal that destroy traditional communities.

But the piece is also available to be read in terms of male/female – the opposition that is probably the most ancient and most fundamental of all and that lurks behind all the others mentioned. (pp. 123–4)

This extrapolation from musical processes to a characterisation of Western thought is comparable with Ford's (1991) reading of the relationship between sonata form and binary opposition. Although he does not suggest that it has any reference to masculinity and femininity outside a particular operatic context, he does extrapolate, from the logic of the Enlightenment, connections between thought about sexuality and musical theory. He identifies the same self-generating series of binary oppositions as does McClary, suggesting that although they pertain particularly to the eighteenth century, the legacy of these associations is still with us today. He seeks to demonstrate that these oppositions were translated into the tension between dominant and subdominant modulation. The former, dominant modulation, seems to go against nature in that it requires an effort, the addition of the dissonant, sharpened fourth degree to form the new leading note, and a large leap to the dominant of the dominant. The latter, subdominant modulation, succumbs to a more natural, seemingly effortless tendency to drop the leading note (which is incidentally in accord with the makeup of the overtone series), and modulate anti-clockwise around the cycle of fifths. Dominant modulation gives a sense of striving, subdominant modulation one of yielding. Thus, in contrast to the view that the first, tonic-key *theme* was seen as masculine, and the second, dominant-key theme as feminine, the process of *modulation from* the tonic *to* the dominant is associated with masculinity (and the other concomitant halves of the binary oppositions), and that of subdominant modulation with femininity (and its concomitants). Linked with these processes is an interpretation of metric dynamism as configuring masculinity, and decorative stasis as connoting femininity. Ford argues, through musical analytical examples, that Mozart articulated such associations in his Da Ponte operas by giving singers particular musical jobs to do, which made use of these musical tensions to either underline or make ambiguous the content of the plot. Putting it crudely, if a character, who may be either a man or a woman, is dominant or in control of a situation, their vocal line will dynamically modulate to the dominant; if yielding to seduction, their line will subside in subdominant modulation.[8]

The identification of alternative strategies

McClary and Citron as well as other theorists[9] do not stop at criticising musical teleology and the narrative paradigm, but go beyond that to

[8] The musicological literature on Mozart's operas is of course extensive, although very little could be identified as feminist, however broadly that term is defined. See Wheelock (1993) for an interpretation which suggests that Mozart's use of the minor mode indicates female/feminine power.

[9] See Cox (1991), and pp. 129–30 below; Wood (1993), (1994), Abbate (1993), Cusick (1993a), (1993b), Rycenga (1994), Lamb (1994a).

offer alternatives. The idea that women may write a different kind of music to men was first mooted earlier in this century. Just as Virginia Woolf had suggested the possibility of a 'woman's sentence', so in 1933 Ethel Smyth conjured up the following scenario:

After all, it must not be forgotten that this hubbub, this bustle, this unrest, consequently in a certain sense this coarseness, are part of a man-made world and constitute an element in which men for the time being seem thoroughly comfortable . . . Now what if women suddenly say to themselves: 'this is blatant, spectacular in the wrong sense, superficial, vulgar; *I don't believe in it*'? Then would my girl student pause a moment, contemplate her half-finished serenade for 8 horns, 8 trumpets, 10 trombones, 12 percussion instruments and two dozen explosive bombs and murmur 'But this is imitative rubbish', tear up her manuscript and throw it into the waste-paper basket. (*Female Pipings in Eden*, cited in Cooper 1977, p. 19)

Systematised investigation of the implications of such a suggestion did not take place until the 1980s. Up until the time of writing *Feminine Endings*, McClary points out, discussions about women in composition had centred on equality of opportunity: the assumption had been that, given the same access, women composers would emerge '*indistinguishable from their male colleagues*' (1991, p. 114). But she argues that a woman can create in a mode that calls upon her experiences as a woman (pp. 115–16). She suggests that it may be possible to show that women composers from Hildegard to Fanny Hensel 'wrote in ways that made a difference within the music itself' (p. 33); and she goes on to show how this occurs in four main contemporary examples, the overall context for whom has allowed them to '*choose* to write music that foregrounds their sexual identities without falling prey to essentialist traps and that departs self-consciously from the assumptions of standard musical procedures' (p. 33). The four are the concert composer Janika Vandervelde, the performance-artists Laurie Anderson and Diamanda Galas, and pop superstar Madonna.

For example, even within the '"non-representational" bastion of instrumental music' (p. 116), as distinct from reproducing the paradigms of musical teleology, Janika Vandervelde has chosen

to deny herself the automatic surge of power it reliably delivers, to analyse its contours, and to embark on a journey in search of alternative ways of organizing sound, ways that correspond more closely to her own values and experiences. By extension it is also the story of any composer – female or male – who has become dissatisfied with implied contents of received artistic conventions and procedures, especially the standard narrative of tonal striving, climax, and closure. (McClary 1991, pp. 113–14)

Vandervelde's search for an alternative mode of musical expression and organisation lead to a series of pieces about genesis (already referred to in a different context above). '*Genesis II* opens with what Vandervelde intends as a musical image of childbirth: the pulsation of a fetal heartbeat, the intensifying strains of labor, and the sudden emergence into a fresh and calm new world' (1991, p. 116). McClary analyses the ensuing organisation of time by the music. On one hand there is a cyclical orientation of time through a clockwork motif which sets up no expectation for change; on the other, there are the more familiar goal-oriented gestures of self-expression and striving (p. 119). She argues that the metaphorical implications of these two types of music allow the enactment of a collision which breaks away from the old narrative paradigms. Furthermore, the traditional order of the first theme as heroic protagonist and the second theme as passive obstacle is reversed. Accepted narrative is disrupted, and finally the cathartic fulfilment of desire at the end is denied in favour of a 'post-nuclear silence' and an 'embryonic promise of a new and perhaps different scenario' (p. 121).

McClary's discussion of Galas, Anderson and Madonna holds in common their challenge to the idea of a unitary male subject, arising both from their performance practices and from their music itself. In ways that are structurally and symbolically akin to the musical processes of Vandervelde described above, their music also presents alternative metaphors in accordance with a non-hierarchical organisation of time, subverting the traditional paradigms of musical teleology and narrative, amd demanding new sets of analytical procedures.[10]

Citron's (1993, pp. 145–64) position is methodologically not dissimilar, but focusses on the work of a nineteenth-century rather than a present-day composer. She analyses the first movement of Cécile Chaminade's Sonata Op. 21 in order to explore the possibility that it challenges the representational model of sonata codes. The movement is a mixture of sonata form, character piece, and prelude and fugue. The idea of tonal progress 'is subverted in favor of emphasis on home key: tonal stasis, if you will. Put another way, a major aspect of desire is being denied' (p. 149). There is structural and gendered ambiguity in the character of the second theme (p. 152), the key of which, unlike that of the masculine

---

[10] On Galas, see e.g. pp. 110–11 and Chapter 4; on Anderson, pp. 141ff *re* the song 'O Superman' and Chapter 6; on Madonna, pp. 158–61 *re* the song 'Live To Tell', and Chapter 7. McClary also analyses alternative, non-teleological procedures linked with the construction of subjectivity in resistance to mainstream notions of male heterosexuality, with reference to Tchaikovsky (1991, pp. 69–79), Brahms (1993) and Schubert (1994).

first theme, is never clearly established (p. 154). The feminine is a notable presence, 'but it is configured as a diffuse gesture that will not let itself be a tonal Other. The masculine is unproblematic in its construction and behavior' (p. 154). Overall, there is resistance to the hierarchical relationship between masculine and feminine: a refusal to play the rules laid out in ideology. Later there is some sensuous luxuriating in pure sound, which also challenges ideologies of sonata form as it was understood at the time.

Both McClary and Citron declare that they do not wish to invoke any concept of a 'woman's music' (e.g. McClary 1991, p. 131; Citron 1993, p. 159). But Renée Cox links the idea of alternative compositional strategy to the concept known as *l'écriture féminine*.[11] Building upon a McClarian type of position, Cox cites Hélène Cixous' depiction of female experience as fluid, diffuse, effervescent, abundant (Clément and Cixous 1985, pp. 90–1, in Cox 1991, p. 334). She links this depiction to 'feminine writing' and suggests a type of music 'modeled on feminine writing' (p. 334). Such music

would engage the listener in the musical moment rather than in the structure as a whole; would have a flexible, cyclical form; and would involve continuous repetition with variation, the cumulative growth of an idea. Such music would serve to deconstruct musical hierarchies and the dialectical juxtaposition and resolution of opposites, disrupt linearity, and avoid definitive closures. In sung music, vocalization would be relaxed and make use of nonverbal or presymbolic sounds. (1991, p. 334)

Comparable invocations of femininity in compositional procedure are made from a lesbian perspective by Rycenga (1994). Although by no means all feminist musicologists subscribe to this type of view, the notion of a 'woman's music' is clearly important and must be indicated as a possible endpoint and radical position in contemporary feminist musicology.

In summary, McClary's important and influential theory of gendered meaning arising from absolute music is characterised by the location of teleological musical drives towards satisfaction, and narrative structures of domination over a submissive or wayward musical Other. These two concepts are bound together through their shared articulation by intra-

---

[11] For a helpful secondary explication of 'feminine writing' see Moi (1990) esp. Chapter 6; also Wolff (1990, pp. 131–2). Also see Cixous and Clément (1985), Cixous (1990). This concept has also influenced women working in the visual arts, rendered as 'la peinture féminine'. See Parker and Pollock's (1987) collection on women's art-works, and also Pollock (1988). Also see Wolff (1990, pp. 82–5) and Battersby (1989, pp. 146ff) for further discussion of feminism and postmodernist art and literature practices.

musical hierarchical relations. The processes of teleology and narrative, and the hierarchical relations through which they are articulated, are not only deciphered in music but are linked to patriarchy and, beyond that, to the binary oppositions which, it is argued, underpin the very fabric of Western thought. Women composers are identified who are seen to have questioned the teleological striving and patriarchal narratives of Western music. They have employed alternative musical strategies which challenge or disrupt these musical processes through techniques of stasis, non-linear progression, circularity, reversal of narrative role, or refusal to forefront any domineering musical motif.

A critical appraisal

The approaches described above contain many helpful elements. Any enquiry into the links between gender and music must question whether patriarchy has led to the employment of particular, commensurate musical techniques and, if it has, whether women composers have avoided or even challenged those techniques. It is also necessary for such an enquiry to consider how music constructs notions of gender and sexuality. Absolute music provides the most pertinent, as well as the most challenging, testing-ground for these questions. Through exploring them, it is possible to open new avenues for evaluating and re-evaluating women's work, understanding our achievements in a fresh light, not as compared with those of men, but as exhibiting strengths of a different order. (There will be more discussion of this in the final chapter.) But at the same time as confronting these salient issues and opening up new avenues, the ideas described above bring with them a host of other questions. In what follows, I hope to locate some of these questions and identify some of the further issues on which they throw light.[12]

The first issue that seems pertinent, with reference to McClary, is whether Western music from c. 1600 to 1900 and thereafter does have a teleological drive that is endemic and powerful enough to support her theory. The idea of musical teleology suggests that some or even most moments of musical experience are ultimately subordinate to the processes in which they are functionally exhausted, that the only musical present which exists as a present is the last moment. Yet if music were

---

[12] For other critiques from within musicology, see Treitler (1993), Bohlman (1993); and for a heated exchange, Toorn (1991) and Solie (1991). For a helpful appraisal of McClary's position from the point of view of the sociology of music, see Martin (1995, pp. 148–60).

thoroughly exhausted in the pursuit of its own end, then the listening experience would have only very limited qualities. Even the sonata principle, which is perhaps particularly vulnerable to the description of teleology, is partially dependent on the retrieval of past events, on stasis in the moment, on the expansion of the listener's sense of time to encompass a wide field of presence. Without these aspects of the listening experience, there could be no teleology either. I am dubious of any suggestion that the teleological element should be given quite such overriding significance.[13]

Not only is musical experience more various than the theory of musical teleology allows, but, as McClary herself observes (e.g. pp. 126–7), a variety of possible types of erotic experience is open to both men and women, and there are also many different kinds of orgasm experienced by both sexes. The fact that she only treats the male, teleological, thrusting sort again seems rather to over-emphasise something which is only partial. Furthermore, if it is appropriate to criticise a musical construction as a symbolic orgasm, then surely it must also be necessary to criticise orgasm itself? Otherwise why should we assume the biological thrusting of male orgasm to be a problem? Yet McClary does not enter into any discussion of ways in which orgasm is related to patriarchy. Although she declares (e.g. p. 8) that she is exposing a historical construction of specifically Western patriarchal mainstream male sexuality and that of course she is not treating this sexuality as essential, in the absence of any discussion of the social or historical construction of sexuality or of the links between orgasm and patriarchy, one's *impression* is of the opposite: teleological orgasms, and their patterning in music, *appear* to be cast as immediately expressive of patriarchal attitudes and as essential attributes of masculinity.

In some ways, McClary's understanding of the teleological musical patterning of desire and the narrative powers of music appears to be Langerian, although McClary does not mention that philosopher. Langer's formulation of musical meaning involved the idea that music 'articulates', or 'composes', an inner life which, as in McClary's thesis, has clear kinaesthetic properties (1955, p. 180):

---

[13] There is a more detailed critique of the tendency to over-emphasise teleology in music, with reference to Meyer's theory of affect and meaning, in Green (1988, pp. 21–5). Many of the same points would again apply here. McClary herself writes with great empathy about various non-teleological qualities in the music of Beethoven, Mozart, Schubert and many other composers. See (1991), (1993), (1994). In so doing, her claim is that the non-teleological elements are present in the music, but that they have been overridden by musicology. I would agree with this, but it seems to entail a shift from her argument that the music itself organises time teleologically.

there are certain aspects of the so-called 'inner life' – physical or mental – which have formal properties similar to those of music – patterns of motion and rest, of tension and release, of agreement and disagreement, preparation, fulfilment, excitation, sudden change, etc. . . .(Langer 1955, pp. 183–4)

This yields a 'connotative relationship', a 'similarity of logical form' between music and subjective experience (p. 185). Thus far, Langer and McClary seem to be remarkably close. But Langer (like Hanslick before her) stops at that point, refusing to specify any content to the structural similarity. 'For music has all the earmarks of a true symbolism, except one: the existence of an assigned connotation . . . Its import is never fixed' (pp. 194–5). This is where McClary begins to part from this approach, for she does identify a content for absolute music. On one hand, the teleological drive which she locates is at times characterised as a trait of Western civilisation, and is at other times linked to male orgasm; on the other hand, the narrative processes which she identifies involve, amongst other things, the masculinity of the domineering elements, and the femininity of the submissive ones. It is this attribution of content to the location of teleology and narrative in absolute music that, in my view, raises the most difficult questions, and poses an urgent need for clarification about the status of the claims being made.

To employ the terms with which I have been working throughout this book, the problem can be stated as the need for a distinction between inherent, symbol-free, contentless, virtual intra-musical meaning, and the social-historical processes which go to make up the delineated content of musical meaning. Otherwise, writing about musical meaning, whether with reference to patriarchy and orgasm or tulips and dragons, falls into the trap of what I have called musical fetishism: making it look as though socially, historically constructed delineations are somehow inherent in the musical notes and processes themselves. Unless all the meaningful content which McClary so eloquently identifies is understood as some sort of delineation, the emphasis which she places on its articulation by absolute music *appears* to be a fetishistic position on musical meaning. McClary, Citron and Cox do conduct pertinent discussions of musical delineations. Furthermore, despite many differences in their individual approaches, they all reveal diverse ways in which gendered meanings surface in particular performance and reception contexts, in pedagogy and in criticism. But they do not reveal how gendered meanings surface in that which is absolute about absolute music. In so far as they claim to do so, my contention is that, in line with the argument that I have made throughout this book, they are allowing musical delineations to influence the way that they hear inherent meanings.

This problem is perhaps particularly clearly illustrated by the citation below, which appears in an endnote during McClary's discussion of Vandervelde's *Genesis II*:

Authorial intentions are especially important in feminist art and need to be taken into account when they are obtainable, so long as we keep in mind that intentions do not necessarily communicate and certainly do not comprise the only possible reading. For instance, in the recording of *Genesis II*, the Mirecourt Trio perform this opening section as a classical 'beanstalk' [i.e. teleological] gesture. An earlier, taped recording (not publicly available) conveys far more successfully a sonic metaphor of childbirth, in part because in refusing to accelerate to its conclusion it avoids the impression of excitement and desire. (1991, p. 198, n. 16)

But this innocuous note causes great problems for me. No, I must contend, authorial intentions are no more important in feminist than in any other art. The whole point of McClary's argument was that Vandervelde's music presents a challenge to the ' "non-representational" bastion of instrumental music' (p. 116): what a let-down it then is to discover that this message is even slightly enhanced if we know that the composer intended the music to mean childbirth and not male orgasm! That a particular performance can reverse such meaning! Where now is the challenge to the bastion of absolute music?

The challenge that McClary has located relies on and is contained within the feminist intentions of the composer.[14] Such intentions do indeed enter the delineations of the music. But the ability of these delineations to affect our perceptions and our performance of inherent meanings is a process that is no different from the way that feminine delineations affected the reception of music by women composers in the nineteenth century: the way, for example, that the femininity of the composer caused contemporary critics to hear her music as in some way inherently feminine (see Chapter 4). This tendency could just as well be described as an attribution of *essential* properties to music, because it makes it look as though the historical, contextual meanings of music reside as an essential property of the notes themselves. Looked at in these terms, this twentieth-century feminist critique of gendered musical meanings in absolute music appears to be a reaction to the nineteenth-

---

[14] McClary also makes claims for the importance of intentions with relation to Madonna (1991, p. 150).

century masculinist construction of sexual musical aesthetics. The two approaches seem to be merely two sides of the same coin, one positive, the other negative, but fundamentally operating on the basis of similar assumptions. Far from 'deconstructing' the 'binarisms of Western thought', the critique would then seem to be adding to them.

The lack of any distinction between different meaningful processes in music, such as I have called inherent and delineated meanings, creates not only the danger of appearing to attribute essential properties to music but also the appearance of the attribution of essential properties to gender. In the case of femininity, an essentialist notion would imply that there is something integral to women, something unchanging, free of historical and social determinants, which was somehow immutably embedded in their biologically determined nature. This essential element would then be at the root of whatever feminine qualities might be heard to emerge in women's music. In disclaiming such a postion, McClary says, for example, that Vandervelde's significance

is not *simply* that she has revealed as phallic and sexually violent many of the 'value-free' conventions of classical form . . . Nor is it that she has introduced for the first time some universal, essential woman's voice. For even though our obsession for classifying all music stylistically might make us want to jump impulsively at the chance to codify the distinctive characteristics of a 'women's music', there can be no such single thing, just as there is no universal male experience or essence. What Vandervelde has accomplished is an approach to composition that permits her – expressly as a woman – to inhabit a traditional discourse, to call into question its gestures and precedures *from the inside*, and to imagine from that vantage point the possibility of other narrative schemata. (p. 131)

McClary, Cox and Citron all consider the question of whether it matters if the 'alternative music' which they discuss is written by a man or a woman, and they all deny that it matters, arguing in several places that the critical strategies which they describe are available to both men and women.[15] For example, McClary acknowledges that as well as female composers, males such as Steve Reich and Philip Glass also present us with what she calls 'deconstructions of this sort' (pp. 122–3).

But the deconstructive methods of postmodernism – the practice of questioning the claims to universality by the 'master narratives' of Western culture, revealing the agendas behind traditional 'value-free' procedures – are also beginning to clear a space in which a woman's voice can at last be heard *as a woman's voice.* (p. 123)

---

[15] E.g. McClary (1991, pp. 122–3), Citron (1993, pp. 156, 144), Cox (1991, pp. 334, 336).

Cox says:

This predilection for musical organicism, for continuous growth and development, can also be found in the music of men, of course, and it is not found in all
music by women. But it is especially meaningful in the music of women, for it
has been associated with the female or feminine since ancient times. The
goddess principle involves the continuous cycle of birth, growth, death and
rebirth, gestation and nurture, proliferation and development. Although these
are natural processes that apply to and can be observed in all living forms, they
are processes that women, who give birth and nurture children, can experience
directly and attentively. (pp. 336–7)

With reference to her analyses of the Chaminade movement, Citron
says:

By choosing a work by a woman I am not implying that such challenges
are available only to women. On the contrary: they are available to any composer, male or female. Nor am I suggesting that there is some essentialist relationship between a woman composer and woman-as-Other in the codes of
sonata form. What I am suggesting is that this is a work that exhibits distinctive behavior in its treatment of themes, and this could signal a
reconfiguration of the ideological relationship between masculine and feminine. No doubt there are many sonata movements in the nineteenth century,
including many by men, that could be analyzed in this way. The fact that they
have not been approached from this standpoint does not mean that they
do not mount similar challenges. But given the makeup of the current canon,
I believe it is especially vital to place women's works into analytic discourse.
(p. 144)

But what *is* it to inhabit a traditional discourse expressly *as a woman*
(McClary 1991, p. 131, cited above)? What is it for a voice to be heard as
a woman's voice (p. 123, cited above)? Why is musical organicism especially meaningful in the music of women (Cox 1991, p. 336, cited
above)? Why is it vital to place women's works into analytic discourse
(Citron 1993, p. 144, cited above)? The answer is that once again the
feminist, critical content which is attributed to the music relies on
delineations, contexts, the intentions or otherwise programmatic ideas
of the composer, the overt challenge to a particular political context, or
whatever other social and historical factors may be pertinent before the
fact of femininity can actually be of any relevance to the musical
meaning. Yet the appearance is unintentionally given that femininity
somehow inheres as an essential characteristic of the notes. Whereas
disclaimers are issued about the attribution of essentialism to femininity, it is actually the attribution of essential properties to music, through

the confusion of delineations with inherent meanings, that is causing the problem.[16]

The identification of gendered meanings or any other meanings in absolute music is viable and pertinent. But the meanings must be understood as not only arising from but also contingent upon music's social and historical contexts. This understanding then allows us to conceptualise the power which these contextualised, delineated meanings wield over our responses to intra-musical, inherent processes. It is precisely because social, historical delineations have the capacity to appear as if they were inherent in musical processes themselves that delineations present themselves to us in musical experience, as if they were autonomous, immediate, truths. The disentanglement of different levels of meaning therefore seems to me to be helpful. I would suggest that it is pertinent to say that music can come to delineate a notion of femininity or of masculinity, amongst other things, owing to the gender of the performer, or the gender of the composer, or a radical performance practice, or the words, or the composer's intentions, or a programmatic content, or a challenging public image or whatever context is afforded within the overall historical situation that governs the production and reception of the music. But unless we are careful, the fetishistic tendencies of musical thinking will make it appear that the music is somehow inherently, essentially feminine, or inherently, essentially masculine.

One project that feminist musicology has taken on board is a continuing onslaught on the notion of musical autonomy, an onslaught mounted from all those fronts that have in recent years been concerned with dismantling elitist assumptions of classical musical supremacy. The concept of autonomy presupposes that no *one* created the music, that no historical subjective ear is located in it, that the music arose naturally: but through what vessel? Man. When music is thought autonomous, with a logic of its own, dependent on historical subjects only for the realisation of its latent, natural properties, then it is inevitably assumed that the composer is male. This assumption, in combination with the cerebral delineations arising from the notion of composition, leads to what I have referred to in Chapter 4 as the 'masculine delineation of music'. The

---

[16] Treitler (1993, p. 41) locates a comparable problem. E.g: 'communication requires a context of basic agreement about what will signify what'. But he appears to lack the conviction that such agreement already does exist. Martin (1995) sheds a particularly clear light on the social construction of musical meanings, and relates this to feminism (pp. 148–60). Also see N. Cook (1994) for a clear analysis of the construction of general cultural meanings or values by television commercials and the relations between those meanings and the 'notes'.

idea of music's autonomy from social and historical circumstance is challenged by feminism. But in challenging the truth of autonomy, we must be careful not to go too far in the opposite direction, and totally forget that music has any autonomy at all. To do so would be to raise delineated meaning to a level which virtually obliterates the symbol-free status of inherent meanings, giving the appearance that delineations are somehow lodged in the intra-musical syntax of even absolute music. I would rather understand the relationship of music and gender in terms of musical stylistic development that is charged on one hand by the relative autonomy of inherent musical processes, and on the other by the aesthetic, cultural and economic changes of the era of the music's production and reception. The position of women within musical stylistic development is a product of the symbiotic relationship between music and society, part and parcel not just of the changing social identities and roles of women or only of changing compositional practices, but of both of these acting upon each other in the changing social construction of musical meaning.

TOWARDS A MODEL OF GENDERED MUSICAL MEANING AND EXPERIENCE

I have argued that it is helpful to posit and keep open a level of virtual musical meaning which is conventional but free of symbolic content: what I call inherent meaning. As well as inherent meaning, whenever we hear music we link it with sets of values and relations which exist outside, or beyond, the musical sounds themselves. These connections are what I have termed delineated musical meanings. Among several available delineations, including those of class, ethnicity, sub-culture, age, religion or nationality for example, there is the delineation of gender. I argued in Chapter 2 that the gender of the woman singer enters into the delineations of the music she sings, normally as an affirmative gesture that concords with patriarchal definitions of femininity. Chapter 3 presented the view that women instrumentalists invoke delineations on a sliding scale, from those that retrieve the affirmation of singing to those that present an interruption to conceptions of femininity. In Chapter 4, I suggested that the woman composer delineates an even stronger threat, because her presence in the musical symbolisation challenges both the historical positioning of men as composers and the masculine cerebral connotations of the act of composition.

History causes us to assume that behind music there is a male creator.

Partly by virtue of this simple fact, and partly by virtue of the delineation of mind which is conjured up by our notion of a composer, music itself has come to imply a male creator and, through him, masculinity. This causes all music, at some usually sublimated level, to delineate masculinity: not 'machismo', but masculinity in the vast complexity and diversity of its understandings and construction. Masculinity is often most revered when marked by the discursively constructed feminine characteristics which characterise the genius. Thus the masculine meaning of music may, and at its most powerful does, conjure up feminine attributes in a genius; but it will never conjure up that aberration, a female genius, a powerfully creative real woman. The masculine meaning of music has been thought about less often than its class, ethnic, sub-cultural or nationalistic meanings; but I have suggested that this is because of its ubiquity, its indelible presence in the listening experience. It exists as surely in musical meaning and in our understanding of what music is as does our very concept of music as an artefact; and it forms the unquestioned backdrop in front of which affirmative, interruptive and threatening feminine delineations all play out their roles.

The masculine delineation of music is not a merely political label, but it affects our musical experiences. I wish to explore this notion through a discussion of various 'ideal types', or exemplars, of musical experience.[17] I will focus first on the experience of the listener. In the terminology of Figure 1 (p. 134), listeners can have a relatively 'fulfilling' or, at the opposite extreme, a relatively 'dissatisfying' experience of inherent meaning, according to their subject-position, their knowledge and their experience in relation to the particular music in question. The more knowledge and experience, the more fulfilling the response will tend to be; the less knowledge and experience, the more dissatisfying. In a similar way, listeners can have a relatively 'positive' or a relatively 'negative' relationship to the delineated meanings, according to whether they feel at home with those meanings and can appropriate them as their own values, or whether they feel embarrassed by them or otherwise antipathetical towards them.

The experience of some listeners with relation to certain pieces of music will be what I have called 'alienated': the listeners do not feel at one with the delineations, and are dissatisfied with the inherent meanings. At the opposite extreme, listeners find themselves 'celebrated'

---

[17] See Green (1988) for a more detailed discussion of this chart, and of the interface between social, individual, delineated and inherent musical factors in musical experience. Two of the terms in the chart have been slightly modified to avoid some overlaps with the current text.

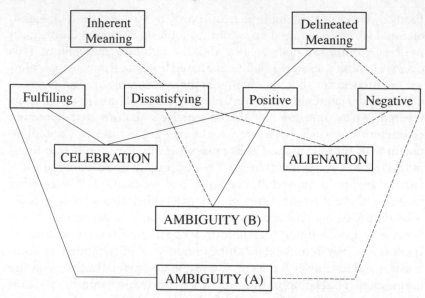

Figure 1. Adapted from Green 1988, p. 138

through a positive relationship to the delineations, and a fulfilling response to the inherent meanings. Clearly, there may often arise situations in which a listener's responses to inherent and delineated meanings do not necessarily tally. The resulting ambiguity occurs in two ways. First (ambiguity B), a person may respond positively to the inherent meanings of, say, Mozart's operatic music, on the basis of a lifetime's listening experience; but he or she may at the same time feel negative about the delineations of the libretto, or about the social milieux in which the operas are perceived to circulate. Secondly, vice versa (ambiguity A), a person may be dissatisfied with the inherent meanings, unfamiliarity with which produces difficulties in even distinguishing salient elements; but he or she might nonetheless feel entirely positive about the narrative contained in the libretto, or about the social function of going out to the opera. In ambiguous musical experience, there is then a contradiction between the quality of experience in relation to the two virtual aspects of musical meaning.

In the case of gender delineations, the presence of the masculine delineation in music provides access to an unmitigated celebratory response for those listeners who are fulfilled by the inherent meanings of the music at the same time as being positively disposed towards its delineations. But where there is an interruptive or threatening, feminine delineation in music, this disrupts the cosy and unquestioned familiarity of music's masculine delineations. Disruptive feminine delineations contain an element of negativity, making an uncompromised celebratory response to any music in which they are present unlikely. This is something which I have argued and illustrated throughout the book. But here I wish to take it a little bit further: for not only does the presence of masculinity or femininity in musical *delineation* affect listeners' overall responses to the music; so too does the *gender of the listener* him- or herself. I have argued that the musical experience of men and women will normally be subject to the taken-for-granted masculine delineation of music. If so, men and women must have a slightly different type of musical experience resulting from their gender. Men, I would argue, have access to a thorough sense of musical celebration; but for women this access is liable to be blocked to some extent, because there must always be a degree of negativity to overcome in women's response to delineation. A woman cannot so readily find herself positively reflected in the delineations of the vast majority of music: her gender is shunned by its masculine delineation. When people listen to music and hear themselves reflected in it, men are engaging with something which is in tune with their gender, something which positively delineates their gender, even if only implicitly; but women are engaging with something the production of which is either practically or symbolically denied them, something that delineates an alien, masculine quality. Even for women who are fulfilled by the inherent meanings of a piece of music, therefore, their experience will have a degree of negativity about it. They are therefore less susceptible to an experience of musical celebration, and more liable to one containing some ambiguity (type B).[18]

It is not only listeners who acquire a knowledge of musical meaning, but performers and composers too, because they are all, already, also listeners.[19] How, then, does the gendered meaning of music affect the performer and composer? I would suggest that if we have relatively celebratory, alienated or ambiguous musical experiences as listeners, then so

[18] For other discussions of gendered listening, see Citron (1994, pp. 26–7) with reference to Schweickart (1986) and Culler (1982); also Citron (1993, pp. 174–8, 188). Also see Pegley and Caputo (1993, pp. 299–300) on, amongst other things, male and female ways of hearing and responding.

[19] See Kallberg (1992, pp. 116ff) on the woman composer as listener; and Rycenga (1994) for an argument about lesbian compositional processes, which is necessarily also bound up with listening. Griffiths (1994) provides an interesting analysis of the insertion of gendered subjectivity into composition.

must we have relatively celebratory, alienated or ambiguous relationships to our own compositions and the products of our own performances. Whereas musicians are unlikely to be wholly alienated from
the music that they perform or compose, there are several reasons why
many musicians should be ambiguous towards their music. For women
musicians, this ambiguity is likely to result in part, *from their gender*. The
female performer, especially one who branches out into playing an
instrument or playing in a musical style which overwhelmingly delineates masculinity, has to overcome –and to go on overcoming – the delineated disruption which her own performance will produce. The female
composer might also be to some extent negatively positioned with relation to the delineations of the music which she composes herself: as
Chapter 4 shows, once it is produced, even if her product is recognised
and valued for its inherent qualities, credit is taken away from her as a
woman; if her product is perceived to have weak inherent meanings, this
is attributed to her femininity.

Throughout history, women composers have felt the need to defend
their activities from public disapproval. In so doing they have frequently
cited either the value of their work itself, or their social standing as a
composer, or both. Expressions of a lack of confidence in presenting
compositions, even by successful women, have been incorporated into
compensatory history by numerous writers.[20] Certainly, any composer of
either sex may be seen as prone to the crisis of confidence which is
indeed a defining characteristic of the 'artistic temperament'. We must
be careful not to act as though only women composers have had such an
experience, and we can only speculate about how much they have
'really' suffered in this respect compared to their male counterparts. But
where we can go further is in understanding their lack of confidence not
only as a part of the gendered social organisation of musical production
or of gendered musical meaning, but also as a product of their gendered
musical experience itself. If, as Chapter 4 argues, the ears of critics are
influenced in their perception and interpretation of inherent meanings
according to the delineated gender of the composer, then the ears of

---

[20] See esp. Ammer (1980), Neuls-Bates (1982), Citron (1993), Bowers (1986), Brown (1986), and many
others in the collections edited by Bowers and Tick (1986) and Pendle (1991b). In the jazz and
popular realms, see Dahl (1984), Steward and Garratt (1984), Grieg (1989), Gaar (1993), Bayton
(1990), (1993a). Citron (1993) suggests that one reason for focussing on a work by a woman is 'the
possibility that the subject positions and socialization of women may inflect their challenges to
codes of representation' (1993, p. 145). It is women's historical subject positioning that makes
them more likely than men to 'mount strategies of resistance to gendered codes in music that
suggest women's domination by men' (p. 156).

composers themselves must also be susceptible. The masculine delineation of music, its insinuation into listeners' perceptions of inherent meanings and the threat which is posed to it by the femininity of a composer: these factors must cause not only critics but many women composers themselves to hear their own music in terms not of the autonomy delineated by the male mind but of the threat to it posed by the female.

Therefore I would contend that the experience of the woman composer is liable to be ambiguous, by virtue of her own femininity; and that this ambiguity will affect not just her approach to the possibility of composing but also the delineations which her own product then carries for her. As soon as the woman composer alienates her skill in a musical composition, the inherent meanings of her music will tend to come back at her, accompanied by her disruption of the normative, masculine delineation. Just as it is through the music itself that the critic or lay listener learns that 'feminine women' cannot compose autonomous music, so it is that women composers learn this from their own music. In order to compose autonomous, 'good' music, the woman composer must either overcome the feminine delineations that are already a part of the very object which she creates, *as she creates it*, or renounce her femininity. In the very pursuit of composition, there is a resistance put up by women not only to musical meaning but also to discursive constructions of gender. This ambiguous relation to music, that of other people and that of her own creation, is, I would suggest, one of the reasons why throughout history women have performed as well as composed certain types of music so much more than others: it is the result not only of some extraneous social convention, but of the fact that the array of music that is open to women is already circumscribed both by musical meaning and by musical experience themselves.

To summarise this argument so far: in order to perceive ourselves as potential musical agents (performers and composers) in the world, especially the public world outside school or home, female and male musicians must hear the possibility of our potential creative power resonate in our musical experiences. As performers, Chapters 2 and 3 argued, the gender of a male has been questioned only in certain areas, such as the salon or the school choir, where femininity is the norm. As composers, Chapter 4 indicated, the gender of a male has hardly ever been questioned. For these reasons I have suggested that, when men listen to music, they can hear themselves reflected and at best, celebrated as activators, as controllers, as potential or actual performers or composers, of the music, in the music. But for women this resonance is to some extent blocked. The gender of a female performer in many contexts, and of a female composer in most contexts, unlike the gender of the male musician, becomes an object of interest, an overt, and often problematic, part of the musical meanings themselves. It is thus not easy for women to find themselves celebrated in music in such a way as to assert or project a positive image of themselves as musicians, and the overall patriarchal situation makes this projection even more difficult when it is directed onto a public plane. Unlike men of the same class or ethnicity or otherwise defined social grouping as themselves, women musicians have first to overcome not just external prejudice, but internalised negative positioning in relation to musical delineation. This negative positioning may, furthermore, colour women's relations to the inherent meanings of the music with which they are involved. Our beliefs and assumptions about gender are not only formed socially outside music, to be then applied to music post hoc; they are also formed through our very experience of music itself – as apparently autonomous truth.

Is there any possibility of an alternative to the normality of the masculine delineation of music, and its near hegemony over our experiences? I want to suggest that, as distinct from the search for a somehow critical inherent syntax articulated through compositional strategy, the masculine meaning of music can be, more simply, challenged through the very disruptive nature of delineations, especially when that disruption is harnessed into interventionary social action. The possibilities here include delineations of an overt nature such as feminist lyrics, and of a more covert nature such as radical performance practice.[21] They also include what has been my main focus of attention: the delineated fact of a female composer, a female improviser and in some cases a female instrumentalist, or a powerful woman singer behind the music. The delineation invoked by the presence of these women in the music's production can have interventionary possibilities, most strongly through the experience of ambiguity (type B), where the listener is already fulfilled by inherent meanings.

In this type of ambiguous experience, the disruptive content of the feminine delineations can have a fetishistic effect on the listener's experience of the inherent meanings. Such an effect can be discerned when listeners evaluate the inherent meanings of music by women in terms of

---

[21] E.g. of the sort located by McClary (1991) with reference to Galas and Anderson, or the sort illuminated by Wood (1994), Abbate (1993), Pope (1994) and many other theorists referenced throughout Part I. Also see Chapter 9, below.

the music's delineated femininity. For many such listeners, even their personal fulfilment by inherent meanings is adversely affected by their negative response to the interruptive or threatening delineations of the music. But there is no absolute necessity for this fetishism: the flow of direction, the negative influence of delineations over our response to inherent meanings, *can* be reversed, so that the fulfilling experience of inherent meanings causes us to re-evaluate the negativity of delineations. If, for whatever reason, we have come to appreciate and value the inherent meanings of a piece of music that is composed or performed by a woman and that carries disruptive delineations, our fulfilment can cause us to re-evaluate the threatening or interruptive qualities which accompany the feminine delineation.

In such a case, as we become aware of our re-evaluation of the feminine delineation, so we are made aware of the normative masculine delineation of music. At the same time we must replace this masculine delineation with a new delineation. In so doing, we not only disrupt our assumptions about the gender-related characteristics of the music itself; we begin to realise that these assumptions have affected our very understanding and judgement of the way we actually perceive femininity too. When the masculine delineation of music is disrupted by the knowledge that it is a female musical creator (and incidentally when the Black meaning of music is disrupted because we find out it was a White band, or when an assumption of maturity behind music is disrupted because we find out the composer or performer was a child), this may not just cause us to rethink who created the music, or to rethink the musical sounds themselves: it may also cause us to think again, even in a minute way, about what femininity and masculinity (or Blackness and Whiteness, or adulthood and childhood) have come to mean to us. Such a re-evaluation of the interruptive or threatening effects of feminine delineations is hard to achieve and rare. But it is more than a mere possibility, for it is what must surely have happened on many occasions, step by step through history, as women performers and composers have broken through to achieve acclaim, *despite* taboos, despite prohibitions, despite all manner of adverse circumstance.

SUMMARY

In this chapter I have explored some questions concerning whether absolute music can carry gendered meanings, and whether women composers have been able to challenge any such meanings. I have

argued that gendered musical meanings are articulated, with both positive and negative connotations, by absolute music; and that this articulation is contingent upon the social, historical context of the music's
production and reception, which becomes wrapped up in what I call
delineated meaning. Yet, because of the power of delineations to overcome our experience of musical inherent meanings, these gendered
delineations tend to appear as if they were an essential part of the very
musical notes themselves. This appearance gives gendered delineations
a powerful sway over our experiences, not only as listeners but also as
performers and composers. Because of the normality of the masculine
delineation of music and the disruptive connotations of many feminine
delineations, men and women are differently positioned with reference
to music. It is relatively difficult for women to achieve a sense of musical
celebration, and this may even include some women musicians' experience of their own music. But disruptive feminine musical delineations do
contain interventionary possibilities, if they can be exposed and re-eval-
uated by the fulfilment of the listener in the experience of that virtual,
symbolically content-free moment of inherent musical meaning. In the
closing chapter of the book I will return to the theme of the interventionary possibilities of musical meaning, to assess how far education can
make a contribution to those possibilities.

PART II

Gendered musical meaning in contemporary education

CHAPTER 6

Affirming femininity in the music classroom

INTRODUCTION

In this second part of the book, I will enter the classroom, viewed as a microcosmic version of the wider society, to consider how gendered musical meanings, as discussed in Part I, can be seen to arise from and affect the practices and experiences of girls, boys and their teachers in the contemporary production and reproduction of gender through music education. First of all I will introduce the broad conception of schooling with which I am working, and then the general characteristics of music education within that conception. My focus will be on English secondary school music education, which I hope will provide an example from which implications for other countries, other systems of music education and other areas of musical life may emerge.[1]

In Chapter 1, I briefly introduced the concept of 'historical grouping', to imply both a verb and a noun: 'grouping' (or 'to group') is something that we do collectively; 'a grouping' (or 'a group') is something to which we belong (see Chapter 1, n. 1, p. 4 above). There is a circular relationship between the reproduction of historical groupings (including class, ethnicity or gender) at the societal level and the formation of identity at the individual level. The one feeds into, and helps to shape, the other. Historical groupings are reproduced partly through an ongoing, collective, discursive construction in which each individual takes part. Because of the interplay between the inertia of the social totality and the caprice of individual human agency, the reproduction of what exists goes hand in hand with the production of what is new – new structures, meanings, relationships, things. The school, amongst other institutions, is a major

[1] England, Wales, Scotland and Northern Ireland, although (currently) all parts of the United Kingdom of Great Britain and Northern Ireland have different education systems and curricula, as well as different musical cultures outside schooling. My use of the word 'England' rather than 'Britain' is intended to be sensitive to these differences, rather than Anglo-centric.

site by virtue of which the reproduction and production of historical groupings occurs, through practices and meanings which are constructed and negotiated between teachers and pupils in the formation of personal identity.[2] In this and the next two chapters, I wish to focus on the reproduction of historical, musical gender groupings in relation to the formation of individuals' gendered identities through musical practices and musical meanings. I will look to the school as an overall framework in which gendered musical practices and gendered musical meanings are played out, in a microcosmic replication of their reproduction and construction in the wider society. Most fundamentally, I will attempt to locate the seeds of this reproduction and construction within musical experience itself, as it is configured for girls and boys in the context of the classroom.

There are several factors affecting English music education, both internal and external to the education system, which must provide a background to the discussion. Internal factors include the relationship between different musical styles within the curriculum; the position of music history, performance, composition, and listening; the resources available; the type of instrumental tuition provided; and the nature of any extra-curricular activities. Although there is significant variation between schools, music education in England has overall undergone a considerable amount of change in the last decade or two. Only fifteen or twenty years ago the curriculum was based largely on singing and appreciation, involving the works of the 'great masters' of classical music, and presupposing the acquisition of classical instrumental skills by a minority of pupils, normally through specialist study outside the classroom.[3] Today there is widespread recognition of the value of pupils'

---

[2] The literature on social reproduction, cultural production and schooling is, of course, vast. I cannot do any justice to it here, but I have been influenced by work in this field, and have used some of the concepts and strategies associated with it in working out the arguments that follow. For standard background literature, see Bourdieu (1973), (1974), Bourdieu and Passeron (1990), Young (1980), Whitty (1985), Willis (1977), Wexler (1987). For feminist education work, see Weiler (1988, pp. 1–66) which provides a clear, succinct introduction to theory; Wolpe (1978), (1988), MacDonald (1979–80), (1980), Arnot (1982), (1984), Deem (1980). There are also the very helpful readers Arnot and Weiner (1987), Weiner and Arnot (1987) and Stone (1994) and the informative general introductions Measor and Sikes (1992) and Weiner (1994). Also see Walkerdine (1990), McRobbie (1991), Thorne (1993), Lather (1991) for diverse approaches and issues. On the interaction between gender, class and ethnicity in schools, see M. Fuller (1980), (1983), Brah and Minhas (1985), Amos and Parmar (1981), Carby (1987), Arnot (1986), Woods and Hammersley (1993), Singh (1994).

[3] For information and different perspectives on the development of music education in England over the past twenty years or so see Swanwick et al. (1987), Fletcher (1987), Rainbow (1989), Plummeridge (1991), Green (1984), (1988), Spruce (1996), Vulliamy (1976), (1977a), (1977b).

compositional capacities, shifting the focus away from specialist instru-mental skills. There has also been a fast-growing inclusion of popular music, the music of many indigenous ethnic groups within 'the West' and music from other parts of the world. These new perspectives stem from the work of educators in what is known as 'creative music' such as John Paynter; of those who have considered child development as a key factor alongside the acquisition of balanced musical skills, including Keith Swanwick; and of those who have been concerned with the imperatives dictated by an increasingly pluralistic society, about which I will say more in a moment.[4] The changes have been formally under-written and implemented on a national basis, through the music syllabus for the sixteen-plus General Certificate of Secondary Education (GCSE), which started running in 1986, and through the National Curriculum for Music for ages five to fourteen, which began its develop-ment in 1992.[5]

One of the most significant areas upon which I will dwell in subsequent discussions is the relationship between classical and popular music, broadly defined, in schools. The incorporation of popular music in the curriculum undoubtedly represents a far-reaching change over the last few years, but at the same time the extent of the change should not be overestimated. Most secondary school music teachers, although they have willingly and enthusiastically embraced new values and skills, remain classically trained themselves, and their backgrounds inevitably influence what is at the centre of their educational projects. In this sense, it is not so much the *content* of what they teach as the pedagogy itself which is affected by their training. When classically trained teachers, like myself, include popular music in their curricula, they are likely to introduce it through skills and concepts that arise from their own backgrounds, such as notation-reading or functional diatonicism. Such procedures may

---

[4] Paynter and Aston (1970) made a significant impact, as did the Schools Council Project described in Paynter (1982). Also see Paynter (1992) and other work associated with this area including Schafer (1967), Self (1967), Dennis (1970). Swanwick was the first British music educator to pub-licly support the use of popular music in schools (1968); he made a significant impact on the development of the music curriculum nationally through his later work, especially (1979), and on music education studies through (1988), further followed up in (1994). Burnett (1972), Farmer (1976), Vulliamy and Lee (1976), (1982) were also early supporters of popular music in the curricu-lum, providing some excellent classroom resources and teaching methods. For current practice in the primary school see Her Majesty's Inspectorate (1991), Mills (1991), Glover and Ward (1993).

[5] For GCSE, see the School Curriculum and Assessment Authority (1995), and for discussion, Green (1988, pp. 74–80), Shepherd and Vulliamy (1994). For the National Curriculum see Department for Education (1995); also, as a precursor, the work of Swanwick (1979), HMI (1985); and for commentaries on the National Curriculum itself, Swanwick (1992), Shepherd and Vulliamy (1994), Gammon (forthcoming).

differ widely from the ways in which those musicians who are responsible for the styles of music being taught originally learnt their skills themselves.[6] Furthermore, the Advanced Level eighteen-plus exam and the majority of university music departments and conservatoires still focus on traditional music-educational paradigms, making it necessary for many secondary school teachers to prepare their pupils in these terms. Although there is considerable variation from school to school, classical music and classically derived pedagogic approaches to music continue to be the mainstay of music education in the majority of schools, with popular and other world music making very significant inroads.

Not only do the practices of teachers tend to lean towards classical techniques and thus blur the boundaries between styles, but the conceptions of musical styles held by pupils become detached from their commonsense connotations in the wider society. For example, as will be illustrated, pupils in a school are quite likely to tell one that they are exclusively taught classical music. One then walks into their classroom, only to discover that the teacher is playing 'Eleanor Rigby' (by the Beatles) on the piano, as an inspiration for pupils' song-writing on the theme of loneliness. To many pupils, 'Eleanor Rigby', especially when played on a piano in a classroom, *is* classical music. On one hand, many pupils, especially those under the age of about fourteen, tend to be confused about technical musical features and find it hard to distinguish them, or even to grasp technical concepts in relation to musical style at all. Quite often they will associate the classical style with any music which is slow or which has violins and cellos in it, and popular music with any music which is fast or which has drums in it. On the other hand, the mere fact that music is in the curriculum affects pupils' judgements of its style, such that any music which the teacher requires them to study is taken to be classical. Popular music, contrastingly, is *by definition* music which the teacher does not require them to study, and, in the minds of many pupils, as soon as the teacher does make this requirement, the music will cease to be popular. Some of the most salient characteristics of much popular music are its spirit of rebellion, its sexual innuendoes and its rejection of authority, a rejection in which education forms a very central target.[7]

---

[6] Vulliamy's work (1976), (1977a), (1977b) was the first to raise awareness of this problem amongst educationalists, specifically focussing on teachers' approaches to structured listening/analysis of popular music in class. For further discussion of differences between studying classical and popular music see Middleton (1990, Chapter 4).

[7] See Green (1988, pp. 141ff), Vulliamy (1977a), (1977b) for further discussion of the way popular music takes on classical contours in the educational context.

Therefore, even though some areas of popular music have entered the curricula of many schools, there will always be a pop–classical split engrained in the music-education system as a whole; or rather, engrained in the relationship between what the music-education system includes and what it leaves out. Concepts of 'classical' and 'popular' in schools are associated not so much with musical styles as they are constructed in the society at large as with notions of 'what counts as music' for teachers and pupils within the particular school. In the rest of the book, I will continue to use broad definitions for musical styles, not only as a matter of convenience, but as a necessity. When I use the words 'classical' and 'popular', I intend to invoke them as counters in the discursive mechanisms of the school, rather than as indicators of conventionally understood stylistic musical boundaries outside the school.

Factors external to the education system that impinge upon my discussion of music education include the social class, ethnic origins and gender of the pupils and teachers, as well as their religious and sub-cultural affiliations, all of which can have significant effects on musical practices and on the meanings with which music is invested. Previous work in the sociology of music education interpreted the content and practice of music education as having implications for the reproduction of social class, concentrating on the split between classical and popular music. More recently, issues of ethnicity, religion and gender, as well as many further musical styles and sub-styles that these imply, have started to be examined.[8]

In considering the relationship between ethnicity and music education in contemporary England, it is necessary to distinguish between two perspectives: one examines the position and meaning of music in different ethnic groupings of the world; the other examines the position and meaning of music for different ethnic groupings living in a 'host' country. It is important not to confuse these two perspectives. Whereas music may involve certain practices and meanings within a given ethnic grouping, if members of that grouping move into a different 'host' culture, new practices and meanings may arise. Regarding religious affiliations, whether or not the people concerned are of ethnic origins

---

[8] On social class, again see Vulliamy (1977a), (1977b), Green (1988); also see Small (1977) for a critique of Western scientist and imperialistic assumptions in music education. On ethnicity and multicultural music education see Kwami (1996). For more recent developments see Keil (n.d.); Jorgensen (forthcoming). There was an early symposium on the sociology of music education in the United States in 1995, and there seems to be increasing interest in this area within music education studies generally.

outside a 'host' culture, there are a number of fresh issues to be tackled. One is that there are some religions to which large number of pupils in English schools belong – for example Islam and Judaism – which in some of their manifestations consider music to be dangerous or even immoral; it may therefore be forbidden to pupils of either sex by their families. Yet according to the English National Curriculum since its inauguration in 1992, all children are required to sing, play, compose, improvise, appraise and listen to music in school. As yet, little has been done about this problem.[9] Regarding sub-culture, although a large number of school pupils are involved in various sub-categories of listening, the majority of those under the age of about fourteen rarely have the maturity, the wherewithal, the freedom or the financial means to be thoroughly immersed, tending to rely on vicarious involvement in sub-cultures such as is available through broadcasting mechanisms. Those older pupils who are more deeply involved in sub-cultures are liable to make this fact apparent in the subtle use of insignia, and are unlikely to allow risky aspects of their affiliation, such as drug usage, to enter too boldly into their projected self-images at school.

In the remainder of this chapter and in the next two chapters, I will make no particular reference to class, ethnicity, religion or sub-culture: many of the issues which I will address are repeated, and often repeated with greater force, within the discourses of and about many different social-class, ethnic, religious and sub-cultural groupings in this country. While I do not wish to reduce the importance of the distinctions in musical practices and musical meanings within and between these groupings, in the context of the present book it is impossible to consider them in any detail. Rather, I will attempt continually to bear in mind many of the issues which they raise, and allow them to provide the context for my main concern: gender.

I undertook some questionnaire research during 1992, involving music teachers in seventy-eight state secondary co-educational schools in the North, South and Midlands.[10] The questions that are of relevance to the present discussion are reproduced below. For each question, teachers were asked to put a ring around either 'Girls', 'Boys' or 'Both equally', and to give reasons for their answer.

---

[9] J. M. Halstead (1994), Murphy (1993) provide helpful discussions of this. Also see the ethnographic literature, especially Koskoff (1987c), Herndon and Ziegler (1990). On issues concerning multicultural music education, see Elliott (1989), (1990), (1995), Kwami (1996).

[10] A fuller description of the qualitative methodology and further responses from the questionnaire are available in Green (1993).

A. In general, throughout the school, which group is the most successful at:
  5. Playing an instrument
  6. Singing
  7. Composing
  8. Listening
  9. Notation-reading and -writing

B. Which group generally speaking prefers to engage in:
  10. Classical music(s)
  11. Popular music(s)
  12. Other world music(s)

   . . .

18. Add any further comments about gender and music which are of general interest and/or relevance to your answers:

The questions were phrased in an open and even deliberately ambiguous way, designed to reduce to a minimum any rhetorical implications and any nudging of answers. My interest lay not in collecting facts and figures about pupils' behaviour but in discovering what unprompted thoughts would surface in teachers' minds, what assumptions and definitions of terms would make themselves apparent. When a number of teachers happened to raise a particular issue, they did so without prompt and without consultation. I then took that issue to be a significant reflection of their collective views, impressions and concerns. Even though as a commentator upon the teachers' perspectives, I must to some extent stand outside them, that does not mean that I cannot myself be implicated in them. Indeed, many of the impressions that teachers report are ones that I recognise and share from my own experience. Teachers' impressions arise from powerful, collective, historically informed perspectives on musical practices and musical meanings. It can never be a question that people are simply wrong or right in such matters. During what follows, I have indicated how many teachers agreed or disagreed on any particular point, or in a few cases I have simply provided all the relevant comments made. This is partly in the interests of accurate representation, and also because I feel that too much generalisation will reduce the impact of the comments; but more than that, the teachers' words evoke the colours and sounds of classroom life.[11]

[11] I would sincerely like to thank all those teachers who gave their time and concentrated their thoughts in responding to the questionnaire. Many teachers were extremely generous in the amount of detail they provided, and many wrote encouraging comments about the work, often providing further unelicited information, all of which greatly helped to spur me on. I am also

At the same time as examining teachers' responses it is helpful to consider pupils' views. I undertook a small amount of interview work, also in 1992, collecting tape recordings of pupils talking about their musical interests and their music lessons. The interviews were informally structured, using open questions which covered five areas, only one of which directly concerned comparisons of boys and girls. The first and main question in this area was: 'Do you think that boys/girls feel the same way about music lessons as you do?' Over two days I recorded conversations with twelve groups of pupils: six groups of girls and six groups of boys aged eleven to fifteen (forty-eight pupils altogether). The school was a large co-educational comprehensive in central London, which took pupils from several different social-class, religious and ethnic groupings. I had visited the music department on fifteen prior occasions over the course of the preceding two years, in order to supervise beginner-teachers. During these visits I worked with pupils in small groups and observed lessons, becoming familiar with the department's Scheme of Work and Music Policy. The curriculum included practical and written performance, composition and appraisal activities involving classical and popular music of many sub-styles, including music from around the world. A peripatetic team supported the department with specialist tuition on several orchestral instruments, guitar and drums. There were a number of extra-curricular options, including a jazz band, a swing band and a large choir, some of which I observed in rehearsal. A selection of pupils' ensembles and rock groups also practised on the premises after hours. The school had a history of considerable musical success and activity; but the Head of Music confided to me during my last few visits that she had become gradually disillusioned, and felt that the department was being run down. In my job at that time I was visiting between eight and twenty different schools in the Inner and Greater London area every year. This particular school seemed to me to have no outstanding properties in one direction or another: I selected it because I saw it as a normal London school, in so far as such a thing can exist at all.[12]

grateful to the Local Education Authorities and head teachers for permitting me to carry out the work in their schools. I have left the comments intact apart from making a few spelling corrections and losing the occasional abbreviation. The responses in any one category are listed here in the order by which they arrived through the post. Further details and more responses are available in Green (1993).

[12] I would like to record my deep appreciation of the two teachers in the department, who showed me a great deal of consideration and kindness. I would also like to thank the pupils for their interest in the project and their willingness to talk about their opinions. I am grateful as well to the

Table 1. *Questionnaire responses: category 1*

Question		No. of ringed responses		
5. Playing	35	0	43	0
6. Singing	64	0	13	1
7. Composing	5	10	63	0
8. Listening	11	0	67	0
9. Notation	27	0	57	0
10. Classical	19	1	56	2
11. Popular	1	12	64	1
12. World	5	1	65	7
	Girls	Boys	Both equally	No response

Source: Green 1993, p. 223

GIRLS SINGING AND PLAYING MUSIC IN SCHOOLS: TEACHERS' AND PUPILS' PERCEPTIONS

My interpretation of the questionnaire responses falls into two categories, which run alongside each other. The first of these concerns the responses that involved putting a ring around 'Girls', 'Boys' or 'Both equally'. These responses can be readily quantified, and are shown in Table 1.

The majority of ringed responses overall indicated that boys and girls are seen to achieve equal success or else prefer to engage equally in music. Two questions in particular, no. 5 on playing and no. 6 on singing, indi-

Local Education Authority and the Head of School for giving me permission to carry out the work.

I had originally intended to replicate the study in other schools in different parts of the country. To judge by my questionnaire results (and personal experience), I surmise that there would have been significant geographical variation that would have strengthened rather than weakened my case. However, the work was cut short by thirty-six weeks of unrelenting pregnancy sickness. I am satisfied that what I did achieve represents a valid case study in itself, whilst at the same time recognising that this area is wide open for further research. (I was able to extend the work in another school in 1995, which will be explained and discussed in Chapter 8.)

The conversations are transcribed as exactly as possible, without getting into minutiae. I have left out interjections such as 'um' and 'er', and I have used standard spelling for almost all pronunciations. Punctuation is standard, but is also used to indicate pauses in speech. Ellipses usually represent irrelevant events such as a new person entering the room, the tape-recorder falling off the table, etc. Occasionally they represent the omission of parts of the conversation which I have considered to be wholly irrelevant. The group situation contributed to an apparent consensus between participants. Whereas such a consensus does rule out individual differences of opinion, it at the same time represents the coercive power of discourse. Because of this consensus, and in the interests of reducing unnecessary information, I have erased the individual identity of speakers (Chapters 6 and 7 only), leaving only my own identity, as LG, intact.

This work is also reported in Green (forthcoming). For an interesting and in many ways complementary approach which takes in issues of gender, class and race with relation to pupils' self-presentations concerning music listening habits, see Richards (1997).

cated an impression of overwhelmingly greater success on the part of girls rather than boys; and girls were also ringed in modestly greater numbers than boys with relation to questions 8 on listening, 9 on notation, 10 on classical music and 12 on other world music. Boys, on the other hand, were only ever ringed marginally more than girls, and only with relation to two questions: no. 7 on composing, and no. 11 on popular music. My second category of interpretation concerns teachers' further comments. Even though in most cases boys' and girls' musical achievements or tastes were ringed as equal, there was an overwhelming consensus among teachers,in their further comments, that the sexes are equal but different. Indeed, many if not most of the ringed responses indicating equality were qualified by comments. It is actually these qualifications, the wealth of other reasons which teachers gave for their ringed responses and the many thoughts which they volunteered, that form the greater focus of my attention. The significance of all these answers, and their relationship to the ways in which pupils talked about the same issues, will be explored during the course of Part II of the book. In the current chapter, I will attend to those areas in which girls are perceived to be deeply involved, and in the next chapter to those areas which are more closely associated with boys.

Singing

As Table 1 shows, sixty-four out of the seventy-eight teachers indicated that girls are more successful at singing than boys. Many of these volunteered the further information that more girls take part in choir or other extra-curricular group-singing activities, often to the total exclusion of boys. Thirty-one teachers commented that boys are shy, reticent or awkward about singing in ways that are connected to puberty or to difficulties caused by the voice breaking. Only thirteen indicated that boys and girls are equal in singing, and none indicated that boys are more successful at singing than girls. In the case-study school, I found that these views concurred with the views of the pupils: all of the girls I interviewed expressed at least a readiness to sing, many of them said that they enjoyed singing, and some said that singing was considered to be a girls' activity, or, in the words of one eleven-year-old: 'singing is girls' jobs'.

Orchestral instrument, guitar and piano playing

Girls were also perceived to be more active than boys as instrumentalists in schools. Thirty-five teachers indicated that girls are more successful, forty-three that both sexes are equal, and none that boys are more successful. Twenty-nine teachers further commented that more girls than boys play instruments, often outnumbering boys by two to one and in many cases in significantly higher ratios. Not only do more girls play instruments, but overwhelmingly teachers said that girls play a certain *type* of instrument, often described as traditional or orchestral, most notably the flute and violin. One teacher commented that out of fifty flautists in her school there was not a single boy. The guitar and piano were also mentioned by several teachers, although less frequently than orchestral instruments. I think the reason for this is that many Local Education Authorities subsidise orchestral instruments only. Therefore the guitar and piano, although they are abundantly played by girls nationwide, are not available on the peripatetic roster of several musically active schools. A great deal of piano tuition, in particular, remains private.[13] As well as specific involvement with instruments, a further nineteen teachers indicated that girls 'prefer to engage in' (see question 10) classical music more than boys, and only one suggested that boys prefer classical music more than girls.

During my interviews with pupils this picture of girls' involvement with orchestral instruments associated with classical music was underlined again and again. For example:

A group of four Year 8 boys (age 12–13):
– LG: . . . I mean do you think that girls like to play the same instruments as you?
– All: No.
– Most girls like to play the violin and the cello.
– Most girls – yeah.
– There are two girls in our class who play the cello I think it is.

A group of three GCSE boys (age 14–15):
– LG: . . . Do you think girls have a similar approach towards their music lessons as you do?
– No, not at all.
– It's funny, there's a lot more of them that actually take music, but they're not quite as interested.
  . . .
– Mostly they, like, they take music lessons, they play flute, violin.
– Violin.
– They don't branch out much from classical music.

[13] These reports can readily be backed up with staggering effect by collections of figures from almost any mixed secondary school or Local Education Authority in Britain which provides (or used to provide) instrumental lessons.

Attitude

Girls' attitudes and approaches to music were understood by teachers to be linked with a willingness to express their feelings, with delicacy or with decoration.

Which group is the most successful at singing?
- Girls . . . see singing as an extension of their feelings, I believe; something they are more in touch with than boys.

Which group prefers to engage in classical music(s)?
- Girls. Classical music seems to affect the feminine principle of anima as outlined by Jung . . .
- Girls. Particularly higher up the age range. Respond more easily to emotional stimulus.
- Girls. I think the boys tend to prefer loud, electronically produced sounds, with that constant electronic drum beat in it!
  Girls seem to be prepared to play more 'delicate' music. Both, however, are happy to play classical music adapted for keyboards.

Which group is the most successful at listening?
- Both equally. (GCSE) Just a comment: Girls tend to be more 'flowery' in approach to answering questions and analysing, boys seem more 'to the point'. (GCSE level) . . .

Girls were understood to possess more highly developed communication skills and cooperative attitudes than boys:

Which group is the most successful at playing?
- Girls . . . More oriented towards group behaviour in many ways.
- Girls . . . (2) In the early years at Secondary School, *team support/* attitude amongst girls is stronger . . .

Which group is the most successful at notation?
- Girls. Girls have the deeper sense of the need for communication and therefore give more time to this aspect of music.

Which group prefers to engage in classical music(s)?
- Girls . . . I feel that because much of the classical music performed here is SOCIAL ie where no *ONE* player takes the limelight – the girls, seemingly more egalitarian, are more suited to this than boys!

Girls were seen to be more open-minded, in a series of answers that merge mostly on classical and on other world music. Below is a sample taken from eight comments:

Which group prefers to engage in classical music(s)?
- Girls. Girls seem to be more open and prepared to listen to a wider range of music.

– Girls. Not sure why. Possibly it may be that girls are more open-minded or more amenable – or perhaps they respond more easily to music . . .

Which group prefers to engage in world music(s)?
– Girls. They are more tolerant & understanding. Can appreciate other faiths & customs.
– Girls. Appear more responsive and 'open' about cultural variety.
– Girls. In the Lower school I find girls generally have a more open mind to listen to unfamiliar sounds, rhythms, scales, instruments etc.

There is only one contradiction to the impression that girls are more open:

Which group is the most successful at listening?
– Both equally . . . the girls are *always* better prepared and therefore more aware of what they are listening for but seem to have more of a problem with concentration span than boys. Boys are generally less well prepared but have a longer concentration span and are more broad-minded and open minded about what they listen to!

The statement above, that girls lack concentration, also contradicts the much more popular idea that girls concentrate better, work harder, or are more mature, motivated, reliable and/or persevering than boys. This is expressed in strikingly similar terms by teachers, many of whom used a vernacular term, 'stickability'.

Which group is the most successful at playing?
– Girls.
 More motivated
 " mature

– Girls.
 Persevere for a longer period
 Punctual at lessons . . .

– Girls . . . All pupils have equal opportunity to take part but girls tend to favour and work harder at their studies . . . Girls tend to be more successful academically.

– Girls.
 1. Girls generally have more stickability.
 2. Boys generally get disheartened very quickly if they don't make rapid progress and consequently give up easily . . .

– Girls are more reliable; remember lessons, instruments, times. Practise harder.

– Girls. Apply themselves to practice, more organised, not so easily influenced by peers or other activities i.e. sport.

– Girls. In classroom projects it is equal – boys and girls but many more girls are prepared to persevere and join in extra curricular activities

– Girls . . . Less peer-pressure on girls.

– Girls. . . . Girls tend to have greater 'stickability' than boys – possibly peer pressure on boys to do other things.

– Girls. More girls than boys opt into our instrumental tuition scheme and tend to continue playing for a longer period of time . . .

– Girls. They seem to persevere more. Stickability.

– Girls. Girls seem generally keener to learn and produce completed performances. Many lads tend to mess around with equipment.

– Girls. There is a greater numerical take up amongst girls and they tend to stick at it better . . .

– Girls. More girls elect to play an instrument and continue to play whereas boys have a go and give up more readily . . .

– Girls . . . Outside the classroom, a few more girls than boys seem to continue playing an orchestral instrument once begun.

– Girls. They seem to have more staying power and have a desire to improve in orchestral instrument situation.
  On classroom instruments the boys come closer, probably because the work is achievable within a short space of time and needs no sacrifice of 'own time' . . .

– Girls . . . The boys that do have lessons seem to drop the commitment more easily . . .

– Girls . . . (3) Girls more mature earlier, and have a corresponding commitment to their work.

– Girls. Girls on the whole 'stick' at an instrument, therefore overcoming the difficulties of learning and moving on to the more satisfying stage. Boys on the whole tend to give up much more easily . . .

– Girls . . . The boys who have attempted to play, tried brass instruments. They gave up within weeks . . .

– Girls.
  . . . (b) 'Staying power' . . .

– Girls.
  . . . 2. I find that girls are more prepared to stick with the instrument than boys . . .

– Girls.
  . . . 2. Poor motivation [on the part of boys] . . .

Which group is the most successful at singing?
- Both equally . . . at the last concert there were 3 Girls 1 boy but that's because those were the people who obeyed their instructions.

- Girls. Clearer sight of how enjoyable it can be . . .

- Girls. In the 1st two years girls + boys sing equally well but by 9th [i.e. 3rd] year some boys seem to think it's below them.

- Girls. In the lower age range 11–13 I would suggest that the groups are equal . . . Overall the girls still show a consistent commitment throughout the process.

- Girls. Although many boys enjoy singing particularly in the lower years, girls work harder at it and so generally produce a better sound . . .

- Girls.
  (a) confidence in themselves.

- Girls. Girls are more confident, especially by year 8 and 9 [i.e. age 12–13 and 13–14]. Both equally in year 7 [i.e. age 11–12].

Which group is the most successful at composing?
- Girls. They get down to work faster and see the task through.

Which group is the most successful at listening?
- Both equally . . . . Sustained listening is best completed by girls.

- Girls. They seem to find it easier to concentrate and think more carefully about presentation of ideas.

- Both equally . . . In some Lower school classes, I would say that girls have a longer concentration span, but many boys are v. imaginative.

Which group is the most successful at notation?
- Girls. Again, because concentration spans seem longer.

- Girls. Happier to learn systematically the rules and facts. Boys can't be bothered.

Which group prefers to engage in classical music(s)?
- Girls. They seem to obtain a grasp of its message at an earlier age.

Further comments
- . . . Girls are more reliable and consistent . . .

Six teachers said that girls are better than boys at notation, for the reason that more of them play instruments whose traditions involve musical literacy. A further thirteen teachers indicated that girls have superior writing abilities, which they sometimes attributed to greater pride in the presentation of their work. Here is a sample:

Which group is the most successful at composing?
- Both equally . . . The boys do well using an improvisatory approach – they are less inclined to want to produce a 'score' for their work. The girls work more methodically, and like writing things down. They take more pride in presenting a well-written score.

Which group is the most successful at notation?
- Girls. Take more pride in how their work is presented therefore try hard to write notation, complete evaluation sheets.

- Girls. Generally like to present their work in a neat & orderly fashion, they enjoy making their work presentable.

Only three teachers disagreed. For example:

Which group is the most successful at notation?
- Both equally. Perhaps there's a myth that girls are neater and more methodical. In my experience it is not so.

Teachers' perceptions about girls' attitudes to musical practices were echoed in interviews with pupils. First, pupils frequently referred to a preference on the part of girls for love songs, soft or slow music, which was sometimes associated with classical styles. For example:

Four Year 8 boys (age 12–13):
- There are two girls in our class who play the cello I think it is.
- LG: Why do you think that is?
- 'Cos they like slower music.

Four Year 8 boys (age 12–13):
- I don't think girls really like fast dancing.
- They like sort of slow music, what you can just groove to.
- Just, really slow music.

Secondly, some of the boys characterised girls as shy or embarrassed, and this was also more than once associated with classical music. For example:

Four Year 8 boys (age 12–13):
- What happens in class is, like, the girls –
- Most of the boys I know like to express theirself, and the girls, like Kerry-Ann, they're too shy, but I say if they're too shy, they should learn classical music.

Five Year 7 boys (age 11–12):
- LG: Are girls as good at music as you?
- No. I think half the girls in our class, maybe even three quarters, are embarrassed.

Thirdly, even when boys challenged the idea that girls were cooperative, they nonetheless could not help at the same time confirming the fact that girls *appear* to be cooperative, or are thought by teachers to be cooperative:

Four Year 8 boys (age 12–13):

- LG: ... Do you think girls feel the same way about the music lessons as you do?
- No, 'cos the girls I think get more of a chance.
- All: Yeah.
- If they say to Miss, 'Miss, can I work with so-and-so?', Miss'll say 'yes', straight away without an argument. When we say to Miss 'Can we work with so-and-so?', she says 'no'.
- [General consent]
- LG: Is that so?
- It seems sometimes like, it's a bit sexist, but –
- I reckon it is a bit, actually.
- LG: In favour of the girls, you mean?
- Yeah.
- That happens in every lesson.
- LG: Does it? And why do you think that happens?
- Because, right, the girls muck about really bad, but the teachers don't actually see them muck around.
- LG: Why is that, then?
- [Despairingly] I don't know!
- Because, like, the girls always get sent outside in the corridors.
  [This is a common practice in many schools with insufficient space, to enable pupils to work in small groups.]
- Yeah.
- And Miss never goes out there, she always stays in here to supervise us.
- The teachers don't supervise them.
- The girls.
- Yeah.
- And they're always mucking about outside.
- Laughing.
- And, like, when Miss goes out there to go and check up on them they always seem, sort of, seem quiet.

AFFIRMING FEMININITY IN THE MUSIC CLASSROOM

These comments by teachers and pupils can be understood as participating in the over-arching discourse on music, and in the reproduction of gendered musical practices and meanings which I have discussed in previous chapters. I argued in Chapter 2 that singing involves a type of display which is relatively affirmative of traditional definitions of femininity, and that this affirmation helps to explain women's extensive involvement in singing throughout history. Here we see that this involvement is repeated in the contemporary school, where singing is by far the most audible and visible musical practice of girls. I also argued that the historical success and predominance of women as music teachers in the home, convent and school are understandable as reflections of an affirmative definition of femininity which is articulated in women's musical 'enabling roles'. The definition of femininity as enabling carried on into debates about women's instrumental abilities in the nineteenth and twentieth centuries, such that many people who defended women classical and jazz instrumentalists appealed to notions of feminine sensitivity and cooperation in their playing (pp. 71 and 74 above). This musical expression of femininity as enabling is also perpetuated in the school, as exemplified in the comments of teachers and pupils above concerning girls' sensitivity and their cooperative attitudes in relation to music.

In Chapter 3, I suggested that women's use of technology breaks away from patriarchal conceptions of femininity, and that in musical performance the presence and manipulation of an instrument symbolically interrupts a feminine delineated display of the body. The extent of this interruption, I argued, is dependent upon a number of factors. Here I wish to concentrate on the least disruptive level of interruption, a level which even allows for a retrieval of affirmation. This occurs when the performance is in the realm of classical music, the discourse surrounding which eschews any recognition of delineation in the first place, insisting instead on the autonomous sovereignty of inherent meanings. Interruption is also reduced when the performance context is domestic or educational, which detracts from the sexual connotations of display. Certain instruments, notably plucked strings, keyboards and a few orchestral instruments, have been particularly susceptible to a reduction of interruption. Women's access to these instruments in the private sphere and later the public sphere has a long history and is today an unremarkable fact. The reduction of interruption which they offer has even been harnessed by some contemporary classical soloists into a publicity image that promotes a strong affirmation of patriarchal conceptions of femininity. Overall, the instrumental performance of classical music, especially in the domestic or educational sphere, especially solo, on keyboards, plucked strings and certain orchestral instruments, is relatively affirmative of femininity. Like singing and 'enabling', this affirmation is also reiterated in the contemporary school, as is evidenced by the overwhelming impressions of teachers and pupils regarding girls' instrumental performance.

Discursive constructions do not merely describe and reiterate 'reality', but they also produce reality. This is how it is possible for some of the boys, cited above, to say:

- Most girls like to play the violin and the cello.
- Most girls – yeah.
- There are two girls in our class who play the cello I think it is.

Two girls in a class of around thirty can hardly constitute 'most girls': but discourse is concerned less with empirical reality than with affirming stereotypes that exist as symbolic constructions of what we assume is and ought to be the case. What the boys mean is that when girls do play instruments, they play classical instruments; and when they play classical instruments, they play the violin and the cello. There is a constant slippage between empirical reality and discursive construction in what the teachers and pupils say. At the surface level, no one would dispute the readily verifiable fact that abundant numbers of girls take part in singing and playing classical instruments, compared to very small numbers of boys. At a deeper level, however, what is of interest and significance is not this mere fact so much as the way that this fact is put into discourse, and the effects that this discourse has on reproducing the fact.

The characteristics of girls' musical practices, as described by teachers and pupils, do not merely represent conventions of female behaviour, but perpetuate *discursive constructions of femininity itself*. Girls taking part in musical performance activities in schools are not just learning to perform music; they are also negotiating a gender identity. They are able to adopt certain musical practices and musical styles, like a mantle or a piece of clothing which helps to define their gender, or to constitute their sexuality. Singing and playing orchestral, plucked or keyboard instruments in areas largely associated with 'classical' music in schools offer girls a means by which symbolically to *affirm* their femininity in conformity with the perceived expectations and norms of the wider society, of the school, of the teachers, of other pupils and of themselves. Most significantly, this symbolic affirmation of femininity does not stop at the level of the discursive constructions surrounding girls' musical *practices*: it becomes a part of the very delineated meanings of the music that girls perform. Thus the music which girls sing or play, the music over which girls are seen to cooperate together, itself comes to delineate femininity within the school.

By drawing attention to their search for an affirmative symbolisation of femininity through music, I am not criticising girls, but rather attempting to recognise what is an inevitable and vital part of being a teenager: a part, indeed, of being human. Music can play a vivid role in the search for gendered as well as sexual identity. One of the reasons why it is so powerful a force is that it enables us to experience its delineated meanings as though they were the direct, unmediated truths of our own subjectivity, carried along by the temporal organisation of the music's inherent materials. By virtue of the affirmative feminine delineation that is afforded to girls through their musical practices in schools, I wish to suggest, their musical experiences themselves can be enhanced: the musical experiences of girl musicians, like those of women musicians as discussed in Chapter 5, can acquire a power and apparent truth-value that is unavailable to them through many other musical channels. Girls and women engaging in affirmatively feminine musical performance practices can find themselves positively reflected in the performance delineations of the music they sing or play; and their manipulation of the music's inherent meanings can afford them that type of familiarity which coincides with fulfilment. Because their femininity is affirmed in the performance delineations of the music, and reflected back at them in combination with a fulfilling grasp of inherent meanings, delineated and inherent meanings together can afford an apparently unitary experience of relative celebration by the music.

For many girls this celebratory musical experience will generate an unmitigated pleasure when, for example, they enjoy their affirmative display, enjoy the inherent meanings of the music which they perform, enjoy finding themselves reflected as girls in the overall musical experience. At its most powerful, such an experience can connect with those alternative images of femininity suggested by the role-models of the diva or the classic blues singer, as discussed in Chapter 2.[14] For other girls, such a celebratory musical experience may provide a welcome means to act creatively in the musical arena, whilst at the same time retarding their entrance into the world of sexuality. On one hand, the educational setting affords the privacy of practice-rooms, or the familiarity of the classroom; and even when girls appear on the school stage, the educational overtones of the performance context reduce the sexual connotations of display which are invoked by more public, professional settings. On the other hand, girls' performance frequently takes place in large groups – the school choir or orchestra – which, again, allow for a reduction of the display element delineated by the solo performer. The cooperative feminine characteristics that are associated with girls' musical

[14] Pegley and Caputo (1993) make an appeal to such an 'empowering' possibility through girls' singing activities, and connect this to the very centrality of the body in the act of singing. They also cite Giles and Shepherd (1990) on singing as an 'active affirmation of self through the "other" – the text – of music' (Giles and Shepherd 1990, p. 20, cited in Pegley and Caputo 1993, p. 304)

practices in schools can also help in the articulation of a space in which girls are able to negotiate their gender with each other and with their teachers.

One further aspect in which such musical performance experience is empowering for girls lies in the possibilities it affords for the development, and potentially the display, of musical skill through the manipulation of inherent meanings. In the realm of classical music, or of 'what counts as music' in schools, problematic sexual aspects of the delineations of display are reduced, not only because of the educational environment, but also because of the seriousness with which the 'music itself' is intended to be taken. Girl performers in such a context are less legitimately to be considered as 'sexually available' or 'sexually suspect' by the discourse surrounding the music. Rather, the discourse will tend to deny delineation at all, eulogising instead the performers' skilful control of inherent meanings. Just as their classical foremothers, in singing from the sixteenth century and in instrumental performance from the eighteenth century onwards, were able to reach the pinnacle of achievement partly by virtue of the construction of relative autonomy of the music they performed, so exceptional girl classical musicians in schools today can attain the highest acclaim for their musical skills, whilst transcending any potential limitations imposed by the delineations of their femininity.

Resistance

In the teachers' and pupils' comments above, girls are constructed as conforming to teachers' expectations, standards of behaviour, and musical values.[15] This conformity is expressed not only through the perceived greater perseverance and harder work of girls, but also through their involvement with what is referred to as classical music, or with 'what counts' in English secondary-school music education. Girls can symbolically affirm their femininity through singing, playing classical music and working in ways which conform to the schools' norms and standards. Any mention of potential non-conformist signs of femininity is noticeably absent from the discussions of teachers and pupils. Non-

---

[15] The issue of girls' and boys' inclinations towards conformity or resistance has been the subject of considerable debate. See Willis (1977), Kessler et al. (1985), Walkerdine (1990), Wolpe (1988), as well as other sources cited in Chapter 6, note 2, p. 144 above. So far, I have been describing the discourse of teachers and pupils on gender and conformity. This discourse does not necessarily correlate with various relatively unnoticed practices of girls and boys, which, as we will go on to see, often present contradictions.

conformist femininity with relation to music is discursively constructed, negatively, as non-existent. Indeed, girls who are definable as 'naughty', who may be sexually active or sub-culturally involved, are liable to find classical music, singing, orchestral instruments, 'perseverance' and 'hard work' more problematic. What musical performance activities, if any, are available to such girls?

Valerie Walkerdine (1990, pp. 116ff) draws on what she characterises as a group of 'bad' girls and a group of 'good' girls in the upper years of a primary school where she was engaged in research. The terms with which she is operating, 'good' and 'bad', are never clearly defined attributes, but are positions which can be taken up and dropped at different times. For all the girls, popular culture with its fiction of romantic heterosexuality was 'present at the interstices of the practices (in the denied and marginalized spaces) where the sanitized images of children's fiction cannot reach' (1990, p. 123). The girls sang pop songs, talked about television programmes, watched films. One song and act which was in the charts at the time, Toni Basil's 'Oh Mickey', presented Basil as the epitome of the sexualised schoolgirl-turned-vamp. Not only the 'bad' but also many of the 'good' girls sang it, and in so doing, they became transformed:

Another 'good' girl, Janie, is transformed in minutes from 'good' to 'bad' girl. The rendition of 'Oh Mickey' is sung in the privacy of the toilets. There in front of the mirror she sighs and poses: the child, the woman, the virgin, the whore, the harlot.

As she leaves the classroom she crosses the hall. In the toilets the suppressed aspect, that which cannot be revealed in her 'good girl' position, is the fantasy of being the object of that other look: the sexual gaze. She sighs in front of the mirror. Then, told to stop messing about, she returns to 'normality'; she steps out of one fiction and into another. As she crosses the hall to her classroom, some children from another class are dancing to a piece of classical flute music. The teacher shouts to a boy: 'You're not supposed to be running, you're a jumping frog – jump!' (1990, p. 123)

In the vocal performance of popular music, girls invoke relatively risqué, dangerous or sexually suggestive display-delineations: for popular music is by definition, to some extent or other, accompanied by the discursive construction of delineations as salient aspects of the overall musical meaning. The female popular singer cannot so readily claim the autonomy of the inherent meanings of her music as a distraction away from her display-delineations. On the contrary, she is liable to invite specific attention to her display, an attention which is not necessarily aggressive, rebellious or counteractive, but which is a perfectly normal part of any audience stance towards popular music. As soon as the girl popular vocalist starts to sing, attention is likely to be paid to the nature of her display, the level of 'attractiveness' which she signifies. Beyond that, her private sexual life – or at least its potentialities – is held open for questioning. The extent to which this occurs in school settings will of course vary considerably from school to school, according to what type of popular music is being performed and whether it is sung before a mirror in the toilets or before an audience in the school concert. In schools where popular vocal performance by girls is a common-place, the familiarity of the feminine delineation, combined with the acceptability of the music, will already have gone a long way to diluting the problematic connotations of the sexual element of the display. In schools where such performance is rare, the display will be the more risqué. With reference to the performance of types of popular music that are often sung by women, such as solo voice and acoustic guitar, the display will be less suggestive; with reference to popular singing that delineates promiscuity, or that is male-dominated, the display will be more problematic.

Music delineates meanings, and allows us to invest in those meanings, wordlessly taking up symbolic postures with relation to how we understand ourselves. In educational environments this symbolisation can become particularly poignant as we cross from style to style, from classical music to popular music, from relative conformity to relative deviance, from madonna to whore, from educational success to educational failure, from femininity to masculinity. The schools' discursive mechanisms involve pupils' adoption of dominant, mainstream musical practices and meanings, but they can also involve allegiance or attraction to alternative musical practices and meanings. These alternatives may run counter to teachers' definitions of good and bad behaviour, or good and bad music in any particular school. But in either case, conforming or not conforming, the search for gender-identity is an inescapable part of being a girl or being a boy. The girl in Walkerdine's cameo above, although she may have resisted some definitions of femininity in her transformation from 'good' to 'bad', nonetheless adopted others which just as securely allowed her to take on the features of patriarchally defined femininity: the tension between the 'good' side of a girl who sings in the choir and the 'naughty' side which turns into a vamp in front of the mirror in the toilets reproduces that age-old definition of the woman as madonna/whore, which her role as singer symbolically encapsulates.

Although the 'feminine' attributes of girls do contribute to the perpetuation of classical music as a conformist aspect of school life, these
'feminine' characteristics are also able to countenance non-conformist
attitudes to the school in general and to school music in particular. The
most readily available musical performance channel for such non-conformity exists in the vocal performance of popular music. But even when
girls attempt to counter teachers' definitions of good behaviour or good
music, by for example invoking risqué display-delineations associated
with popular singing, they are not avoiding the affirmation of femininity
which has been delineated by vocal performance for millennia. As we
will see in the next chapter, the availability of other musical channels of
resistance for girls only rarely extends to the instrumental performance
of popular music.

SUMMARY

In this chapter I have suggested a view of the school music classroom as a
microcosmic version of the wider society, containing a variety of musical
practices, wherein the discourse on music and musical meanings themselves are reproduced in combination with the formation of personal
identity in terms of gender. I have then gone on to examine teachers'
and pupils' discursive constructions of the musical practices of girls in
schools. These practices are overwhelmingly understood to include
mainly singing and orchestral instrument, plucked string and piano
playing in the realm of classical music. Also, girls' attitudes towards
school music and towards each other as musicians are constructed as
being cooperative and conformist. I have linked my arguments to some
of the concepts introduced in earlier parts of the book: in particular, the
concept of affirmation regarding women singers, women musical
'enablers' and women classical instrumentalists; and the concept of the
symbolisation of affirmative femininity in musical delineation. Through
these concepts, I have argued that not only girls' musical practices but
the music with which girls are involved itself come to take on affirmative
feminine delineations within the school.

With relation to 'classical' music, or 'what counts as music' in schools,
this symbolic affirmation contributes to a vigorous discursive construction of femininity. It also enters the musical experience of girl classical
musicians, and from there affords a potential sense of celebration (as
discussed in Chapter 5, pp. 134f), in which positive identification
with performance delineations combines with fulfilment by inherent

meanings. Although girls are largely perceived by teachers and pupils as conforming to the mores of the school, the affirmative delineations of girls' musical practices can countenance girls' resistance to the school. This is exemplified particularly when girls are involved in singing popular music, an act which may invoke dissension from some definitions of what counts as music in a particular school, and which may involve counteraction to how girls are 'supposed' to behave, but which just as surely affirms patriarchal constructions of femininity.

The school aids in the continuation of the long history of girls' and women's performance on the symbolically private side of the private/public dualism that marks the patriarchal organisation of music. Girls taking part in musical activities in schools are overwhelmingly engaged in activities which symbolically affirm their femininity, an affirmation which is reiterated not merely in the reproduction of historically gendered musical practices but in gendered musical meanings and, beyond these, in gendered musical experiences themselves. The musical practices, meanings and experiences surrounding girls in contemporary schools reach out to pick up threads of the history of women in Western music.

CHAPTER 7

From affirmation to interruption of femininity in the music classroom

GIRLS AND BOYS MAKING MUSIC: TEACHERS' AND PUPILS'
PERCEPTIONS

In the last chapter I concentrated almost entirely on the discourse surrounding the musical practices of girls in schools. Here, I will continue to
invoke that discourse as a background to my discussion. Against this
background, I will examine ways in which teachers and pupils wrote and
talked about those areas of school musical life which girls are seen to
avoid, but around which boys are perceived to congregate.

Attitudes

Teachers' views of girls' 'enabling attitudes' towards music, as described
in Chapter 6, contrasted strongly with their characterisations of boys'
attitudes. Whereas girls were seen to use music to express their feelings,
to be cooperative and persevering in their musical practices, boys were
understood characteristically to denunciate the majority of musical
activities that are on offer in the school. The teachers saw this denuncia-
tion as being expressed in several ways, of which four notable ones are as
follows. First, boys prefer sport to music, a choice between the two being
a frequent necessity in schools where they often compete for extra-
curricular time. Secondly, boys create and succumb readily to heavy
peer-group pressure against school music. Thirdly, they lay emphasis on
what is musically 'fashionable' or 'in at the moment', which by definition
does not include music that is in the school curriculum. Fourthly, they
avoid certain musical activities for the reason that these are seen to be
'cissy' and 'un-macho'.[1] I have reproduced all the relevant comments

---

[1] Koza (1994a) analysed a selection of choral methods texts, which bore distinct similarities to the
teachers' opinions cited here. The texts gave four explanations of why boys do not attend choir,
including the observations that boys find it cissy and that they suffer negative peer-group pressure.

below. This is again partly in the interests of accurate representation, and also because I find that the build-up of comments, the independent reiteration of similar fundamental notions by so many people, provide the best available illustration of the workings of discourse within common sense.

Which group is the most successful at playing?
– Girls ... 'Image' – Girls music, Boys sport

– Girls. More socially acceptable for girls to play instruments ... Social stigma very powerful. Last week one pupil doing GCSE refused to carry his guitar outside while his peers were at games. He did not want them to know. We have a significant number of boys who don't care what others think – they do have to be quite strong. Don't know how to change the situation ...

– Girls ... 3. Boys are more aware of peer group pressure – it is still not seen as to give one 'street cred.' if one plays an orchestral instrument ...

– Girls. Peer pressure on boys – negative

– Girls ... Less peer-pressure on girls.

– Girls. More girls show an initial interest in playing an instrument ... – possibly peer pressure on boys to do other things.

– Girls ... Despite continued efforts to promote equal opportunities attitudes boys do generally see music, particularly 'orchestral' instrumental tuition as a 'female' un-macho pastime.

– Girls ... The boys that do have lessons seem to drop the commitment more easily, possibly due to peer pressure and the idea of being a sissy for playing an instrument.

– Girls. (1) Seen as an acceptable activity by peers ...

– Girls ... Boys in *general* still feel more pulled to sports activities and some still suffer torments from other boys about music being 'cissy'. This has improved greatly in recent years but there is still an undercurrent.

– Girls ... The boys who have attempted to play, tried brass instruments. They gave up within weeks. Possibly fear of peer group pressure.

– Girls ... The reasons I think we have more girls is ...
b) boys prefer sport
c) boys bow to peer group pressure.

(Koza criticises the texts for suggesting solutions to the problem of boys' participation not in terms of changing boys' attitudes but in terms of changing the musical activities on offer: e.g. persuading masculine role-models to join the choir and choosing music that boys will like.) Cohen (1991, p. 222) also mentions her own findings and other work, concerning the associations between sport and rock as fantasies of masculinity and power.

- Girls . . . I suspect it's a question of 'image' – boys can get a considerable amount of mocking from their peer group.

- Girls. Boys at 13–16 years tend to be more bothered about spending time socialising with peers; practising at home and lunchtime interferes with social events, such as football etc.

- Girls.
  Boys more interested in sport in playground
  Girls more willing to learn instrument . . .

- Girls. In the area in which we work there is a very male dominated culture which requires boys to be 'macho' and peer group pressure is strong insisting that this is 'cissy'

Which group is the most successful at singing?
- Girls. Boys have too immature an attitude to this activity probably due to parental opinion and pressure, and also the emphasis on sport . . .

- Both equally. Both are equally capable of singing. Often singing is associated as a female activity though . . .

- Girls. Less inhibited. No stigma attached. i.e. boys think it is 'cissy'.

- Girls . . . Image not 'cool' for boys.

- Girls . . . Some boys are very influenced by the attitudes of their friends.

- Girls. In my present (mixed) school it is fairly apparent that singing is thought of as 'non-macho' by the boys . . .

- Girls. 1. Peer group pressure . . .

- Girls . . . Also I think a lot of boys are put off singing by their feelings that it is a girls' activity . . .

- Girls. Past Year seven [i.e. age 11–12] – boys seem reluctant to join in with general sing: Part of the development of awareness of the 'male' role in society. However Boys have no qualms about 'singing' rap or ragga as it represents most of their 'macho' values.

- Girls . . . The girls are also more confident when singing, on the whole . . . There is perhaps a feeling among boys that singing does not improve their 'street-cred'.

- Girls/Both equally. Boys are successful in main school, though it is hard to get the numbers. Singing seems to have little 'Street Cred' . . .

- Girls. Singing is not seen as an activity for boys and so the girls tend to form the much greater majority of choirs . . .

- Girls. Peer group pressure on boys is a perennial problem. Most see singing as a no-go area . . .

- Girls. In the 1st two years [i.e. years 7 and 8 of secondary school] girls + boys sing equally well but by 9th year some boys seem to think it's below them.

- Girls. Very few boys enjoy singing or come to choir, they feel it is not a macho thing to do!

- Girls . . . the choir is mostly girls because the boys perceive it is a girls' activity . . .

- Girls. X [town] is a rather parochial, male dominated area. Heavy brass band/rugby playing area – rather macho type of attitude towards singing (and music in general).

- Girls. Very few boys make an attempt to sing. It is considered unfashionable . . .

- Girls. Boys decide it is cissy to sing.

- Girls. Again 1. image – . . .

- Girls . . . Our school choir is all girls – two boys joined at the start of the school year, and left after the first rehearsal because they were the only 2 boys.

- Girls. Not regarded as the 'done thing' by boys. Shouldn't be seen doing it!

- Girls . . . Boys . . . seem to be more self conscious than girls and bow more to peer pressure.

- Girls. Presumably as a result of a perception held by pupils that singing is not something that secondary age boys should be interested in . . .

- Girls . . . the physical changes [i.e. voice breaking] which affect boys *PLUS* peer group pressure results in a diffidence not noticeable lower down the school.

- Girls. Inhibitions and peer pressure cause problems for both sexes but boys are worst.

Which group prefers to engage in classical music(s)?
- Girls. Again – classical music is 'cissified' by a lot of contemporary youth programmes so it is difficult for teenage boys to step out of their macho role . . .

- Girls . . . It may be partly to do with the fact that it's not the done thing for boys to admit to liking anything that might loosely be described as 'classical'.

- Girls . . . While it is true that [some] boys respond well I think, again, peer group influence on boys stops this.

Further comments
- There is much peer pressure amongst boys that music still has a 'cissy' stigma . . .

- ... In Orchestral/vocal (classical) performance the trend is to ever increasing female domination – especially where a school has a successful (and sometimes dominating) sports tradition.

- ... Boys do not generally stay with the recorder group for very long. I try to interest them, but I fear peer pressure is stronger. Boys who do not play recorders tend to taunt those who do. 'It's not "macho" to play a recorder with all those girls!'

Pupils' comments closely echoed those of teachers. For example:

Four Year 10 GCSE option-group girls (aged 14–15):
- LG: ... do boys feel the same way about music as you feel?
- No.
- No.
- LG: What is different?
- I think they don't think it's important ... And the kind of music they like is different.
- LG: In what way?
- Well I don't know. Most of the boys that I talk to they don't really talk about music and that; but when you put on your kind of music you like, they say 'Oh turn that off, that's rubbish' and so on.
- LG: What sort of music are they likely to say 'That's rubbish' about?
- Reggae and things.
- Slow songs, yeah, MoTown, love songs and that. They don't listen to that.
- No. They're sort of into, like, the music that's in at the moment.
- Yeah, they have to like what they have to like.
- Yeah.
- LG: Why do you think they don't like slow music and love songs?
- People might think they're soppy.
- They don't like showing their feelings.
- Bit of an unmacho image.
  ...
- It's as though they influence each other, what they're listening to. And if, say, they liked something that the others don't like they say 'Oh you're stupid, you can't listen to, like, that' sort of, you know, and they really listen to what their friends listen to.
  ...
- It might make a difference if the music they [the teachers] played was more for our age group.

Three Year 9 girls (age 13–14):
- Our boys in our class, they look at it as, if you enjoy music, then you're sad; and so they don't, I mean, even if they like music inside them, then they won't show it because they think they'll get cussed or teased, but basically I don't care about that sort of thing.

- LG: Why do you think that they think they'll get cussed or teased?
- Because music's, like, not a particularly big, macho, tough thing to do really.
- In our class I think there's probably more boys that like it, but don't want to admit it.

There are several comments from teachers, in which boys are character-ised as extroverts or show-offs, and to be more confident than girls in practically all areas, sometimes even including singing.

Which group is the most successful at singing?
- Both equally . . . Willingness to sing is, in my experience at this school, often one attribute of an extrovert personality, usually that of a boy with a loud voice . . .

Which group is the most successful at composing?
- Both equally. Boys operate at the extremes. Their work is more extrovert generally but they do tend to misbehave more.
     These comments also apply to questions 8–12 [i.e. the remainder of the questions].

- Boys. Tend to have more confidence and are more willing to 'have a go'.

Which group is the most successful at listening?
- Both equally. Girls often know answers, but don't have the confidence to put up their hand. Boys are quite happy to have a go. On the whole they are equal.

- Girls. Boys often don't have the patience to listen carefully and often think they already know it all!

Which group is the most successful at notation?
- Girls . . . 2. Boys have generally acquired less skills in this area at Junior Schools hence they have to compete with the girls. Consequently their motivation is poor – they prefer to show off [rather] than working at developing their skills.

Further comments
- . . . Boys love to show off on keyboards and guitars . . .
- Recorder and orchestra groups – all girls 50% white/Asian.

Boys are seen to be active and to prefer doing something rather than sitting still:

Which group is the most successful at listening?
- Girls. Sitting still for any length of time is quite hard for most adolescent boys and Music is no exception. Even if it is music they like (again, rap, ragga) they tend to 'move to the music' rather than listen.

- Girls. Boys are often restless.

Which group prefers to engage in other world music(s)?
- Both Equally. (Haven't looked into this closely enough yet) – although boys especially enjoy *rhythmic* music.

Many pupils in interviews again echoed these impressions of teachers, noting a tendency on the part of boys towards over-confidence and showing off in the music lessons, refusing to take part, 'mucking about' with instruments. For example:

Four Year 8 boys (age 12–13):
- LG: Do you think girls and boys are equally able in music?
- The boys like doing all the tunes, but the girls just want to do the tune that Miss gave them.
- What happens in the class is, like, the girls –
- Most of the boys I know like to express theirself, and the girls like Kerry-Ann, they're too shy, but I say if they're too shy, they should learn classical music.

Six Year 8 girls (age 12–13):
- LG: Do you feel that boys behave the same as you in music lessons?
- No.
- No. They show off.
- LG: They show off.
- They mess around.
- LG: Right, what sort of things do they do?
- Talk and muck around.
- They don't take it seriously.
   . . .
- Because they think they're so good, they can do it anytime.

Four Year 7 girls (age 11–12):
- LG: Do you think that boys feel the same about the music lessons as you?
- No, because boys don't like singing because they think it's girls' jobs, and they don't like listening to music and dancing because they think it's girls' jobs.
- The things that boys normally like, I think, is playing the instruments, and mucking around.
- They like all the big ones, and mucking about with the instruments, just banging them and that.

Four Year 8 boys (age 12–13):
- All the girls like playing along with music, and like, when they're doing it I like to show them how to do it, like, show them how to play a tune when they do it wrong.
- LG: Are you saying the girls need your help more?
- We're not saying that, but sometimes the girls don't know what to do and like, the boys have always been there for them.

- We give the girls help.
- They are rather able.
- Yeah.
- Except they're not using their ability.
- LG: You feel you're using your ability more?
- We can't because it's not our kind of music.
- LG: But you would if you could?
- Yeah, but we always get in trouble because when, like, they try and do it I try and whisper across to tell them what to do, but she [the teacher] always shouts at me.
- Very true, very true.

Technology and popular music performance

Girls are seen to avoid the manipulation of technology, but boys feature noticeably in the realm of technology, which is often, but not always, associated with 'popular' music.[2]

Which group is the most successful at playing?
- Girls. Seem generally keener to learn and produce completed performances. Many lads tend to mess around with equipment.

- Both equally. Equally successful at playing when the *commitment* is there, *but* more girls than boys actually have instrumental lessons within school. However, a growing interest amongst the boys in electronics (keyboards, guitars) plus percussion.

Which group is the most successful at composing?
- Boys. The boys seem on the whole to be excited more by the concept of hands-on creativity, although *only just!*

- Both equally. Boys tend to be more keen on electronics and music, girls more notation/written based . . .

- Both equally . . . the boys are more comfortable with the technology required to compose more experimentally. Despite my best efforts, the boys tend to monopolise computers, multi-track recorders, sequencers etc. and girls mistrust the technology.

[2] See Caputo (1994) on gender and technology in music education. She argues that the technology emphasises rationality and mind, which are value-laden as masculine attributes and may be alien to girls. Pegley (1994) has also done some interesting work on girls' and boys' occupation of space around technology in the classroom. Also see Bayton (1990) on female popular musicians' expressed nervousness about music technology; and Colley, Comber and Hargreaves (1993), Hargreaves, Colley and Comber (1995) for a fairly large-scale project on the effects of music technology on girls' and boys' comparative practices and attitudes in music education.

- Both equally . . . boys (unless checked) dominate music technology resources: synthesizers/computer controlled notation; girls therefore veer towards orchestral insts if allowed!

- Boys. Tend to be more interested in technology – computers/sequencers etc. They make more use of this and it aids the compositional process.

Which group prefers to engage in popular music(s)?
- Boys. Interest developed within school through recording studio.

- Boys. Boys have more interest in technical equipment and electric guitars etc.

Further comments
- In the Lower School Females form the majority of musicians due to intake from Junior Schools. Due to inclusion of IT into subject + fully equipped recording studio the bias is redressed by the top end of the school.

- . . . Boys tend to be more interested in Technology and percussion – a number of boys are working hard at these activities.

- Since the option system has changed and we have been able to introduce keyboards in Year 9, the uptake of music has been much more balanced [i.e. more boys take it].

- With the advent of MUSIC TECHNOLOGY – Music (at GCSE especially) has become less of a 'feminine' activity/option choice . . .

- It would appear that in the area of choral/vocal work females are generally more evident than males. But I think the more technological the involvement (i.e. computers, synths etc.) the more the males tend to come to the fore . . .

There are just two comments which suggest a more equal involvement with technology between the genders.

Which group is the most successful at composing?
- Both equally. Both sexes given equal opportunities + equipment.

- Both equally. With the advent of computer assisted work. They are only restricted by the size of their imagination and not their lack of ability on a keyboard.

Girls also are seen to avoid performance on electric or very loud instruments, especially those associated with popular music, most notably electric guitars and drums.[3] Contrastingly, boys are depicted as flocking to these instruments, and to active involvement in popular music:

[3]   See the ethnographic work of Bayton (1990) and S. Cohen (1991), as well as the documentary and interview work of Steward and Garratt (1984), Grieg (1989), Gaar (1993); and Chapter 3 above. Even the gradual incorporation of women as rock instrumentalists in the professional world of music is reflected by very little change in schools overall.

Which group is the most successful at playing?
- Both Equally . . . Boys choose to play drums or guitar more than girls, probably because of the rock band idea, some of them want to be rock stars!

Which group is the most successful at notation?
- Girls. Most of the girls have learnt music from a classical standpoint – A good number of the boys have come to music at GCSE through involvement in a rock band & so their notational experience is not so great.

- Girls. More boys seem to be happy to 'play by ear' and tend to play electric guitars/drums etc.

Which group is the most successful at composing?
- Both equally. Less social stigma, if we can call it that. Boys also tend to form 'pop' groups etc. and suddenly they become interested in advanced chords etc. Quite often, then, the boys veer to that side of things whilst the girls tend to stick to the more traditional output.

Which group prefers to engage in classical music(s)?
- Girls. The girls have had a more classical training – the boys have more of a grounding in rock bands – This is of course a general observation & does not hold true in all cases – The girls already have some affinity with classical styles.

- Girls. Although girls are more tolerant of classical music, both I feel, prefer to engage in different styles of music. More girls *do* engage in classical music, however, because more play orchestral instruments.

- Girls. Boys tend to moan & groan more at the thought of listening to classical music – they more seriously find this unfashionable.

Which group prefers to engage in popular music(s)?
- Boys. Interest developed within school through recording studio.

- Boys. Pop groups mainly boys

- Boys. More likely to know words from existing songs & raps to sing along to & more likely to get up and dance to.

- Boys. Many of the boys who opt for GCSE (not all) have had experience in a rock band.
  It is only natural to identify with what one has had first hand experience of.

- Boys. Like to think they are different – delight in *'shocking'* their parents, friends – who has latest No. 1 etc. Rivalry exists between boys a lot more.

- Boys. Greater direct appeal, *particularly for boys*.

- Boys . . . In the later years (e.g. at GCSE level) boys veer to Pop Music performance – with the willingness to imitate performers/styles on guitar, drums, keyboard. At this stage girl performers tend towards classical orchestral performances *or* pop 'vocals'.

- Boys. All pupils, almost without exception, enjoy performing pop music. However boys generally want to do so exclusively and often have little time for anything else.

- Boys. More extrovert characters involved & required in performing popular music.

- Boys. Because they think it's the fashion to do so.

- Boys. We have a few good guitarists, drummers and a bass guitarist at this school who are all boys. They like rock, and heavy metal music especially. Some girls perform pop songs from time to time, but the boys play popular music more often.

- Boys. Boys tend to monopolise drums, bass and guitar, despite arduous efforts to involve girls (either in a mixed or girls-only group).

- Boys. Boys have more interest in technical equipment and electric guitars etc.

Further comments
- . . . it tends to be the males who form the pop groups, jazz group etc. whilst the string quartets would appear to have a female dominance.

- In my last school Music was definitely not a subject for boys. At [X school], I don't find this as there is a fairly strong brass tradition in the area and also boys enjoy the idea of being in a pop band.

Sexuality or desire are only explicitly mentioned by two teachers in the questionnaire response, and in both cases it is with reference to the interest in them displayed by boys, through popular music:

Which group prefers to engage in popular music(s)?
- Boys. Popular music has a large degree of image projection – Boys seem to identify with alter-egos and thus respond well. Rock music with its sexual emphasis and aggression seems to complement the image many boys seem to need.

- Boys. There is a link between bangra and pop which is immediately identifiable – a lust. [School 85% Asian]

Although boys are not understood to like singing in choirs, and in many cases in class lessons too, six teachers noted that they are willing to sing in popular or rock bands:

Which group is the most successful at singing?
- Girls . . . Top end of school, boys tend to start singing in Rock Groups.

- Girls. Not much singing has been done at this school for some time. Classroom singing worked well with both sexes in yr. 7 [age 11–12]. Beyond that, only girls joined the choir. (Though we have boys who sing in the Rock group)

- Girls. Past Year seven – boys seem reluctant to join in with general sing – Part of the development of awareness of the 'male' role in society. However Boys have no qualms about 'singing' rap or ragga as it represents most of their 'macho' values.

- Girls. Although many boys enjoy singing particularly in the lower years, girls work harder at it and so generally produce a better sound. 'Breaking' voices discourage boys from singing. Rock music is again creating a demand for vocalists, and overall there appears to be a change in attitude towards singing.

- Girls. More girls partake in singing activities therefore more likely to succeed. However, more boys take part in rock band vocals.

- Girls. All students are rather reticent when it comes to singing, but girls are more easily persuaded. I do have a few boys who are excellent singers in the pop style.

A teacher whom I cited earlier wrote:

- Both equally . . . Willingness to sing is, in my experience at this school, often one attribute of an extrovert personality, usually that of a boy with a loud voice . . .

One teacher described girls' reticence to play drums and guitars in front of boys; and two others mentioned that girls can be assumed to be unable to play the drums:

Further comments
- . . . although girls have equal skills in drumming and guitar playing they are loathe to perform for their peer group.

- . . . some of the boys express the opinion that girls are unable to play the drum kit.

- Peripatetic expectations of some staff are questionable – esp. percussion i.e. Girls can't play the drum kit!
  (Our best ever drummer was a girl.)

Some teachers explicitly characterised girls as only passive listeners to popular music:

Which group is the most successful at singing?
- Girls . . . Girls more into singing along to Pop records and have better voices. Boys enjoy rapping though.

Which group prefers to engage in popular music(s)?
- Both Equally.
  Girls more singing-wise
  Boys more on forming groups etc.

- Both Equally. Boys are more likely to perform pop music, but girls listen to it more and talk about it more.

- Girls/Boys. Girls prefer to Listen to Popular music more than boys here – enjoying just sitting and listening or getting involved through dance.
    Boys get frustrated just listening & prefer to be actively involved in *doing* – sometimes playing along – but mainly creating own groups. Much stereotyping here! In spite of encouraging both.

Girls were also said to idolise 'pop stars', rather than to play popular music.[4]

Which group prefers to engage in popular music(s)?
- Boys. In very general terms (in the younger years at sec. school) = boys, because they tend to be less inhibited by the social/pop idol elements in 'pop music'. Young teenage girls often think they like Pop *Music* when really they are captivated by the *performers* . . .

- Both equally. But there is a wide variety of styles: girls seem to like it if it's sung by a nice boy, boys if it suits their dancing skills.

- Both equally. I realise that this is an over-simplification but male pop singers win all round – While appealing to boys' masculine values the girls will probably think the singer is 'cute'. It may be manipulation to trade on this – but it works.

- Both equally. Girls tend to idolise singers and get more involved in the music, boys are more reluctant to show emotion and therefore often embarrassed by pop music sentiments. Rhythms however are appreciated by both sexes.

[4] This positioning of the girl as a passive fan (who is subsumed by making herself up in order to attract the imaginary attention of the active male pop star) introduces, besides the issues of girls' and women's instrumental practices, a whole other set of problems. The depiction of femininity as passive and masculinity as active has been challenged from many directions within feminism generally, as well as within feminist educational studies and popular music studies. With reference to teachers' perceptions in the classroom, see Clarricoates (1978), (1980) for early work, and e.g. Wolpe (1988), Lees (1986), Walkerdine (1990). With reference to girls as fans see McRobbie (1981), (1991), McRobbie and McCabe (1981), McRobbie and Nava (1984), Garratt (1990), Wise (1990), Schwichtenberg (1993). With reference to fans, gender and passivity, Frith and McRobbie (1978) caused a lot of debate, including: Laing and Taylor (1979), Bradby and Torode (1984), Frith (1985), Shepherd (1987), Middleton (1990, pp. 259–60), McClary and Walser (1990), Scott (1993). All of these texts problematise the traditional notion of the fan as a passive consumer, recognising instead that fandom involves investing meanings in the product, which then must cease to be seen as a merely given object. This is a field of enquiry in its own right with a sizeable literature, and although it would have interesting implications for the topics which I am engaged in, I am unable to enter into it here.

In my interviews with pupils, voices in every group of boys to whom I spoke, without exception, said either that they would like to play, or that they already do play, the drums. Many complained that they were not given the chance. This interest in drumming was associated with an expressed involvement in other popular music instruments as well, and in sound-reproduction or amplification technology. In the words of one thirteen-year-old girl, talking about boys: 'Things like drums and electric guitar, you know, *they're* not considered unmacho.' The music in which boys were understood to be interested was considered as 'fast' or to 'have a beat'. Girls, on the other hand, continued to be described as performers in classical music, and only as passive listeners when it came to popular music.

Four Year 8 boys (age 12–13):
– Do any of you play an instrument outside music lessons?
– I'd like to. I asked Miss if I could play drums 'cos I'm really good at it. But she says 'later', but she never gives us the chance.
– 'Cos I asked her whether I could play drums, but she never gives us the chance.
– I'm already good at drums 'cos I got some things at home.
– 'Cos we like putting a beat into it.

Four Year 8 boys (age 12–13):
– I like playing the drums but it's just that we never get a chance to express ourselves. It's just xylophones, xylophones. We would like to play drums, we would like to play guitar, we would like to play lots of things.
– We would like to have a turntable and mix things.
– Like, listen Miss, if we went up to the teacher now and asked her if we can make a mixing record . . . she'd say 'no', she'd just say 'no', I'd say 'please Miss', and she wouldn't even think about it.
– And if we complained it would result in our grades.
– We've done so before, and it resulted in our grades.
– Because all Miss plays is xylophone, and I got bad grades because I didn't want to play it; when everyone had to do a tune I didn't want to play it.
– But if we had a chance to do something else –
– Express ourselves -
– Like play a drum kit or sing in a microphone –
– Yeah, then maybe we'd feel better.
– We'd crack it.

Four Year 10 GCSE option-group girls (age 14–15):
– LG : Why do you think that is? [i.e. boys do not like music lessons]
– Well basically in the music lessons all we do is listen to classical music and we have to write down sort of like the cadences and that sort of thing.
– We don't get much practical done.

– LG: Do you think it would make a difference if the –
– It might make a difference if the music they played was more for our age group.
– Yes, so the kind of things you played were sort of electric guitar and that sort of thing.
– Like not orchestras and that sort of thing; like, I reckon they would be more interested if it was sort of our age-group.
– But we'd have to have the other side to sort of balance it out.

Three Year 10 GCSE option-group boys (age 14–15):
– LG: Why did you opt for GCSE?
– I was best at it. 'Cos I play a lot of instruments.
– Same as Nick. I like music, and when I grow up I want to be a professional drummer. I'm in a couple of bands. That's why I took music.

. . .

– LG: Do you think girls and boys are the same in music?
– No, not at all.
– It's funny, there's a lot more of them that actually take music, but they're not quite as interested.
– None of them play anything in any of the rock groups at all. I don't think there's any of them in the jazz group.
– There's one girl.
– Mostly they, like, they take music lessons, they play flute, violin.
– Violin.
– They don't branch out much from classical music. Some of them are in the Swing band. But that's usually what they learn.
– Most of the people in the class, they like crap – er, rap, sorry! I was just saying that 'cos Nick and I we say rap is crap.
– Yeah, they're into popular music [as distinct from rock] a lot more than we are, but they don't play it and they usually play classical music.

. . .

– LG: Do you think in general, girls are as capable as boys?
– Yes, but they're just not interested in the same things as we are.
– I think so.
– There are some really, really good girl musicians in the school but they just play classical music.
– They used to have one band, one girls' band.
– But that split up quite quickly.
– They didn't have a drummer; but, well they *had* a drummer, but she never came; and I said 'Well, you need a drummer.' I didn't want to chuck the girl out, so I started up and they said 'Oh well, we just don't like the music' and they just –
– They gave up.
– They gave up. But they are capable of doing it 'cos they did play for a while.
– They're capable of playing rock music alright, but it's just that they don't do it.

INTERRUPTING FEMININITY IN THE MUSIC CLASSROOM

As Chapter 6 illustrates, girls' musical practices in schools are typically understood to centre around singing and the instrumental performance of what is often referred to as 'classical music' or 'slow music'. Contrastingly, material in the current chapter suggests that the practices of boys are accompanied by a far-reaching association with drums, electric instruments and other technology, largely in the production of what is called 'popular music' or 'fast music'. I have already argued (pp. 145–7) that the names of musical styles as they operate in the school detach themselves from their connotations as they occur in mainstream discourse beyond the school. I now wish to point to a construction of 'classical music' in contradistinction to 'popular music' which is arrived at *by virtue of gender*. The terms 'classical' and 'popular' are used by pupils as well as teachers, not so much as signifiers of particular *musical styles* or only as currency in the measurement of 'what counts as music' in school, but also as connotations of particular *gendered musical practices*. Further, these gendered associations actually enter into the delineations of the music itself, such that 'classical' and 'slow' together form an affirmative feminine delineation, whilst 'popular' and 'fast' form a delineation that is interruptive for femininity and that is concomitantly more inviting to boys.

In Chapter 6 I argued that girls can symbolically affirm their femininity through singing and through the performance of classical instrumental music in schools. Even the potentially interruptive effects of the instrument are diluted, because the seriousness with which the music is taken, the educational context, and the images of many contemporary classical soloists all allow for a retrieval of femininity. Girls' vocal and instrumental display in this realm, furthermore, coincides with a cooperative attitude, constructed as feminine, which involves conformity to the mores of the school and to 'what counts as music' within the school. Singing and classical instrumental performance by girls transmit musical delineations that are relatively affirmative with regard to constructions of femininity. Contrastingly, popular music practices in schools problematise femininity. As I argued in Chapter 6, even the affirmative practice of singing may, in the popular field, bring with it that side of femininity which conflicts with the 'family values' and code of sexual conduct that the school is supposed to proffer. As a solo popular vocalist in school, particularly when using that technological icon of popular music delineation, the microphone, the girl invokes the problematic dualistic delineation of the madonna/whore. But going further still, instrumental performance which involves the use of technology, drums and electric guitars in the execution of popular music is highly inter-ruptive for a delineated display of femininity within the context of the contemporary English school. This interruption is made particularly noticeable by the nature of the discourse surrounding popular music, which legitimises a consideration of the performer's bodily display as an important part of the total musical meaning.

Teachers' and pupils' notions that girls are passive and boys are active in the realm of popular music cannot be taken as unproblematic descrip-tions of reality. We may wish to challenge these notions as stereotypes that bear no resemblance to what it is really like to be a girl or a boy. But what is of relevance here is not whether these notions are 'true' within the psychology of pupils, but the fact that they are repeatedly put into discourse, forming a salient part of teachers' and pupils' *understanding and depiction* of girls' and boys' musical proclivities. If we look at classical musical practices in schools, the picture of activity and passivity shifts, for here girls are readily perceived to be more musically active than boys. Yet boys are never described as passive! Any explanation for this conun-drum must be sought not only in the discursive construction of feminin-ity and masculinity, but also in the wider delineations of the music with which girls and boys are associated. Through the delineations of classi-cal music, the girl performer affirms her femininity; but with reference to the delineations of popular music, the story is altogether different. On one hand, even if femininity is affirmed by singing in popular music, it is also made risqué and subject to abuse. On the other hand, more strongly, femininity tends to be symbolically interrupted by popular music instru-mental performance. By avoiding a very active part in the performance of popular music in schools, girls avoid a problematisation or an inter-ruption of their femininity. The inevitable consequence of this situation is to force upon girls the continuation of the appearance of passivity. This appearance of the passive female is, furthermore, an explicit part of the delineations of many popular sub-styles, which are dependent on a pervasive image of the sexed female Other as desirable, elusive, and def-initely not an instrumentalist in the band.[5]

Boys in schools are under a great deal of pressure to be 'macho', and part of their response to this involves constructing an appearance that

---

[5] As well as the texts in note 4 above, see Hurley (1994), who did some observation work in media studies in a school, with relation to boys' and girls' relationships to popular music video.

they actively want sex and succeed in getting it.[6] Wolpe (1988, p. 174) describes ways in which boys construct reputations 'of rampant, aggressive sexuality with a James Bond syndrome of numerous sexual encounters'. But she indicates that underlying the appearances is something very different, and she probes the problem of how hard it is for such reputations to be achieved whilst still at school. Girls are under an equal amount of pressure to appear feminine. In many ways they are supposed to want sex, but at the same time to avoid it in order to safeguard their reputations.[7] Whatever the particular details concerning the social class, ethnic grouping, religion, sexual orientation or any other factors in the individual subjective identity of each pupil, music is available to help in the adoption of symbolic gendered as well as sexual personae. In general, when boys in schools perform 'popular music' or 'fast music', play drums and electric instruments, or manipulate technology, they are furthering a symbolic representation of their masculinity. Popular music even overcomes to some extent the 'cissy' connotations of singing, sometimes through highly individualised techniques which are impossible for massed voices, and sometimes through the delineation of a non-singing stance such as in rap, or an anti-singing stance such as in punk, a stance which is also harnessed in the construction of machismo at football matches. Contrastingly, when girls sing, and when they play 'slow' music, or 'classical' music on orchestral instruments, they are furthering a powerful symbolisation of their femininity. Both genders are restricted in their freedom to cross a divide, not only between the discursively constructed characteristics of the two genders, but between their symbolic depiction in delineated musical meanings. For a boy to engage in vocal or orchestral music, 'slow' music or music that is associated with the classical style in school – to join a choir, to play a flute – involves taking a risk with his symbolic masculinity. For a girl to sing popular music in a microphone, to play drums or electric bass, involves taking a risk with the delineations of her reputation, or invoking an interrupted display of her femininity.[8]

---

[6] See Lees (1986), Wolpe (1988) for seminal work on the construction of gender/sexual personae by boys and girls in schools.

[7] For girls of different social classes and ethnic groups, this appearance of desire and its denial features in different ways: as a path towards marriage, or as a strategy in avoiding being seen as a 'slag', for example. See texts in note 4 above; also M. Fuller (1980).

[8] This crossing into the musical territory of the opposite sex would, I imagine, act particularly powerfully for adolescents who are beginning to consider whether they are homosexual. For discussion of the relationship between homosexuality and music see Brett, Thomas and Wood (1994), Gill (1994). On girls and boys crossing gender roles in schools, see Thorne (1993).

The implications of gendered musical delineations have little surface relevance to truth-value: it is not that all boys are 'really' more sexually assertive, confident or active in music, or that all girls 'really' prefer slow, 'classical' music and fear electronic instruments. Whether such appearances are the case or not for any particular individual, the point that I would like to illuminate is that pupils and teachers collude with each other in the perpetuation of the gender politics of music: the construction of a gendered discourse on music that aids in the regulation of gender and sexuality, linked to the reproduction and production of historical musical practices and musical meanings. This discourse bears a deep relation to what we all take to be natural, normal common sense, in that this political gender relationship that is available to us through music acts in the formation of our own identities as gendered beings. Not only does gender reside in musical practices, in extra-musical delineations or in the discourse surrounding music; the delineation of gender works within musical experience itself, and from that position it affects our listening experiences. The delineation of femininity or masculinity enters the experience of pupils and teachers; and according to where each individual positions himself or herself with relation to the music, the delineation gives confidence, or takes confidence away; affirms identity, or interrupts and problematises it.

When we feel negative towards the gender delineations of a piece of music, thrown off or challenged by them, this negativity will pervade the total musical experience. Even if we are fulfilled by the music's inherent meanings, the negative delineations will nonetheless be present in our experience, engendering ambiguity; and if we are dissatisfied with the inherent meanings, our experience will be alienated (see Figure 1, Chapter 5, p. 133 above.) At worst, negativity towards delineations may influence the way we perceive inherent meanings, *causing* our experience to become alienated. When girls avoid drums, it is not just because of stereotypes or conventions concerning musical roles, but because of the performance-related musical delineations of a girl drummer that act back to interrupt not only the listeners' experience of her drumming but also *her own listening experience of her own drumming*. Not only girls but also women teachers working with boys in rock bands find themselves in a position where even a display of competence is at the same time a refutation of their own femininity. The masculinity of popular music's performance delineations will tend to be negative and problematic for girls. Equally, the affirmative femininity of classical music's performance delineations will present problems for boys. In both cases, an ambiguous or alienating relationship is engendered. Contrastingly, when we stand, consciously or unconsciously, in a positive relationship to the gendered delineations of a piece of music, and we simultaneously become fulfilled and wrapped up in the temporal arrangement of the music's inherent meanings, this unified, celebratory musical experience is like hearing ourselves, our gendered make-up: it is like gender-truth. In the context of the school, girls' allegiance to classical music and boys' allegiance to popular music affords them a sense not only of potential musical celebration but of their own gender identity.

Resistance

The discourse surrounding music in school does not operate one-dimensionally: girls and boys do not simply negotiate their musical roles in close accordance with the historically constituted gender politics of music, and the school does not merely reproduce pre-existing musical practices and meanings. Resistance to these is sometimes offered to pupils by teachers, who themselves take up critical practices. As many teachers answering my questionnaire made clear, girls are frequently encouraged to play the drums and the electric guitar, and to engage in other popular music practices. Similarly, many teachers expressed concern that boys are not taking up musical opportunities afforded by the choir or the orchestra. When girls and boys do take up alternative musical practices, they are challenging conventional gender delineations in what may be a courageous gesture that contravenes the stereotyping assumptions of a wider, powerful discourse. Exceptionally competent pupils, who can skilfully manipulate the inherent meanings of the music they perform, are more readily able to cross the music/gender divide than are most pupils. The concentration on inherent meaning which their performance is able to summon up deflects attention away from the delineations and allows for a less problematic listening experience. They can perform the 'music itself', without so much fear of challenging the symbolic construction of their gender either in the experiences of their listeners or in their own experiences. Both girls and boys who can raise musical inherent meanings to such a level by their skill in performance are able to cross the divide. For the vast majority of pupils, this avenue is not open. Teachers should not be surprised if large numbers of pupils so often do not avail themselves of opportunities to take part in practices dominated by the opposite sex: for in offering the opportunities, we ride roughshod over the very delineations of gender differences in which pupils desire to invest, or feel compelled to invest. In the succinct phrase of Valerie Walkerdine, 'offering girls, as is often suggested, Lego and boys dolls, can hardly match the whirlpool of desire' in which they are caught (1990, p. 80).

The girls in the group cited below were more musically active than the majority of pupils in the case-study school, or indeed in the country at large. Two of them played the flute, one the clarinet and saxophone, and they also all played the piano or guitar as second studies. They were members of the school swing band (not the jazz band), they were enrolled on young people's courses at London music colleges and they had all passed Grade IV or V of the Associated Board of the Royal Schools of Music (ABRSM).[9] Their own characterisations of the styles they played do not concur with the characterisations of girls' musical practices and interests that we have so far come across.

Four Year 10 GCSE option-group girls (age 14–15):
 – LG: What kind of music do you play?
 – I dunno. On the piano I play courses, you know piano books; on the flute, Mozart, on the guitar, folk and rock. It's really varied.
 – Most of the time I play sort of classical music, but sometimes it switches to jazz and rock, things like that.
 – On the piano I've just been doing this classical piece but I've got these books called 'Boogie and Blues' and 'Jazz'; and on the sax I do jazz and blues, and on the clarinet it's all mixed. I don't do that much classical on the clarinet.

In line with the overriding discourse on femininity and music, the girls put classical music first, followed by 'But I also . . .' with reference to popular music, as well as folk and jazz. Many of the issues raised by the performance of these styles concern improvisation, which is something that I will return to in Chapter 8. As popular music is so heavily associated with at least some level of improvisation and with group performance, one's inclination is to take it 'with a pinch of salt' when a classically trained player says he or she plays blues or jazz from a book. But I want to suggest that the taste is the saltier when it is girls who are saying this. If a boy says that he plays rock on the guitar, or that he plays from a book called *Boogie and Blues* or *Jazz*, his credibility is already a good deal higher: the masculine delineations of improvisation, and the masculinity of the performance delineations associated with those styles, guarantee this. The girls above are claiming a space for themselves, by

---

[9] The ABRSM as well as Trinity College and the London College of Music run systems of graded performance examinations throughout the UK and Commonwealth countries. (Until the early 1990s when Trinity College introduced a rock and pop syllabus, these have focussed entirely on classical music.) The standard is from beginner (Grade I) to advanced (Grade VIII) and then diploma level. Although the grades are not age-related, within the context of the school, Grade V would be the expected standard for a successful instrumentalist at about the age of fifteen or sixteen.

their references to popular music and jazz, within the more glamorous world of masculinity as it exists within the musical culture of the school. At the same time they are succumbing to the loss of confidence and identity, the potential interruption of their symbolic femininity, that these styles engender. They are protecting the affirmative delineations of femininity surrounding their musical practices, through the very uncertainty with which they approach expression of their involvement in these more interruptive practices. Most fundamentally, I would suggest, it cannot be merely in the way that they insert themselves into the discourse on music that this loss of confidence and identity arises; but it must also be in their very musical experiences themselves.

The association of popular music with masculinity in schools brings with it further associations, as we have seen, with 'showing off' or with being 'unable to sit still', for example. Popular music takes a symbolic role counter to teachers' definitions and expectations: even in my case-study school, where drum lessons were offered free of charge, where rock groups practised without question, where various sub-styles of popular music were included in the curriculum, we have seen that in the conversations of boys and girls popular music took on an oppositional character. Popular music comes to be defined as that music which is not included in the school: in the case-study school, it was the music that boys 'would like to do', but were 'not given the chance to do'. To a large extent, this exclusion from the school has always been and will always be a defining characteristic of 'popular music' in its most desirable manifestation.

Four Year 8 boys (age 12–13):
– I like playing the drums but it's just that we never get a chance to express ourselves. It's just xylophones, xylophones. We would like to play drums, we would like to play guitar, we would like to play lots of things.
– We would like to have a turntable and mix things.
– Like, listen Miss, if we went up to the teacher now and asked her if we can make a mixing record . . . she'd say 'no', she'd just say 'no', I'd say 'please Miss', and she wouldn't even think about it.
– And if we complained it would result in our grades.
– We've done so before, and it resulted in our grades.
– Because all Miss plays is xylophone, and I got bad grades because I didn't want to play it; when everyone had to do a tune I didn't want to play it.
– But if we had a chance to do something else –
– Express ourselves –
– Like play a drum kit or sing in a microphone –
– Yeah, then maybe we'd feel better.
– We'd crack it.

This conversation between boys, reprinted from earlier in the chapter, not only betrays an association between popular music and an anti-curriculum stance, but also suggests that the boys' failure ('it resulted in our grades') was their own *choice*: it was not because of lack of ability that they were awarded low grades, but because the teacher had tried to test them on the *wrong* music. The boys' deviance and refusal to accept the teacher's definitions of music education thus turn ironically into an assertion of their real, closely guarded, musical superiority.[10]

The film comedy *The Blues Brothers* (Universal Studios, 1980) makes an explicit statement of the association of popular music performance with masculine deviance, and an implicit suggestion that surface-level musical incompetence is 'really' a sign of deep-level musical superiority. In the climactic scene the Blues Brothers, who in 'real life' are not musicians but actors, are late arriving for a gig which, without their fictitious but supposedly indispensable musicianly talents, cannot go on. The musicians, who, conversely, are played in the film not by actors but by 'real', male musicians, wait behind the closed curtain on stage, and the audience is getting impatient. The brothers are trying to get into the building without being detected by the police, who are in hot pursuit. They are completely cool, even though everything depends on their being at this gig. The band keeps the audience entertained by rustling up a throw-back thirties number, presented as fantasy. The brothers arrive on stage just in time to save the show, and after a short spell the crowd begins to go wild. This sequence represents for me a multitude of occasions which I have observed, and for which I have myself been responsible, when teachers have given a 'naughty' boy, who may be talented but is inexperienced, the chance to play the drums in the classroom, or even in a concert. For such a pupil to turn up late, cool, indispensable is entirely commensurate with the position of popular music in schools. The Blues Brothers construct an image of desire in the male musician as bad and brilliant, his 'real' musical ineptitude only contributing to his deviance and thus to the total effect. The disruptive boy who is in this position can display characteristics of madness which only feed the similitude of genius.[11]

This similitude and the harnessing of misbehaviour to creativity is

---

[10] On constructions of boys' superiority in the face of girls' higher grades, see Walkerdine (1990). There will be further discussion of this in the next chapter.

[11] This runs so deep in unspeakable ways, and conjoins madness also with war, rape, death. See Walkerdine (1990, pp. 124ff) for an incisive critique of ways in which teachers link boys' misbehaviour with creativity, and girls' conformity with dullness. Also see Chapter 8 below.

denied to girls. Their music, unlike that of boys, is largely associated with being good or conformist; their musical practices allow for the expression of enabling and cooperative attitudes; their hard work and perseverance take place with relation to singing and to the classical music which is the mainstay of music education, the music that is *on offer*: girls are abundantly to be counted in choirs, in orchestras and chamber ensembles, in concerts, in rehearsals, in peripatetic instrumental lessons, in option groups. Those girls who do not conform to school music in this way cannot, like their male counterparts, simulate genius: they are, rather, offered the opportunity to appear as the symbolic harlot in the vocal performance of certain categories of popular music, or they are, in the extreme case, denied any active instrumental involvement in any kind of music at all. Their deviance will prevent them from taking part in classical music; and since instrumental performance in popular music interrupts their femininity, they are thereby deterred from any practical involvement in that music also. For girls, by contrast with boys, being 'good' at music within the school walls usually means being conformist. A disruptive girl cannot at the same time cope with being 'good' at instrumental performance, because at the moment that she is good at the performance, she denies either her deviance or her femininity. Whereas for boys deviance can contribute to the similitude of genius, for girls it blocks them from instrumental performance at all. Only exceptional talent, as I noted earlier, can override this problem.

Deviant girls can take an active part in the singing of popular music, most particularly as a soloist, with a microphone, where femininity is affirmed but sexual licence is risked: in so doing, they continue to affirm an age-old feminine delineation. Likewise, boys who wrest their musical roles away from the surface values which they understand to be propagated by the school – who refuse to take part in classical music or play xylophones, who assert a 'macho' and non-conformist allegiance to popular music – are nonetheless conforming to wider definitions of masculinity. The apparent conflict which some musical gender personae suggest may not be as threatening to the school, to the education system and to the society as they appear on the surface, but may actually harbour a deep conservatism, expressed because of a desire: a desire to *be* a boy, a desire to *be* a girl. The construction of this desire through musical experience in the context of the school aids in the regulation of heterosexuality and of patriarchal definitions of masculinity and femininity.

SUMMARY

In this chapter I have interpreted the discursive constructions involved in the expressed perceptions of teachers and pupils concerning the characteristics of girls' and boys' musical practices in schools. As a background I have provided my argument of the previous chapter, that singing and taking part in instrumental practices associated with classical music in schools affirm femininity. Contrastingly, I have suggested, the performance of popular music involving drums, electronic instruments and other technology is interruptive to femininity, and provides a symbolic space into which masculinity can enter. But it is not only pupils' involvement in musical practices or the gender-stereotyping of musical roles that contribute to the reproduction of this situation. Gender enters the delineations of the music with which girls and boys are associated, and from there gets inside the very listening experiences, and indeed the very performance experiences, of pupils and of teachers.

The school helps in the reproduction of gendered musical practices and meanings which can be traced in the history of Western musical performance. But the school does not achieve this reproduction through a raw offering of opportunity. Rather, it takes part in the perpetuation of subtle definitions of femininity and masculinity as connotations of musical practices, linked to musical styles, in which pupils invest their desires to conform, not necessarily to the school only, but to the wider field of gender and sexual politics. Most profoundly, the school provides a context in which the very musical experiences of girls and boys, reflecting the relative femininity or masculinity connoted by music's delineations and in conjunction with the temporal organisation of inherent meanings, contribute to the construction of a sense of self as a gendered being, a sense which takes on the appearance of truth.

CHAPTER 8

Threatening femininity in the music classroom

INTRODUCTION

Composition as a general classroom activity has only recently been systematically included in the English school. Musicians and educators had begun to argue for its necessity as a part of a balanced music education during the 1960s, and it gradually entered the curriculum through the ensuing decades. The Schools Council project of the late 1970s provided one major boost, and composition was also formally ratified by Her Majesty's Inspectorate in 1985. Following this it was incorporated in the 1986 GCSE *National Criteria*, and finally in the 1992 National Curriculum for Music.[1] In all these contexts, composition has been used as a generic term to include individual and group composition as well as improvisation, notated in any form, or unnotated. I will continue to adopt this broad definition in what follows.

Owing to its relative novelty in the school setting, composition is not bolstered by a long history of educational debate or a variety of recognised pedagogic methods, such as surround performance, music appreciation or many other classroom activities. Nor is it supported by any external, international, graded systems of examination such as those run by the Associated Board of the Royal Schools of Music (see Chapter 7, n. 9, p. 188 above). The notorious difficulty of judging composition, which has often resulted in the demise and pauperisation of composers and improvisers who were to be recognised only after their deaths, has

[1] For early teaching methods, ideas and materials with reference to classroom composition see Paynter and Aston (1970), Self (1967), Dennis (1970), Schafer (1967). Swanwick (1979) was one of the first systematic rationales for composition as an integral part of the curriculum. For the Schools Council Project see Paynter (1982); for the HMI document see Her Majesty's Inspectorate (1985); for GCSE see Department of Education and Science (1986), School Curriculum and Assessment Authority (1995); and for the National Curriculum see Department of Education and Science (1992), Department for Education (1995). A large selection of teaching materials related to composing in the classroom is now available.

made its own contribution to the lack of formal mechanisms or even vocabulary for the assessment of composition in education.[2] Unlike performance, the sight and sound of which immediately offer a feast of impressions on which to feed our assumptions about musical practice, composition's surface appearances are not so revealing. Composition is a relatively private creative act, the nature of which remains largely concealed within the minds of composers, and within the meanings of the music they create.

For all these reasons, teachers' questionnaire responses about composition were thinner and fewer than those about performance. But at the same time, and with an added piquancy derived from this very concision, those comments which teachers did make about girls' and boys' compositional proclivities revealed a high level of consensus and were marked by an unsolicited convergence around a central core of issues. Regarding pupils' views, whilst I was working on a draft of the current chapter, I realised that the interviews which I had conducted in 1992 had not tapped sufficiently into the topic of composition. The novelty and the privacy of composition must again be partly responsible for the fact that pupils had not volunteered any opinions explicitly addressing composition in response to my open questions. Added to this, most of the pupils were from Years 7 to 9, and their compositional experiences largely involved group work integrated with various performance tasks, which I think tended to detract from their perception of composition as a separate activity. It therefore seemed necessary, three years after the original interviews had taken place, to top them up by going back into a school and talking to pupils specifically about their attitudes towards composition. I decided to focus entirely on GCSE pupils (that is, Years 10 and 11), for whom composition has a high profile as one of three more or less equal, distinct, compulsory parts of the course (these parts being performing, composing and listening). I also decided to interview the Head of Music, in place of eliciting a response to the questionnaire. I chose a different school, not dissimilar to the first in that it was a London state comprehensive, but different in that it was less racially mixed and had an exceptionally thriving music department with an outstanding record of extra-curricular concerts. I had made several visits to the school over the preceding five years, in order to supervise beginner-teachers, and – as with the first school, though in a

---

[2] For further discussions of the assessment of composition in education see Swanwick (1990), Green (1990), Music Advisers' National Association (1986), National Association for Education in the Arts (1988a), (1988b), United Kingdom Council for Musical Education and Training (1993).

less concentrated way – had become familiar with the ethos of the department.[3]

Altogether I interviewed twenty-one pupils, comprising thirteen girls and eight boys, in seven single-sex groups. These pupils formed the two GCSE classes, one in Year 10 and the other in Year 11 (not including four girls who were absent). The make-up of the classes was representative of GCSE music classes nationally, in that there were more girls than boys, all the girls were primarily classically orientated, and most of the boys were rock-orientated. The interviews took place at the beginning of the summer term, which is well into the first year of the course for the Year 10 group, and immediately before the end for the Year 11 group. Using informally structured open questions, each interview began with a discussion of pupils' general musical interests and their response to the GCSE course, focussing in on composition later, and including only one question about gender at the end. Because of the smaller number and greater maturity of the pupils compared to those in the previous school, my report and interpretation of the conversations will pay more attention to individual differences than in previous chapters, and will retain the identity of speakers. Pupils taking GCSE music represent a minority of the school population, and their perspectives tend to echo those of a musician, or an embryonic musician, rather than those of the majority. At the same time, GCSE pupils have come through the system shared by all pupils in Years 7 to 9, and this common ground, as depicted in previous chapters, was reflected in the conversations I had with them.[4]

There were two particularly interesting issues which arose in connection with composition, but which I am unable to explore here. First, all the pupils, both girls and boys, stated that they found notation difficult, often strongly implying that they felt it hampered their creativity. Secondly, many girls and boys said that they especially enjoyed group work, and regretted that most of their compositions had been done on an individual basis. Although certain issues concerning notation and group work do impinge on my discussion, I have had to resist any temptation to enter fully into these topics, as they quickly move beyond the bounds of my theoretical framework, into the cognitive pyschology

---

[3] I would sincerely like to thank the two teachers in the school; especially the Head of Music for her willingness to help me out with very little notice at a busy time of year. I would also like to thank the pupils for their readiness to take part and for their interest in the project.

[4] In the transcriptions I have continued to omit interjections such as 'um', 'er', etc.; use punctuation to indicate both grammar and pauses in speech; insert ellipses where parts of the conversation have been omitted; and indicate any significant gestures. I have substituted fictitious names for the pupils.

of music, studies of creativity, child development, curriculum planning and other fields.[5]

THE GENDERING OF COMPOSITION IN SCHOOL

Teachers' perceptions

In their questionnaire responses, as shown in Table 1, Chapter 6, p. 151, teachers had indicated that boys are more musically successful and motivated than girls in only two areas. Popular music was one; the other was composition. The main features of boys' success in composition were depicted as their imagination, exploratory inclinations, inventiveness, creativity, improvisatory ability and natural talent. These qualities were explicitly described as lacking in girls, who were instead characterised as conservative, traditional and reliant on notation.[6]

Which group is the most successful at composing?
- Boys. I would not like to say which are the more 'successful' but on the whole, boys produce more imaginative work than girls.

- Boys.
  1. Girls generally feel less confident in this area than re-creating music.

  2. Boys are more inclined to experiment and have more confidence to assert themselves and their ideas when composing in groups.

- Boys. At this school the boys are more creative and seem more interested in composition. Gain higher grades than girls + are more confident during performance.

---

[5] Another possibility for work in this area would be to analyse pupils' compositions themselves, in combination with closely following individual pupils during the compositional process over an extended period of time, with an eye and ear to the differences and similarities in the approaches of girls and boys. Such work could be conducted along the lines of Bunting's case-studies (1987), (1988) of children composing, in which he incidentally called for more research into the composing methods of girls. Possibly independent judges could be asked to make assessments against each other and/or against the researcher, which could then link into the seminal work of Swanwick and Tillman (1986) in which children's compositions were analysed in relation to a model of musical development. (Also see Swanwick 1988, 1994). Although such approaches would be fascinating, there has not been time or space for them in this project. Anne Penton and Brigitte Charles are currently in the early stages of such work at the University of London Institute of Education.

[6] A great deal of feminist work in education has shown how teachers' perceptions of girls' and boys' characteristics differ in precisely the same terms. For early work in this area, see Clarricoates (1978), (1980). Also see the sources on feminist education work in Chapter 6, note 2 p. 144 above. There is a helpful discussion of sex, gender and creativity with reference to music in J. Halstead (1995, pp. 43ff). On composition, with special reference to the use of technology, see Hargreaves, Colley and Comber (1995), who also say that boys are more experimental, and that girls produce 'safer' work.

- Both equally. Though for different reasons. The boys do well using an improvisatory approach – they are less inclined to want to produce a 'score' for their work. The girls work more methodically, and like writing things down. They take more pride in presenting a well-written score.

- Boys. Not so afraid to be inventive, and experiment. Girls tend to stick to set forms.

- Both equally. No real difference. Girls tend to be more traditional and conservative in their compositions . . .

- Both equally. Given a motivating task, equal amounts of pupils work. Boys tend to need initial starting points. Girls like lots of reassurance.

- Both equally. Although more girls in the upper years study music, much of the creative, adventurous composing comes from boys. Girls tend to be more conservative.

- Both equally. I find each sex has its own problems and strong points. With more girls playing instruments they find composing at a piano or keyboard easier – especially if it is in a 'classical' style. However, boys are much more adventurous and not worried about playing wrong notes or putting unusual sounds together, so achieve some pleasing results.

- Boys. The number of boys composing (1 at GCSE + 1 at 'A' Level) is smaller, but the standard is higher.
    Natural ability – girls seem to have to work harder + don't have as much natural ability. Not sure why!

- Both equally. At GCSE level most pupils are already performers and tend to write music with their instrument in mind. At 13/14 years girls tend to produce more 'serious' compositions. The boys enjoy producing sounds rather than melodic tunes.

- Both equally. Difficult to answer. It is my experience that girls are better when it comes to exercises in composing and getting down to work, but quite a few of the boys show imagination and ability.

- Boys. Generally, boys seem to have a greater creative spark than girls.
    In my experience I have had many better boy composers than girls. The girls seem often to be devoid of ideas, + have a problem developing musical ideas.

Which group is the most successful at notation?
- Girls. Girls are more interested in writing things down & getting it right. Boys would rather be creative & not bother learning how to write/record work.

The Head of Music whom I interviewed in the second case-study school held a comparable view:

I think girls tend to be very traditional in their approach. They tend to, you know, write 'a piano piece' for their instrument. I think boys tend, from my experience, tend to be, well much more keen to use music technology, partly because of the style of musician they have tended to be. I mean the boys in the group you've just talked to are guitarists, and the style of music they're writing doesn't necessarily lend itself to a formal score. You know, they've done much more work with commentaries, and multi-track and things like that, often having to use their own equipment. Whereas with the girls I feel that they've been, felt much more secure about the whole thing if they've just sort of concentrated on, writing 'a piece' in a very sort of traditional structure and using, you know, set ideas.

Another perception included within the statements of many of the teachers cited above was that boys do not work as hard as girls, or do not adopt the paradigms provided by the teacher, such as notation or set compositional tasks. This perceived failure to comply contrasts with the fact that boys are nonetheless understood to produce work that is at least as good as, or even better than, that of the girls. This was also observed by the Head of Music in the case-study school, who said:

- HOM: I do find that when it comes to actually handing in the compositions, boys often produce work in the last few weeks . . . I mean you know they've done things that, it's not always up to the standard they're really capable of until they're under the pressure . . .
- LG: Do you predict the girls will get better grades than the boys, for composing?
- HOM: I don't think so . . .

Walkerdine's analysis of gender in the mathematics classroom can help to illuminate the underpinnings of a discourse surrounding music here. She addressed the fact that girls were for many years understood to fail at mathematics, and argues that this fact was constructed in spite of the extreme ambiguity of the evidence in its favour (1990, p. 61). Girls in mathematics contexts are attributed with qualities in line with those which, as we have seen throughout Part II, teachers attribute to girls in music, such as diligence and perseverance. These same qualities are also seen as the root of girls' failure, because they are used as *causal explanations* for girls' lack of autonomy and creativity. Those estimations that do acknowledge some success in girls attribute it to rule-following and rote-learning, which are distinguished from and even opposed to understanding. 'Hence they negate that success at the moment they announce it: girls "just" follow rules – they are good compared with "naughty" boys who can "break set" (make conceptual leaps)' (Walkerdine 1990, p. 65).

Girls may be able to do mathematics, but good performance is not to be equated with proper reasoning. It is this which is taken into account in relation to later 'failure' where abstract reasoning is required. On the other hand, boys tend to produce evidence of what is counted as 'reason', even though their attainment may itself be relatively poor. This differentiation between classroom performance, its posited cause, and therefore the problem of 'the real', returns again and again. Throughout the age-range, girls' good performance is downplayed while boys' often relatively poor attainment is taken as evidence of real understanding such that any counter-evidence (poor attainment, poor attention, and so forth) is explained as peripheral to the real (Walden and Walkerdine, 1983). It is interesting that in the case of girls (as in all judgements about attainment), attainment itself is not seen as a reliable indicator. In this view, right attainment can, in principle, be produced for wrong reasons. It becomes important, therefore, to establish as permissible only that attainment taken as premissed on 'real understanding'. Only this attainment, then, is *real*. The rest, although apparently real, is actually false. (Walkerdine 1990, p. 66)

Elsewhere (1990, p. 127) she goes further to link boys' naughtiness and even violence with an assumption of masculine creativity. In the classrooms she examined, while girls' complaints of boys' violence were central, equally important was the fact that teachers downplayed and ignored violence – including, for women teachers, violence which was directed at themselves. This denial, she says, is endemic to the pedagogic and child-rearing practices on which it is based.

That is, boys are independent, brilliant, proper thinkers. They are also naughty. There seems here to be a splitting. The teachers constantly downplay the violence of boys, transforming it into words like 'naughty', understood as a positive attribute, or at the very least to be allowed and probably positively fostered as the basis of independent thinking. On the other hand, girls are, by and large, described as lacking the qualities boys possess. They are no trouble, but then their lack of naughtiness is also a lack of spark, fire, brilliance.

So the practices themselves actually and positively permit this violence and, moreover, covertly link it to that other kind of mastery, the brilliance of the omnipotent theorist who can explain the workings of the universe . . . Conversely, the girls appear to live in a chronic state of paranoia. They are constantly afraid to make the challenges to authority which would win for them the accolade 'brilliant'. The female teachers, too, in their adulation of the boys and dismissal of the girls, tell us something about the production of desire and the support of that Other which too claims to possess what we lack. But these are fantasies, fictions lived out in the powerful veridicality of the regulation of the present-day practices. Such practices create truths which are read back on to the boys, girls, men and women themselves, claiming often to be the incontrovertible truths about human nature, rather than elaborate fantasies masquerading as certain and true explanations. (Walkerdine 1990, pp. 127–8)

With reference to musical performance in schools, we have seen in Chapters 6 and 7 that there is an equation of classical music not only with femininity but also with conformity, and of popular music with masculinity and non-conformity. Now I wish to suggest that these performance-related associations are reiterated forcefully in the realm of composition, where feminine conformity is taken to be a symptom of lack of compositional ability and a dull musical mind, whilst, conversely, masculine non-conformity is understood to be a source of inventiveness and creativity. Likewise, girls' diligent hard work is not merely dissociated from but even opposed to attainment in musical composition, whereas boys' lack of studiousness operates as an indication of genuine understanding and creative spontaneity. This is how it is possible for some teachers to link the *outward* signs of boys' failure with their postulated *inward* success. In the first citation below, it is *because* boys play *wrong* notes that they achieve pleasing results; and in the second, it is by contrast to girls 'getting down to work' that boys show imagination and ability.

Which group is the most successful at composing?
– Both equally. I find each sex has its own problems and strong points. With more girls playing instruments they find composing at a piano or keyboard easier – especially if it is in a 'classical' style. However, boys are much more adventurous and not worried about playing wrong notes or putting unusual sounds together, so achieve some pleasing results.

– Both equally. Difficult to answer. It is my experience that girls are better when it comes to exercises in composing and getting down to work, but quite a few of the boys show imagination and ability.

Girls' attitudes

In each of the four groups of girls whom I interviewed, some or all of the group-members expressed a dislike for the activity of composition, and for the compositions which they had produced.

Year 10, Group 1, Girls:
– LG: How about Xena, anything else?
– Xena: I don't like the composition, at all.
– LG: No. Why not?
– Xena: I don't know. I find it very difficult. I feel as though I can't do it.
– LG: Right. what sort of things do you feel you can't do?
– Xena: I don't know, just all of the composing.
– LG: Yes. Is it the writing down, or [pause]?

– Xena: I can do the writing down. I find it difficult sitting down and playing
  something and seeing if it sounds good, then getting the next bit to link in
  with that, so it flows.

Year 10, Group 2, Girls:
– LG: . . . Do you think your compositions are any good?
– Anita: Not really no.
– LG: No. What's wrong with them?
– Anita: Just too simple compared to everyone else in the class, 'cos most
  people are a lot more advanced than I am, so mine are just very simple, just
  sort of the tune and then a single note underneath or something.
– LG: Yes I see. And do you have to play them in front of everybody?
– Anita: Yes.
– LG: How do you feel about that?
– Anita: You feel very sort of [pause].
– Georgina: You feel incompetent, like everyone's better than you, and you
  just [pause] – and that puts you down even more.
– Anita: It does, it makes you feel awful.
  . . .
– LG: Do you feel that you've done any good compositions, Georgina?
– Georgina: No. You sit there and you listen, to everyone else's, but most of
  the class are better than me and you sit there and you listen to them, and you
  think, and then you go up there to play and it's just nothing [inaudible] that
  wants to do this.

Year 11, Group 1, Girls:
– LG: How do you feel about your compositions, Stephanie, do you think
  they're any good or not?
– Stephanie: No not really, I mean I don't, I just don't like the sound of them.
– LG: You don't like the sound of them.
– Stephanie: No I don't like. There's only one that I like, but the rest of them,
  I think they're quite boring.
– LG: Boring.
– Stephanie: Yeah, I'm not actually very pleased with them.
– LG: Were you disappointed when you heard them played, or did you expect
  them to be like that?
– Stephanie: Actually I, when my trumpet duet was played, I thought it would
  sound much worse than it did. But still, like, the tune is quite boring, to me.

Year 11, Group 2, Girls:
– Charlene: Well I like composition when I've done something and I like what
  I do, but sometimes I feel that it just doesn't sound right, and I just can't get
  the motivation to actually sit down and think up something.
– LG: Yes. [To Jaswinda] How about you?
– Jaswinda: Probably the same, I mean, I dunno, it's just, there's always
  something, I dunno, that I don't like, but when I'm doing an actual piece,

and then I hear it afterwards it just sounds awful, it really sounds like, I dunno, I just bang my head; there's always something wrong with it, and it always sounds terrible, even though other people say 'Oh it's alright', I just [pauses, shaking head].
- LG: You don't believe them?
- Jaswinda: It sounds horrible to me.
- LG: Right. In what sort of way?
- Jaswinda: Well I don't know, not horrible, but it just sounds really simple really.
- Charlene: Sometimes they sound kind of silly, like a nursery rhyme.
- Jaswinda: Yeah . . . When other people come up with some really good, like really nice pieces, you know, I like [makes a strangled sound].

Some of the girls said that they disliked theory. On trying to discover more, I found them unwilling to discuss the content of the theory they had been covering, and inclined to deflect attention away from any necessity to use technical terms:

Year 10, Group 2, Girls:
- LG: OK, what about your dislikes? Anita?
- Anita: Probably, the theory side, because I'm not that good at it, and it gets me confused and sometimes [pause].
- LG: Yes. What sort of theory do you do?
- Anita: Well, basically just sort of note-reading, reading music and I had to have extra lessons 'cos I wasn't very good at it and sometimes it gets a bit confusing, 'cos the names are different [pause].
- LG: OK what about Georgina, what do you like least?
- Georgina: Theory 'cos I don't understand it at all.
- LG: You don't understand. Right. What is it, you just don't understand what he's saying, or what?
- Georgina: He just makes it hard to understand [inaudible] attitudes.
- LG: So what sort of things has he been covering?
- Georgina: Just basic theory and he starts from there like the blues and that . . .
- Anita: He goes too quickly.
- LG: So you get left behind?
- Anita: Yes.
- LG: So what do you about that then? [Pause] I mean do you [pause].
- Georgina: You go home and try and make sense of it by myself [*sic*].
  . . .
- LG: How about Caroline, what do you like least of all?
- Caroline: Again it's the theory. I just feel Mr. Q rushes it, and he thinks you know, we're all capable of learning quickly when we're not always, because it's confusing.

It would be quite wrong to give the impression that all of the girls were negatively inclined towards composition. On the contrary, a significant number of them felt positive towards it, and openly talked about their liking for it. These positive responses can be put into two categories. First, for many girls, it was free composition that they liked, and frequently, this went hand in hand with their *dislike* of theory: free composition was welcomed because it was perceived to be theory-free. Most emphatically, it was seen to enable girls in some way to express themselves or their feelings. In addition, four girls said that they enjoyed writing songs and that they wrote the words themselves.

Year 10, Group 1, Girls:
- LG: . . . What do you like most about GCSE?
- Layla: Well, I quite like the composition, when it's doing what you want to do, and what you feel and everything, but I don't so much like the theory because you've got to learn it and it's just not so interesting for me.
  . . .
- Layla: Before I did music GCSE I'd had a go at it [i.e. composing], and things like that. I quite like it, really. It's just like, you just go and sit at the piano and you just play something what you're feeling, and it's quite good really, I like it.
  . . .
- LG: . . . What sort of compositions do you do, can you describe them at all?
- Layla: Well I mainly do them on the piano because I find that easier, and sometimes it's just what I'm feeling, or sometimes Mr Q. gives us set things to do .

Year 10, Group 2, Girls:
- LG: So some of your pieces were free compositions . . . and some of them were where you had set tasks, were they?
- Caroline: Yes.
- LG: Right. What sort of set tasks did you have?
- Caroline: They were more for the history, to do with like, ground bass and things like that.
- LG: What, take a ground bass, and compose over it or whatever, something like that? Which do you prefer, free composition or set tasks?
- Caroline: I'd rather do something of my own.
  . . .
- LG . . . How about Georgina?
- Georgina: I did, I haven't done that much, I've done more at home. I do more at home, just free stuff. It's more, it's easier.

Year 10, Group 2, Girls:
- LG: What do you like most about the course?

- Anita: Sometimes when we're doing compositions and we just get to choose by ourselves, not being told what to do.
- LG: Yes, you like that. Why is that do you think?
- Anita: It gives you more freedom to do what you want; you can put down what you think.
- LG: Georgina?
- Georgina: Same as Anita, just doing your own thing not being told that you have to do it in a specific style.
- LG: Right. Caroline?
- Caroline: More or less what Anita and Georgina have said. I just like playing and doodling around, till I find something [pause].

Year 11, Group 1, Girls:
- LG: What do you like most about GCSE music?
- Stephanie: I like the composing part because, you know, we can do whatever we wanted and stuff . . .

Secondly, some girls said they felt proud of their compositions. This was again linked to their emotional existence, and also to a sense of self-expression. Pride was described more than once, not only with relation to the sound, but also to the sight of the composition on paper.

Year 11, Group 1, Girls:
- LG: Right, what about Shala, do you like your compositions?
- Shala: Well, yeah, I do. I mean, I had a lot of boring, silly ones and I put them aside, I forgot about them, I can't even remember them now. But the ones I always seem to be playing them, even now, like if I'm just sitting at a piano, I just sit and play them, and people say 'Oh that's nice', and I say 'Oh that's my composition', you know. And so, yeah, I do. I only give in the ones I like, really. I can't be bothered to write the silly ones down.
- LG: No. So what do you like about them? What do you get out of them?
- Shala: When I like a piece it's more, like I get this feeling, I know it's really silly but I get this feeling I think, you know, Ah, self-satisfaction, and I sort of like have this big glow on my face, you know I actually – people may not like it, but if I like it, then it's OK.

Year 11, Group 2, Girls:
- Jo: I definitely have got better at sitting down and writing them. I like the feeling that you get when you've written something and someone else plays it and it sounds right, and you just think, 'I did that.'
- LG . . . [To Liz] and Liz, do you like it?
- Liz: I do like it, yeah.
- LG: What do you like about it?
- Liz: Just at the end when you look at the piece of paper and think that, you know, you've written that, and it's not come from a book, it's come from you, and actually you know its yours, yourself.

- LG: Yes, that makes you feel proud? [Liz nods] And what about when you hear it being played?
- Liz: I like that as well, when the teacher plays it, and everyone goes 'Yeah, it's really good.'

Girls also appreciated high compositional ability in one of their peers. Throughout the questionnaire and both case-studies, I only came across one example of a girl being called 'brilliant', and it came from other girls in her class. The girl herself was absent and I was unable to interview her.

Year 11, Group 1, Girls:
- Shala: There's a couple of people who, they find it so easy to do compositions, they don't even have to sit at the piano, they just write them down, like Louise, and she just sits there with this composition, 'Ah I've got a composition', and she just writes it on the manuscript paper, down, and then she plays it, and they're brilliant, you know, 'cos she's just, she's just, superb, and that just makes me think 'Oh I'll never get my composition done' . . .

Year 11, Group 2, Girls:
- Jo: . . . There are obviously people that are better, like Louise, is quite good, is *really* good.
- Charlene: She's writing a fugue for like, three or four voices.
- Jo: But she's just talented, she's really talented, and like, it just depends.
- LG: Is talent the thing that you think makes the difference, or is it technical knowledge?
- All: Talent.
- Charlene: Imagination too.

Boys' attitudes

Although girls and boys shared some views about composition, there were also significant divergences. In addition, the ways in which they expressed their views were different, and they attributed different attitudes to each other.

Year 10, Group 2, Girls:
- LG : [To Anita and Georgina] Do you think that most people in your class feel the same way as you do [i.e. negative] about composition?
  . . .
- Georgina: It's more the girls.
- Anita: Yeah.
- Georgina: Yeah, a couple of the boys, like . . . one of them's very sort of un[inaudible] 'cos he's really good, and the other two are a bit more iffy about their composition, and the girls are definitely more iffy.

- LG: Why do you think that is?
- Georgina: The boys tend to sort of, if someone says something like, you know, you could have done this, that and the other, they seem to shrug it off; whereas the girls have to think [pause].
- Anita and Caroline: Yeah, yeah [inaudible].
- Anita: And they're [i.e. boys] normally the ones making the comments.
- Georgina: They take over.
- Caroline: They're the ones making the comments.

Of the eight boys I interviewed, none was entirely negative about composition. However, two boys, both in Year 11, were less than wholly positive. One of these was immersed in classical music as a trumpeter who had taken several ABRSM grades and was just about to take the final, advanced grade. He said he had not liked composition at the beginning of the course, but that he had come to like it by the end.

Year 11, Group 3, Boys:
- LG: Adam you said you didn't use to like composition; why was that do you think?
- Adam: Well, not really dislike it, but it was a bit monotonous, that sort of area of dislike.
- LG: Right.
- Adam: Because I'm not very good at composing anyway, sort of making up tunes. Like, I just hear all these famous tunes in my head from playing the trumpet, you know.
- LG: Right.
- Adam: It's just getting a tune in your head which isn't already known and putting it on paper and getting it, yeah, and sort of if it's a piano piece, getting the harmony and all that down into the [inaudible] sort of aspect of it really.

In contrast to the attitudes of the girls who were negative about composition, cited in the previous section, Adam's negativity is expressed in terms not so much of lacking confidence or understanding as of their opposites. His explanation appeals on one hand to his lack of *interest* ('it was a bit monotonous'); and on the other hand, to his specialist *knowledge* of 'famous tunes', which got in the way. The other boy who had a relatively negative response to composition was at the opposite end of the spectrum. He was a rock drummer (Pete), who said that although he enjoyed music, he had not opted for the subject. He did not read music and found that the drums were not a suitable instrument for which to compose for GCSE. He was disqualified from entrance to the exam owing to non-completion of coursework. Again his failure was portrayed as the result not so much of his lack of ability as his lack of interest and the shortcomings of an exam system that did not recognise the realities of group composition in popular music.[7]

The remaining six boys all said that they liked composing and that they liked some or all of their compositions. In this liking for composition, their relationship to theory was quite different to that of the girls: they portrayed it as 'easy' and they used technical terms without hesitation. In direct contrast to the girls, some of them even expressed a preference for set tasks rather than free composition.

Year 10, Group 3, Boys:
- LG: What do you like most about the course?
- Henry: Basically it's learning about all the different styles, actually the theoretical side of the course.
  . . .
- Paul: Well, I like learning about new ways of composition, and different styles of writing. Like we've just been learning today about, what was that thing?
- Anthony: Two-part writing.
- Paul: Yeah, and the history is also interesting.
- Anthony: I like the two-part writing as well, and composition. I enjoy writing pieces.
- LG: Right. How did you go about learning the two-part writing today, for example, what did you learn?
- Anthony: About thirds and fourths and [pauses].
- Paul: And about how fourths and fifths sound the same, and thirds and sixths sound the same.

Below, they again stated that they found the set tasks easy, but were this time unwilling to oppose that to free composition: both types of composition were greeted positively.

Year 10, Group 3, Boys:
- LG: Does any of you compose at home?
- Anthony: I do, I compose quite a lot at home, and I base it on chord sequences.
- Henry: Just sort of mucking around, but you don't write it down.
- Paul: Yeah, you don't write it down. I just play around with the chords on the guitar.
- LG: Yes. And how do you feel about the different kinds of composition: some of it is your own free composition that you do at home, some of it is composition that you've been given as a set task, like a ground bass or something?

---

[7] In fact most GCSE syllabuses do allow group composition, but the Head of Music in the school did not go in for it. In my experience very few heads of music do, possibly because it drastically magnifies the problems of assessment.

- Henry: I prefer a set task, it's easier to work from.
- LG: Really?
- Henry: You've got like something that you have to focus on like a ground bass or a chord sequence.
  . . .
- LG [To others in the group]: Do you both agree with that, or do you feel differently?
- Paul: Yeah.
- Anthony: Yeah.
- Paul: It's a lot easier.
- Anthony: Well, sometimes it can be easier for my [inaudible] have some chords, is to make them up, you know; it's easy to make them up.
- LG: Yes. And your instrument is clarinet?
- Anthony: Yes.
- LG: So, you obviously play the chords on something: on the piano, do you, or the guitar?
- Anthony: Yeah I base them on the piano; I don't play the piano myself though.

Year 11, Group 3, Boys:
- LG: Right what about Chris, you say composition's your favourite aspect?
- Chris: Well, yeah, its just it's easier.
- LG: You find it easier.
- Chris: Yes, I just get it done on keyboard.
- LG: Right.
- Chris: I'm just about to take my Grade IV, and it's just getting better and better.
- LG: Can you tell me about the sort of compositions that you do?
- Chris: Well, I've made a couple of classical ones on the keyboard, a jazz duet for trumpet and keyboard, and a popular, or a modern composition on keyboard.
- LG: On keyboard. And you play all of them yourself do you?
- Chris: Yes.
- LG: And do you do them, by, you play it first and then you do the writing down later on, or do you do it by notation?
- Chris: In most cases, I make it up first, then I write.
- LG: Right. And so, have you had any of your compositions performed? . . .
- Chris: Yeah . . .
- LG: And how did you feel about that?
- Chris: It was just nice to hear somebody else play it.
- LG: Yeah, did it surprise you, or [pause].
- Chris: No, it just, sounded the same.

As distinct from the girls' emotional relationships to composition, through which they could 'do what they feel and everything', 'put down what they think', 'do what they wanted and stuff' (p. 203), the boys' rela-

tionships to composition appear more rational, more controlled. Girls'
and boys' expectations about their pieces also betrayed signs, or
constructions of 'irrational reaction' against 'rational judgement'.
Compare, for example, Stephanie with Chris: when Stephanie's
'trumpet duet was played, she thought it would sound much worse than
it did, but it still sounded quite boring, to her' (p. 201, above); but Chris
found that it 'was just nice to hear somebody else play' his composition,
the performance of which did not surprise him but 'just, sounded the
same' as he expected (p. 208, above).

In contrast to those girls who lacked confidence, who felt 'incompetent' and 'awful', who thought that at least some of their compositions sounded 'terrible', 'horrible', 'simple' and 'silly' (pp. 201–2), boys'
apparent possession of confidence surfaced through a light-hearted,
humorous or careless attitude towards their work. The boy in the first
example below is Adam the classical trumpeter, already mentioned, who
felt less keen on composition. Even though in the conversation here he to
some extent adopts the feminine characteristic of being unsure of his
work, he nonetheless 'just laughs' when he hears it performed. The boy
in the second example introduced his compositions, which were a strong
point with him, into the conversation by making a negative joke.

Year 11, Group 3, Boys:
- LG: So when you hear your compositions, Adam, now, how do you feel
  about them? Do you like them, or dislike them or do you think they're any
  good or not?
- Adam: I laugh at them really, saying, you know in a stupid way really, 'cos
  saying this is, 'cos I'm surprised at what I've done, writing them down and
  all these tunes, and how [pause].
- LG: Surprised in a nice way or in a [pause].
- Adam: Yeah, in a sort of nice way really, just someone playing it and saying,
  I sort of laugh really, just whilst I'm listening to it.
- LG: Right. What makes you laugh – I mean is it out of embarrassment, or
  'cos you feel proud of them, or what?
- Adam: No, 'cos I, well, I dunno really, I suppose, I don't think how good this
  was going to turn out like. I had the mind, the ideas in my head, but I didn't
  realise how well it was going to turn out on paper, so that's quite a laugh
  really.
- LG: So you're pleased.
- Adam: Yeah, that's quite funny.

Year 11, Group 4, Boys:
- LG: . . . How about you Adrian, can you tell me something about the
  compositions that you've done? What are they like, for example?

- Adrian: Dreary.
- LG: Pardon?
- Adrian: Dreary.
- LG: Dreary?
- Adrian: No, no. I've tried to vary them as much as I can. I've done one calypso-ey Christmas carol, [this was performed at the school concert] that was one that I did. I've done one jazzy piece on piano, which I can't really play the piano much but I just got past. I've done two guitar pieces, which have got, well, a keyboard and drums and everything.

None of the boys mentioned 'putting what they feel' into a composition, self-expression, song-writing or taking pride in their work.

Conformity / creativity: pupils' perceptions

Pupils are not in a position to make judgements about the comparative level of conformity or innovation which teachers cited as characteristic of girls or boys respectively in composition. The pupils with whom I spoke made no explicit reference to such concepts. But implicit constructions of femininity and masculinity around the opposition of conformity to inventiveness were integrally woven into the common-sense notions with which they described their relationships to composition.

In the conversation below, the idea that girls 'just follow rules' surfaces through barely noticeable nooks and crannies. Undoubtedly no London teenager of the 1990s is liable to write a waltz or a French *Ballet* unless they have been quite formally given the instruction and the rules by which to do so. The conversation also indicates a willingness to convey reliance on the guidance of the teacher.

Year 11, Group 1, Girls:
- LG: You've done four compositions, can you tell me what they're like, what sort of things are they?
- Stephanie: Mostly a lot of them are absolute [sudden and unexplained pause] – three-four time, sort of like waltzes, I don't know why, I just, I find it easier to write them. And that's about it, really. But I don't like them.
- LG: Right. And what are they for – piano, or other instruments?
- Stephanie: No, one of them's, actually one of them's a trumpet duet, and the others are piano. I tried writing a song but I couldn't get the, I wrote the words but I couldn't get the piano part to it.
- LG: Shala, what kind of compositions have you done?
- Shala: I've also done *Ballet* [French procrunciation], *Ballet* or something, a waltz kind of thing.
- LG: Yes.
- Shala: Yes, one of those. Actually I've done them all with my piano teacher

out of school. He helped me a lot with them. Because here I needed a lot, because, like, help with them, not *with* them, with writing them down. I have so many in my head, but just the fact that writing them down is quite tricky for me, but if I'm by myself I'd probably get it wrong, kind of thing.
- LG: I see. And again, are they free style, or are they to do with set tasks, or anything you like?
- Shala: Well, I had, before we, like last year I think, ages ago I had a couple in mind, just like silly things, and then I sort of developed them, this year, sort of, 'cos my teacher said, 'Oh that's nice', you know, 'Maybe you could use that as a composition' and I said 'Oh yeah, maybe', and I confronted my piano teacher out of school and I said 'Look I've got these compositions in my head and I really need a lot of help, like, to perfect them and everything, get them down on paper', and he said 'OK, well do you want me to listen to them?' and I showed them him. I played them to him and he started helping me with them, and we put aside some work that I was doing with him, and he helped me out, and I've given them all in now, so it's a bit of a relief.

Unlike Shala, who got help from outside school by going to another teacher, when boys talked about working on their compositions out of school, as we have already seen to some extent, this was clothed in the guise of 'just mucking around', 'you don't write it down', 'I just play around' (above, p. 207). The example below goes further, in that this boy portrays his composition in a way that is pitted *against* the teacher and the school:

Year 11, Group 4, Boys:
- LG: . . . Do you like your compositions, do you think they're any good?
- Adrian: I could have done better. Because the equipment we have here, it's naff [aplogetic laugh], it's no good at all. I've used Chico's, my friend's; and my brother's got quite a bit of equipment.
- LG: Right. So you've done quite a bit of your compositions out of school.
- Adrian: I've done all of them out of school.
- LG: You've done all of them out of school, right.
- Adrian: Yeah, and I could have done better if I had more time to work on them here.
- LG: Yes, yes. And what do you feel like when you hear the compositions? Do you feel proud of them, or ashamed, or what?
- Adrian: Yeah, some of them, and some of them I don't like, I feel I could have done better. There was one I did originally, but I didn't like it so I scrapped it and did another one, which was [pause].
- LG: Right. What didn't you like about it?
- Adrian: The whole thing. It was just [pause] crap [laughs; general laughter].
- LG: Just crap. In what way?
- Adrian: I dunno, it's just a bit too simplistic, it sounded, like the quality of it, like the four-track packed in half way through the recording of it so, it's just [pause].

– LG: Oh right, that's a shame.
– Adrian: so I didn't run it.

Adrian's appeal puts me in mind of some boys cited in Chapter 7 (p. 189), who portrayed their low grades in performance as resulting from poor equipment and from the inadequacies of the teacher: it was because they were not allowed to play drums and they had to play xylophones that they failed. Here, it is because the school did not have the right technology, or because the technology did not work properly, that Adrian did not do as well as he could. This lack of equipment on the part of the school contributes to and legitimates the lack of school rule-following on the part of the boy, finally serving, without the least conscious intention on Adrian's part, to enhance the construction of his creative inventiveness.

The boys in Adrian's group shared the dislike of theory expressed by some girls, but in a different way. Whereas the girls found theory hard to understand and went home 'to work it out by myself' (above, p. 202), these boys found it hard to understand *because they did not try* to understand it, preferring to do something else instead. They were all rock musicians who portrayed themselves, and were portrayed by other pupils in their class, as having spent most of the course jamming in the practice room where the interviews took place.

Yr 11, Group 4, Boys:
– LG: What do you like most of all about the course?
– Adrian: Practical lessons.
– Pete: Yeah.
– Tom: Yeah.
– LG: Meaning, performance?
– Adrian: Yeah, just playing, jamming.
– LG: Right. Other people?
– Pete: Well, it's the same.
– Tom: It's the same.
– Pete: I can't read music, so the theory side is difficult for me.
– LG: Yeah, so when you have practical lessons, what do you do, are you all three, you play together do you quite often?
– All: Yeah.
– LG: What, you have a band or something, or [pause].
– Adrian: No, but in here we do. [Laughter]
– LG: In here. You just jam.
– Adrian: Yeah.
– Pete: Yeah.
– LG: . . . And what about the bit of the course that you like least of all?

- Adrian: Theory.
- Tom: Yeah, set work.
- Pete: Yeah, theory and set work.
- LG: Yeah. What's wrong with it?
- All: It's boring.
- Tom: And it's hard, dealing with all that sort of, little notes and stuff.

The pop/classical split, discussed in Chapter 7, with its harnessing of popular music to masculine non-conformity and creativity, here operates to legitimate and even glamorise the boys' failure to understand theory, to read music, or to deal with 'little notes and stuff'.

Earlier, with reference to Walkerdine's arguments (1990) I suggested that teachers' perceptions that boys have a careless attitude towards work contribute to the assumption of boys' genuine understanding and creative talent. This was contrasted with the perception that the hardworking attitude of girls proves their lack of true understanding and imagination. Although, again, pupils cannot assess each other in the same way as teachers do, they nonetheless reiterated this theme concerning attitude to work in their own ways. Both girls and boys said that boys 'could have done better' in their compositions, implying that the boys' actual attainment was deceptively low in relation to their genuine, but concealed, ability. Adrian's comments above provide one example of this, and there are further examples below. No one suggested that girls 'could have done better'. In addition, pupils indicated that boys produced good compositions without doing much work, whereas girls were presented as more reliant on hard work and, as has already been seen, on adopting the paradigms provided by the teacher.

Year 10, Group 1, Girls:
- LG: . . . What about the boys in your class. What are they like as composers?
- Xena: I can't say I really heard much of their compositions. Anthony's quite good.
- Layla: Yeah, he's good.
- Xena: Yeah, he's really good at composition.
- Layla: I think Paul could be good. But he doesn't, he just doesn't, he can't write it down.
- Xena: He can't write it down because he plays guitar.

Year 11, Group 1, Girls:
- LG: Do you think most people in your class feel the same about composition, or does everybody feel differently?
- Shala: . . . A lot of the boys, yeah, they just sit here on the drums and they sit and play guitar you know, 'cos they think that music is fun, and everything, and they can play the guitar very well, but they, they do get compositions,

they've got their compositions done already but they could probably have done much better.

. . .

- Shala: . . . With their actual composition, they just don't really take it seriously like everyone else really, apart from a couple of people.
- Stephanie: It's like, everyone's got ideas, everyone, but, they haven't got them, they just don't write them down.
- LG: Yes I understand that. And do you think it's the same for boys and girls?
- Stephanie: Some of the boys got excellent compositions, produced at the very end. Adrian's got a very good one, he wrote a Christmas carol I think.
- Shala: Yes, it was very good, nice composition.
- Stephanie: There's a lot of talent. 'Cos, at this age, I know, I sound like an old granny, [laughter] but at this age usually students, I mean like the boys in our class really, they like to, you know they do subjects for a doss[8] and when they actually do get into actual lessons every week and they just think they can take advantage of the time they have, because they enjoy it so much, they just like to, you know, to sit and play and not work, write down and have that hassle, and the teacher's always with other people who do really want to work, and if they don't then the students will just say, 'Oh yes, I'm just working on it', and then she'll leave them, you know, unless they actually ask her to come, she hasn't got time to see everyone in one lesson . . .

Year 11, Group 2, Girls:
- LG: . . . do you think there's any difference in attitude in the way boys approach composition and the way girls approach composition?
- Jaswinda: The boys just like, tend to just sit down and play something but they're not really thinking about composing.
- Charlene: Yes.
- Jo: It's different on the part of [some of] the boys. You take people like Chris [pause].
- Charlene: Yeah.
- Liz: Yeah, he's really into it.
- Jo: He'll sit down and he'll do it and he comes up with about six or seven compositions to choose from; and Adam does quite a lot. But Adrian and that, they just sort of [pause].
- Charlene: Sit in here.
- Jo: Sit in here, and jam the whole lesson.
- LG: What, you mean they just don't do the composition?
- Jo: They have done them eventually, but it just takes a while.

Year 11, Group 4, Boys:
- LG: Do you think there's any difference in the way girls and boys feel about composition?

---

[8] In British slang, 'to doss' means to sleep; and a task which is 'a doss' is a task that requires very little effort.

- Tom: Girls I think work harder and start right at the beginning of the course, but I did all four in about one half term.
- LG: Right.
- Tom: Like, I wrote a couple of them before, but I recorded them all and wrote them, like, down, and they [i.e. girls] started at the beginning of the two years.
- LG: Right.
- Adrian: And like, we jammed for about one and a half years. [Laughter]

In the final example below, which follows straight on from the conversation above, the boys re-examine their relationship to work, and seem to reiterate the complexity in the constructions of 'reality' represented by this issue. Adrian appeals to the practices of other males in his family, apparently as an explanation or a justification for the fact that he did do some work.

Year 11, Group 4, Boys:
- LG: Any other differences or similarities between girls' and boys' approaches to composition?
- Adrian: They seem to be, get more involved in it, in their pieces.
- LG: Do they?
- Tom: Yeah. They enjoy what they do.
- LG: Right.
- Tom: Probably go home and work quite hard on their pieces. [Pause]
- Adrian: Well so do I! [Embarrassed laugh]
- LG to Adrian: You do too.
- Tom: I'm not saying I *don't*.
- Adrian: Yeah I do. Sod it, I'm in a musical family, so I'm always trying, always been involved with music.
- LG: Right.
- Adrian: My dad plays. You know, it just depends. My two little brothers play.
- LG: Right.
- Tom: The majority of the class is girls.

THREATENING FEMININITY IN THE MUSIC CLASSROOM

The comments of teachers and pupils concerning boys' and girls' relationships to composition participate in an over-arching discourse on masculinity and femininity. Masculinity is characterised by a confident, rational approach to composition based on creativity and genuine attainment through natural talent; femininity is constructed as lacking confidence in composition, as bound up with feelings on one hand and rules on the other, as conservative, traditional and attaining success only through hard work. This discourse does not merely reflect conventional constructions of masculinity and femininity in the society at large, or the overt content of boys' and girls' compositional practices in the school; its influence must also be sought in musical meaning, and in the relationship of musical meaning to musical practice and ultimately to musical experience itself.

I argued in Chapters 4 and 5 that a masculine meaning, or delineation, specifically related to the notion of composition imbues all Western music. The masculine delineation of music is articulated through two channels. One of these is the cerebral control over knowledge and technique which is implicit in the notion of composition, and which is definitively masculine in its connotations. The other channel is historical precedence, which dictates that most music known in the public sphere has been understood to be composed or improvised by men. This twofold masculine delineation of music has marked the history of music, has influenced the ears of listeners and musicians for many years, and continues to have a powerful and pervasive effect on our practices and our hearing today. It presents a filter through which the music of women composers has been measured in terms of its femininity, pitted against a masculinity which is invisible, implicit, unexamined and ubiquitous. Women's music has either been denigrated for being feminine, praised for being feminine, or greeted with surprised approval for being deemed masculine, in which last case the women composers involved have themselves often been accordingly reproved. In all three cases, women's music has been appraised in terms of the masculine delineation of music, the cerebral and historical connotations of which together conflict with conventional constructions of femininity. The woman composer presents a threat to femininity, not only by virtue of her musical practices but, moreover, by virtue of the problematic delineations arising from her music.

The influence of the masculine delineation of music is decipherable in teachers' and pupils' comments above. Teachers' depictions of girls as compositionally conservative connect with the threat posed to femininity by the cerebral connotations of composition: to be innovative in composition is to use one's mind, and to use one's mind is to be not-female. The teachers' portrayal of girls' lack of creativity also connects with the practical position of women composers throughout history which, after Hildegard and until very recently, has been marked by a lack of 'what counts' as innovation. This lack has been partly the result of restricted educational opportunities; but it is also a cause, in that it contributes to the discursive construction of femininity as non-innovatory. Here we see that even when educational opportunity is unequivocally provided, this cannot lead to the automatic adoption of innovatory techniques by female students, or to the automatic recognition of any such techniques by teachers.

Girls' own expressed negativity towards theory, their frequent references to feeling and self-expression even when these accompany pride and pleasure in composition, their denigration of their own compositions or their own feelings: all these tendencies participate in the patriarchal definition of femininity as subject to the body and opposed to the mind, subject to the feelings and alienated from reason. The girls with whom I talked put themselves firmly on the feminine side of the mind/body, feeling/reason split. Contrastingly, boys' positive relationships towards theory in some cases, their superior rejection of it in others, their claims to knowledge even when in a negative disposition towards composition (such as when famous tunes or inadequate technology get in the way), their confidence in their compositional ability, their rational expectation that their piece will sound no different from how they intended, their lack of reliance on the teacher, the absence of self-denigration in their dialogue, their neglect to mention their feelings or to conceive of composition as a form of self-expression: all these participate in the patriarchal construction of masculinity's greater cerebrality, creative autonomy and domination over the body. The masculine cerebral delineation of music and the hegemony of the male composer in history here legitimate themselves.

I have argued that the way in which listeners and critics judge musical value is influenced partly by whether they understand and can achieve fulfilment through the music's inherent meanings, or whether they feel dissatisfied, lost and thrown off by inherent meanings. Listeners' responses to musical inherent meanings are also influenced by their attitudes to delineations. Thus when teachers take up the role of the critic to judge the ability of boys and girls relative to each other, their judgements are made not only in ways that concur with a wider discourse on masculinity and femininity but, furthermore, in ways that concur with wider musical delineations and their effects on musical experience. As is the case for everyone who is operating within the bounds of musical common sense, teachers cannot help perceiving the inherent meanings of a girl composer's music through the gauze of the masculine cerebral and historical delineation, that implicit meaning of all music, which denies and threatens femininity. This, I wish to suggest, is one reason how it comes about that whereas teachers abundantly described girls' composition as diligent, not one teacher described girls' composition as inspired, creative, imaginative or brilliant. Even the possibility that music by a girl could be deemed 'masculine' in its excellence never once arose.

The masculine delineation of music and its threat to femininity must also be at work in the experience of pupils. If there is any root of girls' expressed lack of creative autonomy, confidence or rationality in their approach to composition, and boys' apparent possession of these capacities, then it must lie most fundamentally in musical meaning and in musical experience itself. I have suggested that an experience of full and absolute musical celebration can occur when listeners are wholly cognisant of and responsive to music's inherent meanings, at the same time as being entirely positive about its delineations. For women and girls, I have argued, the most total experience of full celebration must be very rare, and is perhaps almost impossible: because the ubiquitous masculine delineation will always to some extent throw off the female listener, engendering even a slight ambiguity in the relationship. Girl composers as well as women composers themselves must take on board the consequences of the masculine delineation, not only in listening to other people's music but moreover, in listening to their own music. It must be more difficult for them than it is for boys and men to find themselves positively reflected and celebrated in the musical object. This is therefore the case even when women or girls compose or improvise the music themselves, because their own music will come back at them imbued with at least a trace of the masculine delineation and the threat to it which is presented by femininity. This delineation will throw off their gendered subjectivity, expose their femininity in the delineations of the music, problematise it. For boys, contrastingly, the masculine delineation will correspond with, and help to affirm, their sense of gendered identity as they find it reflected in the music.

I would like to illuminate this point by contrasting the two conversations below, one with a girl and one with a group of boys:

Year 10, Group 2, Girls:
- LG: How about Caroline, how much composition have you done?
- Caroline: I've done about two or three brief pieces, but I was supposed to play them to the class, but I haven't actually got around to that.
- LG: No, right. Are you looking forward to that?
- Caroline: Well, I don't really like playing my compositions to the class, but if it's something that I feel is good, like other pieces composed by other people, famous or not famous, then I feel more confident than when I do my own.

Year 10, Group 3, Boys:
- LG: Do you think that your compositions are any good or not?
- Henry: Some.
- LG: Some.
- Anthony: I think they're quite good. I like them.
- Paul: There's room: you can better them, they can be better.
- LG: They could be better. Right. What makes them good, do you think, which ones do you think are good and why?
- Anthony: It's the ones that I think would sound good as something that someone else would have composed, if someone else had done it.

What strikes me is the way that the girl, Caroline, says she does not like performing her own compositions but prefers performing the compositions of other people; whereas the boy, Anthony, says his compositions sound good when they sound as if they have been composed by someone else. Whereas she negatively contrasts her work with that of others, he positively aligns his composition with that of others; whereas she participates in the conventional construction of femininity as lacking confidence in composition, he rides on the assumption of masculine confidence; whereas she does not wish to find herself presented in the music she plays, but would rather present another person, he finds himself reflected as if he were another. And who are these 'other people', 'someone else', 'famous or not famous'? In the curriculum of the school, in the content of the National Curriculum for music and the music GCSE, in the media and press, on audio and visual recordings, in the society at large, in the imprint of history on our musical practices and on musical meaning, these 'other people' may be famous or not famous, but they are certainly not women. They are symbolically masculine in terms of the cerebral delineation of music, and they are actually men in terms of the normative orientation of music history. The masculine delineation of music ensures that when these other people are women, real biological women, this fact is problematic.

I would like to contrast two other conversations which also illustrate the problems girls have in finding themselves positively reflected in their own music, compared to the relative simplicity with which boys project themselves. One of the conversations arises from the first case-study school and was the only occasion when the topic of composition, or as it happens, improvisation, arose explicitly in that school. The other is from the second school and is also about improvisation.

Four GCSE girls, Year 10, first case-study school:
- L G : Do you improvise or is it all done from notation?
- I improvise a bit on the guitar but I hate doing it in public.
- There was a jazz course and a concert at the end of it and we had to improvise. I was really nervous. We had to improvise. It was all out of time and that.
- A special person came into the school.
- I did enjoy it but I just didn't like improvising.
- ˙ L G : Why?
- Because improvisation is, like, something that you make up and you can't really go wrong, really, in improvisation; and it's OK on your own but in front of everyone, people – if you're just on your own it's OK but when you've got those people watching you, you just feel you're going wrong the whole time.
- When you're improvising it's like, your own thing; it's like the music that comes from *you*; and if it sounds really awful that's like, you know; [pause] whereas if you're playing from a sheet of music it's like, what someone else's written, it's someone else's thing.
- They just pointed to you and you just had to stand up and do it.
- I was the first person and then it came round again, so I played an extra time and I just wasn't ready.
- L G : Did you have many boys on that course?
- There was quite a few. Might have been more boys than girls.
- Most people thought improvisation was a pain; most of the people who've never done it before. The ones who are in the jazz band and like jazz, they thought it was OK.

When these girls said that the people in the jazz band thought improvisation was OK, in fact there was only one girl in this large jazz band: it was boys who thought improvisation was OK. Contrast this, from the second case-study school:

Year 11, Group 3, Boys:
- L G : . . . How about Chris, how do you feel when your compositions are being played?
- Chris: Not many people can play mine. Because they don't know how to play the keyboard as well as I do.
- L G : Yes. So you have to only do them yourself. And do you think they're any good or not?
- Chris: Well, yeah. But when I play them, I'm already jazzing it up, so: if it doesn't sound right and I want to do something else to it, like take something off and add something on, and it just ended up as that, and I'm not changing them any more.

What is significant here is not only the lack of confidence that is expressed by the girls or the impression of confidence that is given by the boy, but the way that one girl in particular links her experience of improvisation to a problematic *revealing of herself* in the improvised music, and contrasts this experience to that of playing what *someone else* has written.

When you're improvising it's like, your own thing; it's like the music that comes from *you*; and if it sounds really awful that's like, you know; [pause] whereas if you're playing from a sheet of music it's like, what someone else's written, it's someone else's thing.

But for the boy improviser, other people could not play his music.

It is by no means always the case that girls express such a lack of confidence or suggest this incapacity to find themselves positively reflected in their music. As we have seen, girls are quite prone to express pride in their compositions, and this would seem to contradict, or at least necessitate modification to, my argument that girls cannot find themselves positively reflected in their music: it indicates that some girls at least *are* able to be fully celebrated by their own music, and that they *can* find themselves reflected in it, very precisely and very positively. This looks in two ways. In one direction I feel it does indicate a real chink of light, and I will return to this in Chapter 9. But in the other direction, girls' pride in their composition has to be placed within the overall context of their discursively constructed femininity: the link of femininity to feeling, to lack of creativity, to conformity and artistic conservativism. Girls' pride is expressed in ways that participate in the overriding masculine delineation of music.

Year 11, Group 1, Girls:
- Shala: When I like a piece [of mine] it's more, like I get this feeling, I know it's really silly but I get this feeling I think, you know, Ah, self-satisfaction, and I sort of like have this big glow on my face, you know I actually – people may not like it, but if I like it, then it's OK.

Year 11, Group 2, Girls:
- Jo: . . . I like the feeling that you get when you've written something and someone else plays it and it sounds right, and you just think, 'I did that.'
  . . .
- Liz: Just at the end when you look at the piece of paper and think that, you know, you've written that, and it's not come from a book, it's come from you, and actually you know it's yours, yourself.

Whereas boys are confident of their music as something which someone else might have composed, or as something which no one else can play, these girls express a more dubious relationship: a sense of pride which is at the same time denigrated for being 'silly', which is bound up with feeling, with the body and the body's uncontrollability ('I have this big glow on my face'), with the self ('I did that', 'it's come from you, and actually you know it's yours, yourself'). In contrast to those other girls who lack confidence, these girls clearly can find themselves positively reflected in their own music, and they experience pleasure in doing so. But this self-reflection is nonetheless firmly embedded within patriarchal constructions of femininity.

As I have already indicated, the girls were also able to celebrate the compositional achievements of one of their female peers. But the music itself, both that in which they found themselves positively reflected and that through which they celebrated the achievements of a classmate, was *safe*. Unlike teachers, whose greater experience of music affords a broader and indeed more fully conventional response, pupils are liable to be dazzled by technical prowess. I noted earlier that girls' pride sometimes expressed itself in relation to the paper on which they could see their music written. When they described their colleague Louise as 'brilliant', it is necessary to observe that Louise, unlike all the other pupils to whom I talked, was understood to compose by notation first, then to play her work afterwards.

Year 11, Group 1, Girls:
– Shala: There's a couple of people who, they find it so easy to do compositions, they don't even have to sit at the piano, they just write them down, like Louise, and she just sits there with this composition, 'Ah, I've got a composition', and she just writes it on the manuscript paper, down, and then she plays it, and they're brilliant, you know, 'cos she's just, she's just, superb.

Year 11, Group 2, Girls:
– Charlene: She [Louise] is writing a fugue for like, three or four voices.
– Jo: But she's just talented, she's really talented, and like, it just depends.
– LG: Is talent the thing that you think makes the difference, or is it technical knowledge?
– All: Talent.
– Charlene: Imagination too.

I by no means wish to deny that these girls were inspired, if troubled also, by the achievements of their classmate; and I do wish to indicate the very real promise of this. But at the same time it would be wrong to fail to place these achievements within the overall context of the threat to femininity contained in the masculine compositional delineation, or of the discursive construction of feminine musicality, not only within the school but throughout history. Although the girls in Louise's group found her composition awe-inspiring, to her teacher – as to the questionnaire teachers with reference to girl composers in general – it was *pastiche*: advanced perhaps, well-notated definitely, but lacking inspiration for those very reasons.

The girls' appeals to their own lack of confidence on one hand and to their pride in themselves on the other, to their feelings and to their sense of revealing themselves in their music, can be understood as participating in the over-arching discursive construction of femininity. The boys to whom I talked, on the other hand, presented themselves as overridingly confident about their work. Their conversations contributed to the construction of their masculinity through the postulation of images of themselves which contrasted with those of the girls: images of themselves as creative, imaginative, experimental, images which have been painted by teachers' questionnaire responses and pupils' conversations in so many vivid colours in this chapter as well as previous ones. Instead of feeling pride in *themselves* such as the girls indicate, when boys think their compositions are good, it is because they think they sound good; it is the composition that is good. For girls, it is the expression of self; it is referred back to the girl. Instead of open pride, boys exude confidence. Girls' pride is bound up with feeling, self-expression; boys' confidence eschews the need for pride.

This lack of confidence on the part of girls and its possession on the part of boys are not necessarily authentic 'truths' about the pupils' psychology. They are better understood as discursive constructions, part of the currency through the likes of which we all construct our gender-identities. I by no means wish to argue that girls are always quivering with anxiety, or that boys are unfailingly brazen when presenting their work. But what I do wish to suggest is that girls and boys do not put either their negative or their positive attitudes towards composition into discourse in the same way as each other. When we speak of ourselves, we contribute to the over-arching discourse of our society, a discourse which helps us to define ourselves and to affirm our identity. Gender identity is afforded with reference to musical composition not by any 'real' lack or presence of confidence, of autonomy, of creative spark, but by the putting-into-discourse of these attributes or their lack.

Partly because of their discursive construction, femininity and masculinity are spaces into which girls and boys can cross. Music is one of the most readily available vessels in which to effect such a crossing into the gendered territory of the other. This was illustrated by one of the boys I interviewed: Adam, the trumpeter. We have seen that, unlike the other boys, he was immersed solely in classical music, he was an exceptionally advanced performer, and he was not terribly keen on composition, finding it difficult to '[get] a tune in [his] head which isn't already known . . . ' (p. 206 above). He also expressed uncertainty about having his compositions performed. The Head of Music described his work thus:

I think if you talk to Adam Wilson, who's the trumpeter, he's had a very sort of formal upbringing in music, and he's been much more traditional in his approach. You know, he's done everything a little bit like the old system, very much based on his theory lessons and things like that . . . He's a brilliant performer, but his compositions are a little bit contrived, you know? . . . whereas the 'lads' have tended to be much more doing things like rock bands and their own stuff, where they're composing anyway, so they improvise and are much freer in their whole approach to music, and in many ways they're not so restricted by the sort of formal [trails off].

Boys such as Adam challenge and cross the musically delineated divide between anti-conformist, innovative masculinity and conservative, uncreative femininity. The fact that he was a 'brilliant' performer meant that he was able to distract listeners and observers away from the delineations of his performance and onto the inherent meanings. This will have helped him to ride what otherwise, in the context of the school, would risk being taken for 'feminine characteristics', for effeminacy, for being cissy, and all the other derogatory labels which we have seen applied to such practices.[9]

As for girls who cross the divide, I believe that I did not come across any signs of this in my interviews; and no teachers indicated any such signs in their questionnaire responses. This does not mean that none of the thousands of girls attending the seventy-eight questionnaire schools or the two case-study schools ever crossed into symbolically masculine compositional territory or composed original music. It means that no one responding to my questions articulated such a crossing or such a compositional achievement. I too can think of only one girl who has ever struck me as displaying 'masculine' compositional traits, and whose approach to composition seemed to challenge the symbolic threat to femininity posed by the masculine delineation of music. She was a pupil in a school where I used to

[9] Again the issue of homosexuality and the symbolic space provided for homosexuals by music, pitted against the normalisation of heterosexuality by music, is brought to mind. See Brett, Thomas and Wood (1994), Gill (1994) on homosexuality in music. Also see Kemp (1982) on androgynous personality traits among musicians; and J. Halstead (1995, Chapter 2, esp. pp. 94ff) on crossing gender-stereotyping with reference to music. On girls and boys crossing gender-roles in schools, see Thorne (1993).

teach, and I can only say that she composed music which, in the context of that school, was original and spontaneous; it was full of youthful joy, composed without using notation; she performed it herself in front of the whole school, and she did so with prowess and to acclaim.[10]

I have argued that a discursively constituted lack of confidence or creativity in girls coalesces with the masculine delineation of music, and feeds into the experience of composing or improvising music, in so powerful and threatening a way as to imbue girls' musical experience itself with the sense of ambiguity and even alienation that arises from negativity in one's relation to delineations. Even when girls are positive towards their compositions, this positivity is expressed as a feeling, an emotion, a revealing of self. This, I wish to suggest, is symbolic of the revealing of femininity by the fact of composition, the exposure of femininity against the unexamined assumption of masculinity. For boys, the opposite occurs, as they find themselves reflected back at themselves from their own music, in which the masculine delineation affirms their identity, connects with them as individual gendered beings, all the while unnoticed and unremarked. Girls and boys thus constitute themselves not only in their experience of the work of others but in their experience of their own work. Again, this does not mean that girls 'really' feel any less confident, or that boys 'really' feel more confident about composing and improvising or about the music they produce; nor is it to suggest that girls are really more proud and boys are in any way less pleased with their work. But what I do wish to suggest is that girls' and boys' attitudes, and the attitudes of us all as composers or improvisers, are constructed as lacking in confidence or confident, proud or unconcerned, self-expressive or rational, conformist or deviant, conservative or creative, through the gendered discourse surrounding musical practices: this attitude then turns around to become a delineation of the music that we compose or improvise, so that the music itself finally constitutes such aspects of our gendered identities for us.

The masculine delineation of music and the gender politics of music in schools

Even in the face of boys' explicitly acknowledged lack of interest or hard work, they are nonetheless understood by teachers to be ultimately more musically successful than girls, or at least equal, in realms that burst the banks of composition alone.

---

[10] The girl, now a woman whose identity need not be suppressed, was Lorraine Spaine. Her work is also treated in Green (1990), where it is accompanied by a recording of one piece.

Which group is the most successful at playing?
- Both equally. Throughout the school this really does break down quite evenly. There are some variations from class – class but not I think necessarily a gender bias. But when I look at Yr 10 and 11 there is a difference, with generally the boys being more successful.

- Girls. There is a greater numerical take-up amongst girls and they tend to stick at it better.
  The good boys tend to achieve a higher standard.

- Girls on the whole 'stick' at an instrument, therefore overcoming the difficulties of learning and moving on to the more satisfying stage. Boys on the whole tend to give up much more easily.
  However those boys who *do* play instruments overall do so very successfully, whereas many of the girls, despite their work, are only average performers.

- Both equally . . . Here, at present the ratio of Girls/Boys learning to play is approximately 3 Girls to 1 Boy, but those going on to achieve success in the sense of standard achieved (grades etc.) provide a more equal balance of Boys and Girls.

Which group is the most successful at listening?
- Both equally. Boys tend not to listen carefully enough most of the time, but when they do can make more sense of what's happening more easily than the girls.

Which group is the most successful at notation?
- Both equally. Boys begin more slowly but soon catch up and often but not always become better.
- Both equally. Girls are neater, but not always technically correct. Boys are more untidy, but precise when work is legible.

Further comments
- . . . In the lower school groups (years 7–9) there is quite a balance in terms of music achievement – and gender is something I'm aware of when I'm looking at placements for instrumental tuition.
  But very definitely in Years 10 & 11 it is the boys who are the highest achievers – and there are considerably more boys in the Year 11 option group.
  The numbers balance out more in the Year 10 group, but again the boys are the highest achievers . . .

- There is much peer pressure amongst boys that music still has a 'cissy' stigma. Boys that do have the character to resist the pressure tend to achieve highly.
  Girls are more reliable and consistent but tend to fill the rank and file desks . . .

This understanding of teachers helps to unravel the conundrum that whereas girls appear to be so much more successful and numerous as musicians in schools, boys go on to become so much more successful and numerous in professional musical life. From what we have seen throughout Part II, for many boys conformity to school music and especially to the classical music that is the mainstay in most schools represents a symbolic threat to their masculinity. Only those who are exceptionally good at classical music, such as Adam in this chapter, whose control of inherent meanings can therefore override the gendered delineations of the music, are able to rebuff such a slur and cross into the delineated musical territory of femininity. The ultimate success of male classical performers is partially explained by this very fact: for it means that there is a process of self-selection taking place among boys at an early age. Only boys with exceptional talent or interest are likely to persevere, and they are concomitantly less likely to be 'de-selected' at a later stage. This is expressed by some of the teachers above as well as these below:

Which group is the most successful at performing?
- Both equally. By the time the pupils have opted for GCSE, they seem more sure of their future plans/needs, and want to succeed despite gender. Although more girls than boys *play* instruments, the boys who choose the course are usually the better players (i.e. better than the other boys) with more dedication, and so they tend to have gained C grades and above.
- Girls . . . We have a significant number of boys who don't care what others think – they do have to be quite strong. Don't know how to change the situation . . .

But it is not only this self-selection process that can throw light on the hegemony of men in music. At a deeper symbolic level, the endemic influence of the masculine cerebral and historical delineation of music, seen as a dual delineation as discussed in Chapter 4, moves beyond the bounds of the compositional arena whence it springs, to infiltrate and colour the relative position of boys and girls in the whole musical spectrum. Although girls are granted enormous success in a variety of musical practices, it is boys whom teachers perceive to be musically superior in an all-round way. This perception is made possible through boys' possession of those attributes of creative genius which are, by definition, denied to girls. The affirmation of femininity through singing and playing classical music, the interruption posed to femininity by popular music instrumental practices, and the threat to femininity which is inveigled by composition are all re-enacted in the school under the overriding sway of the masculine delineation.

SUMMARY

Teachers view the compositional abilities and attitudes of girls as conformist, conservative and wanting in those attributes of autonomy and creativity which are definitive aspects of the construction of genius as a male prerogative. Ironically, it is the very *fact* of girls' hard work that *proves their lack* of that attribute which history has made possessable only by males. But it is not only that girls are seen to lack the cerebral qualities that are necessary for genuine attainment: more than that, this lack *constitutes* their femininity.

this proof of the existence of the Other, girls' performance as difference, is a constant reassertion that 'woman' exists in her difference from and therefore deficiency in contrast to those rational powers of the mind that are a constituent of 'man'. (Walkerdine 1990, p. 62)

Boys, on the other hand, are understood to be inventive and creative, their possession of these traits being proven by the very perception of their anti-conformity and reluctance to work hard. Teachers' characterisations of girls and boys as composers reveal deeply entrenched assumptions, in which I would suggest we all share, not only concerning the nature of composition or that of gender but, moreover, arising from the transparent masculine delineation of music that imbues our musical experiences. The masculine delineation of music contributes to the perpetuation of the appearance of feminine musical conservatism and lack of talent, through its imposition of cerebral, creative masculinity as the normal and unquestionable backdrop to all musical experience, and the insertion of compositional feminine delineations as a threat to conventional patriarchal constructions of femininity.

Although pupils do not adopt the same terminology as their teachers, they nonetheless participate in the same over-arching discourse on gender and musical meaning with relation to composition. Girls express both a lack of confidence and a sense of pride in their composition, but in either case they operate within the bounds of the patriarchal discourse on femininity and the masculine compositional delineation of music: they oppose themselves to music theory, they declare that they cannot understand it, they attach significance instead to the expression of their feelings through composition, they find themselves subject to emotional responses concerning their composition which they cannot always control, they shrink from presenting themselves as composers, they characterise themselves as lacking in confidence, and they denigrate their own work or their own feelings about it. Contrastingly, boys present themselves as more positive about their composition, more confident, more carefree, less hard-working, less attentive to the paradigms provided by the teacher, yet more conversant with what is appropriate, less concerned with their feelings; and rather than expressing themselves through their work, they tend to position their work with positive reference to that of other people. In all these respects, girls and boys do not merely relate to composition; they experience their own music as a reflection and legitimation of their own gender identities.

Music's incorporation of gender does not reside in musical practices or musical meanings only, for gendered musical practices and meanings affect our consciousness and experience not only of music but, through music, of ourselves. Gendered musical practices and meanings participate in the construction of our very notions of masculinity and femininity. This means that we can use music to affirm and perpetuate our concepts of ourselves as gendered beings. Such a use of music lies behind many of the teachers' and pupils' perceptions of girls' and boys' musical abilities. Thus teachers may be right that girls are more interested in violins than drums or that they are conservative in their approach to composition; that boys are more interested in popular music than classical music or that they have a spontaneous approach to composition: what is crucial is that such judgements are combined with a consideration of girls' and boys' own musical experiences, which themselves cannot be separated from the influence of gendered musical meanings and the overriding sway of the masculine delineation of music. The school has a hand in the perpetuation of the gender politics of music, not only through gendered musical practices but also in the discourse surrounding music and, most fundamentally, in the very meanings and experience of music itself. Gendered musical meanings are not only handed down through history; they persist in the organisation of musical production and reception in present-day society at large, and they are also re-enacted daily in the life of the music classroom as a dynamic, microcosmic version of the wider society.

CHAPTER 9

The music curriculum and the possibilities for intervention

Until recently, the field of music education has ignored gender. Countless books and articles *about* music education, syllabuses and curriculum materials for use *in* music education, have been produced as though women have played barely a part in the history of music other than as the wives, mistresses, mothers or sisters of famous male musicians; as though the musical practices of girls and boys in schools were to all intents and purposes indistinguishable; and as though any differences in the educational value and availability of music for girls and for boys were wholly inconsequential. Not only such pragmatic issues but more ephemeral questions surrounding gendered musical meanings have also been unapologetically ignored by a field which has largely understood itself to be concerned with transmitting the supposedly autonomous and universal content of musical value. These observations are by no means intended to criticise my colleagues as though I were myself wholly exonerated. My earlier book (1988) presented an analysis of the interpenetration of aesthetic ideology and musical meaning in the discourse of music education. Even though I have always considered myself a feminist, I ruled out any consideration of gender in that book because I could not at the time see how I could relate it to a theory of musical meaning. Yet once one starts to enquire into some of the issues surrounding gender in music education, they become so compelling that such a refusal is no longer possible. Essentially what I have tried to do in the present book is to expand the purview of that earlier theory in order to bring it to bear upon gender. Like a *trompe l'œil*, first one sees no gender issues, then one sees them.

In Part II so far I have presented a picture of musical practices on one hand and musical meanings on the other as inseparably combining in classrooms to participate in the discursive reproduction of the gender politics of music. This would therefore seem to present a very bleak outlook for the role of music education. If, indeed, deeply entrenched gendered musical meanings are impinging in ways which reproduce the historical precedents of men's and women's musical practices as defining characteristics of gender, then there would not seem to be a great deal that the school can do to intervene. Any reorganisation of girls' and boys' musical practices within the school, or of women's and men's musical practices in the society at large, would seem to be blocked by the need for the redefinition of musical meaning itself. However, the fact of this blockage is not the end of the story. Gender studies related to education have burgeoned over the last two or three decades, and now form a major field of enquiry covering sociological, psychological and philosophical issues as well as subject-specific factors operating in different curriculum areas from science to sport (see Chapter 6, note 2, p. 144 above). Although music was not on the agenda to begin with, music educators gradually began to take an interest in gender during the seventies, and their resulting work has increasingly made inroads within music education studies.[1] In this chapter I will discuss some of the pragmatic concerns which have marked gender studies in music education, relate these to the arguments surrounding gendered musical meaning that have been discussed in previous chapters, and offer some perspectives concerning the potential and relevance of education as an interventionary force in the reproduction of the gender politics of music.

---

[1] English-language research concerning gender and music education began first in North America, growing rapidly during the 1990s. See Trollinger (1994) for a helpful review of the research from 1968 to 1992; Porter and Abeles (1978) and Abeles and Porter (1979) for early empirical work on girls' and boys' choices of instruments; Lamb (1987), (1991a), Jezic and Binder (1987), Koza (1992), (1994a) for early text-analyses; and Lamb (1991b), (1993), (1994a), (1994b), (1996) for feminist critique. In Britain isolated explorations began to appear in the eighties, and interest has grown ever since. See Kemp (1982), Cant (1990b) for early forays. Four recent journal issues have been devoted to gender and music education. These are: *Music Educators' Journal*, 78/7 (1992); *Quarterly Journal of Music Teaching and Learning*, 4/4 and 5/1, (1993–4); *British Journal of Music Education*, 10/3 (1993); and *Philosophy of Music Education Review*, 2/3 (1994). The first British conference on gender and music education took place in March 1992, organised jointly by Women in Music and Bristol University; and an international conference on music, gender and pedagogics took place at the University of Gothenburg, April 1996. There are active Music, Gender and Education networks such as GRIME (Gender Research in Music Education) in North America, and the WIM (Women in Music) Education sub-committee in Britain. Work is also on-going in Australia (thanks to Maree MacMillan for contacting me about this), and New Zealand, for which see Harper (1986) and, no doubt, in many other countries too. A résumé of some of the arguments put forward in this chapter is available in Green (1996).

GENDER AND THE MUSIC CURRICULUM: A PRAGMATIC VIEW

Curriculum content: the balance of men and women

The under-representation, or more often total neglect, of women musicians in text-books and other curriculum materials has been a subject of concern to many music teachers in schools and musicologists in higher education.[2] It is believed that standard texts misrepresent the historical and contemporary make-up of the musical world, sending the 'wrong' messages to girls and women students, and perpetuating a misleading appearance that the professional musical sphere in particular is largely unavailable to them. At present publishers are beginning to take an interest in alternative curriculum materials, and some teachers and lecturers are actively developing their own.[3] There are several possible alternative strategies regarding the content of such materials, of which I would like to mention three that together provide a representative span.

First, as an extreme position, alternative curriculum materials could positively discriminate in favour of women's musical practices, placing greater emphasis on women whilst representing men in a lesser capacity. This would offer a counter to the exclusive emphasis on men's practices which marks standard texts. But, at the same time, like them it would give a misleading appearance, making it seem that more women have taken part in a greater variety of musical practices than is factually justifiable from any vantage-point.

Secondly, curriculum materials could focus solely on women in music, with the intention that they be used alongside standard texts on men in music. Texts such as the many compensatory histories that I have cited throughout Part I or school books for secondary pupils such as Aelwyn

---

[2] The rather oddly termed practice of 'text-analysis' involves counting up e.g. the numbers of men and women mentioned, the roles in which they are portrayed, etc. For an early survey of text-analyses in gender and music education curriculum materials, see Pucciani (1983). For text-analyses themselves, see Lamb (1987), (1991a), Jezic and Binder (1987), Koza (1992), (1994). The standard texts of music history are so lacking in any mention of women as to make any analysis of them, such as Jezic and Binder's, starkly revealing.

[3] See Lamb (1991a, pp. 692–702) for details of a curriculum materials project designed for use in schools; and Wilkins and Askew (1993) for a project at university level. The London-based Women in Music (WIM) Archive and Resource Centre, and the WIM Education sub-committee are developing materials for use in schools. See S. Fuller (1994b), Women in Music (n.d.). A very useful source is Brisco's (1987) anthology of music by women. See Zaimont et al. (1991) for extensive information on publications, recordings and other materials. In Britain, the Birmingham-based Women's Revolutions Per Minute (WRPM) is a helpful resource-centre.

Pugh's *Women in Music* (1992) are already available. But this option also contains a disadvantage, for however well written such publications are, their authors are abundantly aware that they suffer from the marginal-isation which has been forced upon them by the need to present their subject-matter in a separate text to begin with. This marginalisation then serves to perpetuate, rather than challenge, the position women have occupied in the history of music for several hundred years.

Thirdly, curriculum materials could give a factually balanced picture of the achievements of both men and women throughout the history of music up to the present day, showing that women musicians have always been active, although with restrictions. Koza (1992) analysed a number of texts in which attempts had been made to address what she terms 'equity issues', focussing on their pictorial content. She was concerned that in spite of their gender-awareness, they portrayed men and women unevenly. Texts such as these, she argues, will ultimately transmit con-flicting messages.

While attempting to show that girls and women are free to pursue whatever career they wish, including becoming composers or conductors, the books simultaneously send the message that the musical world is predominantly a male world in which some women participate, to a greater or lesser degree, depending on the activity in question. Most teachers would agree that the latter message is inappropriate and counterproductive. (1992, p. 32)

The problem of sending conflicting messages is genuine, but it is not restricted to texts: it is a contradiction of contemporary musical life, which does indeed, as I have argued, offer every musical opportunity to girls in schools, whilst at the same time channelling them into the rather narrower tracks of their foremothers. I therefore believe that women musicians should be included in texts, precisely in such a way that their minority status in most musical fields, or their tendency to be concen-trated in a few musical practices, are made manifest. Ideally, but not nec-essarily, these restrictions would moreover be examined as topics in themselves, as integral parts of a text's presentation, of a teacher's han-dling of class discussion, or of further work. The perpetuation of gen-dered musical practices is not something that we can avoid or something that we should play down, but rather something that we can come to recognise and understand as an influential aspect of our music history and of ourselves as musicians, listeners, teachers and learners. Whilst the first option, of developing misleading texts, is clearly out of the question, the second option, of using texts that focus on women alongside stan-dard texts, does provide not an end in itself so much as a necessary and important step *towards* a different position for the future. This future position would be represented by the third option.

Curriculum content: music and words

Not only the balance of men and women musicians represented in the curriculum but also the characterisations of masculinity and femininity carried by the linguistic or otherwise referential aspects of musical works themselves must come under scrutiny. Particularly pertinent here is music that is programmatic or that is set to words: mainly operas, liturgical or other sacred settings, and songs in styles ranging from classical music to folk, jazz and popular music from all around the world, including nursery rhymes and playground songs. For example, the contemporary critiques of gender-constructions in central icons of the canon such as operas by Mozart or Bizet may cause some teachers to re-inspect their presentation of such works.[4] With reference to children's music, in the lyrics of the many collections of songs used by primary school teachers in Britain, women are both seriously under-represented and stereotypically portrayed in menial, domestic or romantic roles, in contrast to men, who are numerously represented through a great variety of active personae.[5]

Most teachers and lecturers would presumably refuse to teach music representing topics or possessing lyrics that they thought were prejudicial or symbolically violent towards any social grouping. But it is not always easy to decide which music is so. Upheaval and misunderstanding can arise between groups who interpret the symbolic import of operas or other works in different ways. An example of the pragmatic consequences of this occurred recently in Liverpool with reference to racial issues, when a planned collaborative community performance of Gershwin's *Porgy and Bess* by the Royal Liverpool Philharmonic Society was blocked by the Liverpool Anti-Racist and Community Arts Association (Horn 1994). Again with reference to race, I was once asked by a worried Head of Music in a school whether a student who was on teaching practice there had received any advice on equal opportunities.

---

[4] See for example Ford (1991) on *Così*, McClary (1991), (1992) on *Carmen*, Abbate (1991), (1993) on various operas, Bradby (1990), (1992) on popular lyrics; and Chapter 5, notes 2 and 3, pp. 116 and 117.

[5] The full scale of this, and its extraordinary anachronism in an age of equal opportunities policies in schools, has been brought home to me by research on children's song-books in primary school usage currently being undertaken by Heather Brewer at the London University Institute of Education. See Brewer (1995).

The reason for the question was that the student had used Debussy's 'Golliwogg's Cakewalk' in class, which was deemed to have a racist title.

Whether with reference to an opera or a nursery rhyme, teachers and lecturers cannot throw out the materials they already possess, for economic reasons, nor can they merely disregard a vast proportion of music from either the past or the present in the hope that whatever problems its lyrics present will go away. Rather, we can introduce even problematic pieces, not in all circumstances but with sensitivity to whatever cultural or political situation we are in; and we can re-examine them to gain a deeper understanding of the ways in which they symbolise gender, race or other constructions of difference through the use of linguistic or programmatic representation, to raise awareness in ourselves and our pupils or students, and to stretch horizons. Where programmes, libretti or lyrics cause concern, very often we can legitimately bring these concerns into our courses as cross-curricular themes, points of discussion, or the starting-point of projects, creative work or dissertations.

Curriculum content: the role of the canon

Traditionally music education, both in schools and in higher education, has assumed and helped to perpetuate a canon of 'masterworks'. At its most rarefied level the canon includes only a few works by a handful of great Western composers. At a more general level the canon is represented by a large number of pieces of classical music, very loosely defined. Citron's (1993) wide-ranging discussion covers a number of social influences on the formation of the canon. These include, for example, the fact that in order to enter the canon, music must have been published, reviewed or otherwise publicly recorded and distributed, or the fact that canonisation relies on a linear view of musical development according to principles of innovation. Factors such as these, she argues, mean that men's work has been more likely to be canonised than women's, for reasons concerning men's and women's social and historical positions and opportunities rather than their ability as composers or the quality of their compositions. But such social determinants have been concealed because the greatness of the canon is held to be above social or historical considerations.

She reviews various alternative bases for the valuation of music, revolving around the contextualisation of music within the era and place whence it sprang, in relation to the social position and identity of its producer. With reference to gender, she suggests, such alternative bases require the re-definition of several current assumptions, of which I wish to mention three. First, she questions the validity of accepted historical periodisation. For example the Renaissance has long been hailed as a time of artistic and scientific expansion and development. This may be true for men's work, she argues, but for women the Renaissance was an era of increasing oppression and restriction. Dividing history up according to men's lives may serve to conceal developments in women's lives.[6] Secondly, she suggests that the relative value attached to various genres as well as recognised genre-boundaries themselves require re-definition. For example the symphony, a form predominantly composed by men, has very high canonic status, whereas the monophonic folk lullaby, normally sung and passed on by women, has virtually no canonic status at all. Any re-evaluation of genres will include re-examining unnamed and unwritten traditions, which will impinge on women's music such as lullabies, nursery rhymes and various types of folk, ritual and domestic music. Thirdly, she argues that the individualist concept of the great composer must be re-examined, allowing in its place a more positive evaluation of collective achievement, which again is more inclusive of women's contributions.[7]

Battersby (1989, pp. 10–11, 154–61) argues that feminists should not throw out the term genius and, by extension, the idea of the great composer and the canon, but that such concepts should be appropriated and redefined in order to include women. Women artists have been concealed from history, she says, because they have been viewed from a perspective of Otherness, as not fully individual. But their work can be constructed into individual *œuvres* and situated within traditions of female creativity.

These traditions will be different from the traditions of male achievement, because males did not have to confront the rhetoric of sexual exclusion each time they tried to create. In calling a woman a 'genius', feminist critics (collectively) reconstruct history from the point of view of their own value scheme. (1989, pp. 10–11)

Citron counters Battersby's plea for feminists to appropriate the term genius, on the grounds that the term will inevitably continue to be associated with the concept of the transcendent individual, contrasted with her preference for a 'de-centered subject' (1993, pp. 225–6). But, with

---

[6] See esp. Citron (1993, pp. 210–19). The historical work of Joan Kelly (1984) has been seminal in the development of this debate.

[7] On women's musical traditions see Marshall (1993b). On the great composer, also see Tick (1986), Battersby (1989).

Battersby, she does support the construction of alternative evaluations of women's work.

The music curriculum tends to reiterate the canon, not only in higher education but even, although to a lesser degree, in the primary sector: a fact of which the British government recently demonstrated a keen awareness through its attempts to reinstate the great masters of Western music in the National Curriculum from ages five to fourteen.[8] However, the younger the age-range of pupils, the less canonic the curriculum is likely to be. Secondary teachers and lecturers will find far more women's works, such as the many compositions and arrangements of folk songs for children by composers such as Ruth Seeger and Grace Williams, or women's genres, such as lullabies, in materials for the early years than in those for their own students.[9] Such curriculum materials do represent women's work and for that reason make a refreshing change; but at the same time it must be acknowledged that this in itself cannot exonerate them from critique. First, as I have already mentioned, their representational content can be very far from interventionary. The lyrics of folk music and music for young children are potentially just as capable of perpetrating narrow perspectives, including nationalism, racism and sexism, as are the lyrics or libretti of the more rarefied contents of the university sector. Secondly, as I have argued in Chapter 2, women have for a long time been recognised for their role as music educators in both professional and mothering capacities, a role whose enabling characteristics are affirmative of traditional definitions of femininity. Whilst the importance and power of this role can and must be celebrated, its interventionary possibilities are bound up in very complex ways with the perpetuation of conventional, patriarchal constructions of femininity.

Popular music, jazz and many other musical styles from all around the world, which have only quite recently entered the formal educational scene, also represent new possibilities for challenging the hegemony of the classical canon. But in many ways, canonic principles continue to operate in non-classical music: a fact which can be discerned for example in the existence of a fast-expanding critical literature on popular music, in the marketing of a search for authenticity as demonstrated by the valorisation of 'classic rock', or in the increasingly panoramic historical purview which the sheer durability (and the CD re-issue market) of so much popular music is now affording. Canon-formation in

---

[8] For analyses of the cultural politics involved in the inauguration of the National Curriculum for Music in Britain, see Swanwick (1992), Shepherd and Vulliamy (1994), Gammon (forthcoming).

[9] On Seeger see Gaume (1986); on Williams, Jill Halstead (1995, p. 178), Boyd (1980).

popular music occurs with particularly detrimental consequences for girls in schools. As we have seen, many girls are already excluded or discouraged from practising popular music, because its delineations within the school context either conflict with conventional constructions of femininity or suggest an overwhelming masculinity.

Those teachers and lecturers who wish to include women's work in their courses are faced with a variety of choices about how they employ the canon: whether to 'infiltrate' the existing canon by including the works of individual women in their teaching; whether to seek alternative standards by which to judge women's work so as to present a separate women's canon alongside that of men; or whether to attempt to dismantle any concept of canon at all by purposefully excluding the 'great masterworks', however those are defined. But in practice, all three strategies are interrelated, and none would be possible without to some extent involving the others. It is only by allowing individual women's work to enter into our courses that canonic presuppositions can begin to be revealed as having been biased towards men; it is only by re-evaluating women's contributions within the paradigms of an alternative canon that women's work can be adequately represented; and at the same time both these practices must involve dismantling the appearance that musical greatness is an ahistorical, natural phenomenon, an appearance which has been an intrinsic part of the very notion of canon.

The tendency towards canonicity is integral to any systematised form of education in a complex society. It is only as a part of canon-formation that most music has ever got as far as entering any curriculum in the first place, and without some kind of canon we would hardly have any music curriculum at all. In our fervour to be aware of the presuppositions on the basis of which a canon comes into being, and in our desire to consider the historical context of the work and the social class, ethnicity or gender of the author, we must not go too far and forget to listen to the works themselves. If works of art have no life of their own whatsoever, then they can be nothing more than idealised manifestations of our imagination, devoid of qualities. To deny the last shred of autonomy to music would be as ridiculous as to deny its historical context: it is surely in the very tension between these that what we call 'art' is born.

It would be madness to suggest re-writing music history in order to present an *equal* balance of men and women musicians or of their work. In the teaching of music history, given the time and resource restrictions that dog all formal teaching, it is not merely understandable but entirely pertinent to concentrate on canonic works. But there are two vital qualifications to this. First, we do not need to present the canon unquestion-ingly as though its formation was entirely autonomous from the kinds of social and historical conditions to which Citron and Battersby point. On the contrary, teachers and lecturers might explicitly weigh up the social context of the production and reception of the music which they use, as an influence upon its received musical value. These conditions can at the very least be allowed to surface in the presentation of works; and at the most they may form a focus of enquiry in themselves.

Secondly, we might benefit from asking ourselves precisely what, in each case, we are using a particular piece of music *for*. Presenting music which is at the forefront of innovation and historical development can by no means be the only aim and object of anyone's teaching. From the university to the nursery, in the teaching of stylistic markers, conven-tional figurations, instrumentation, instruments of the orchestra, music and mood, music and narrative, music and movement, or in the produc-tion and reception of music through pastiche composition, analysis, structured listening, kinaesthetics, social history, aesthetics – in all such cases, we must surely be open to the possibility that a piano trio by Clara Schumann might be as capable of demonstrating characteristic Romantic piano writing as one by her husband; that the early seventeenth-century solo song could be just as well exemplified through a piece by Francesca Caccini as through one by her father; that Ruth Seeger's use of note-clusters could provide as pertinent an example of this technique as any; or that women's involvement in the salon is worth men-tioning as a factor in the organisation of nineteenth-century music. Likewise we can illustrate many teaching points in popular music, folk or jazz through examples drawn from women's music; and the possibilities begin to seem quite endless.[10] Even though scores, recordings and other materials including such works may still be unavailable in many institu-tions, it is only if music educators as well as listeners demand them that publishers and recording companies will ever make them more accessible.

Assessment

The field of assessment with reference to gender in music education pro-vides, so far as I know at the time of writing, an unexploited goldmine for research enquiries. Educationalists working on assessment in other

---

[10] See Lamb (1991a, pp. 692–702) for some curriculum materials using women's music along these lines.

subjects have found that girls and boys respond differently to test questions, for example according to whether the wording of the question
implies a masculine or a feminine pastime. Caroline Gipps illustrated
how this can happen in mathematics and science.[11] Pupils taking part in
an experiment were asked one question about how much water was
absorbed by a set of paper towels, and another question about how
many nuts and bolts were present in a tool-box. There was also a question about how many hours' work were completed by a secretary. Boys'
and girls' results were significantly different, the boys getting the answers
to nuts and bolts correct, the girls those to paper towels and secretaries.
There is work crying out to be done in music here, some of which could
be carried out experimentally.

For example, pupils could be asked formal test questions, in a replication of the sort of listening test to which they might already be accustomed in any particular school, or one similar to the listening test of the
GCSE. Questions might relate to music played by different instruments,
or to different musical styles or particular pieces which, to adopt the
terms I have suggested in this book, are particularly affirmative, interruptive or threatening for femininity. It would be interesting to see
whether any significant differences according to gender would surface in
the responses. Pupils could also be played examples of music composed
or improvised by women and examples of music by men, making it clear
which was which, in an attempt to find out whether pupils would evaluate the music according to principles which I have dubbed the masculine
delineation of music. Listening is a very private activity. Conducting
small experiments such as these would represent one way in which to 'get
inside' the gendered listening experiences of boys and girls.[12]

In previous chapters of Part II, I have illustrated the dramatic differences that are discernible between girls' and boys' performance and
composition practices in schools. I argued that there is a need to overcome a loss of confidence for a girl in musical realms where her feminin-

---

[11] The following information was conveyed in a lecture given by Caroline Gipps to Post-Graduate
Certificate in Education students at the London University Institute of Education in 1992. She
discusses other related work in (1990, p. 56) although without mentioning these particular examples.

[12] See Tagg (1990) for an illuminating project which reveals listeners' verbal and visual associations
with television music. One of the most overwhelming areas, which was completely unsolicited,
concerned the association of masculinity and femininity with particular types of music. The
content of the associations was very much in line with gendered delineations as discussed in this
book, the difference being that the television associations were related to general contexts without
specific reference to the gender of the performer or composer. Work of this nature could usefully
be extended to the school situation and the responses of girls and boys to music used in tests.

ity is interrupted or threatened, and likewise that there is a need to over-come taunts which are faced by a boy who joins in musical practices that affirm femininity. Such factors must adversely affect the development and manifestation of pupils' abilities. Conversely, the affirmation of femininity that offers itself to the girl in the choir, the machismo that is delineated for the boy on the drum-kit, or the celebration of self afforded to the boy composer in listening to his own work – such experi-ences must help in the positive self-fulfilment of their capacities. When we assess what we think is a fair representation of pupils' musical abil-ities, we may be more accurately assessing a gendered musical ability that is limited and misleading, an ability straitjacketed by pupils' sense of the need to conform to gendered musical practices, and by pupils' self-fulfilment of gendered musical delineations.

It is not just that pupils are constrained in their capacities to reveal their musical abilities, but also that teachers' judgements are affected by our knowledge of a pupil's gender. As revealed in Chapter 8, even though girls are portrayed as overwhelmingly more committed and active in school music than boys, teachers nonetheless find girls to be ulti-mately less successful as musicians. When we hear a boy take up a Schubert melody on a violin, we understand that he is fighting potential taunts, we view him in the light of his commitment to music, and we are likely to be well-disposed towards him. This predisposition will enter the delineations of his performance, inclining us to pay serious attention to his manipulation of inherent meanings, and even to overlook errors, which can anyway be taken as evidence of creative spontaneity. When we hear a girl embellish a funk riff on an electric bass, we understand that she too is stepping out of her conformist, affirmatively feminine dis-cursive position; but unlike the boy, she presents a challenge, perhaps a challenge to ourselves, to the school, to convention, or to her own sense of gendered identity. I have suggested that the symbolic import of the delineations which will surround her performance are likely to predis-pose us in such a way as to deafen us towards, or even prejudice us against, her handling of the inherent meanings of the music that she performs.

In particular, teachers in my survey portrayed girls' and boys' compositional abilities very differently, emphasising the perceived super-ior creativity of boys in comparison to the inferior, rule-bound conform-ism of girls. Pupils themselves also adopted conventional constructions of gender in their own portrayals of their compositional capacities and inclinations. Boys presented themselves as confident and talented without the aid of hard work, able to find themselves positively reflected in the music they had composed. Girls tended to shy away from such self-presentation, freely admitted their hard-working conformity to the teachers' paradigms, and were reluctant to position themselves in the role of the composer. How can we really know whether we are allowing our *preconceptions* or our *expectations* of boys' and girls' compositions to affect our judgement? Or whether boys and girls themselves are fulfilling not so much some impossible natural musical leanings as their own expectations of themselves, constructed in accordance with age-old, restrictive and wholly unimaginative gender stereotypes? In the area of composition, where the masculine cerebral delineation of music has so powerful and so well-concealed an influence, I think it is particularly difficult to know whether we are judging what we think we are judging. Only teachers' self-awareness and a profound sensitivity in interacting with pupils' existing tacit awareness of gender issues and in introducing pupils to the potential power and depth of gendered musical meanings can ever intervene in such problems.

Role-models

Many of the teachers who responded to my questionnaire mentioned that they considered the sex of the teacher to act as a role-model in influencing the pupils' perceptions of musical practices.[13] With reference to performance, a number of teachers commented that pupils follow or are in some way influenced by role-models provided by the teachers themselves, by other musicians within the school or community, or by rock stars in the case of boys. Here is a sample out of fifteen such comments:

Which group is most successful at playing?
– Both equally . . . (2) A new resource (brass instruments) has appeared and been seized upon by boys, following a recent concert by an all-male brass quintet . . . (3) Confidence of boys to imitate or identify with male-only music staff.

Which group is most successful at singing?
– Girls. Boys . . . lack role models.

Further comments
– . . . I'm pleased to note that quite a few girls are now opting for sax & keyboards, you will have noticed that those two are taught by ladies . . .

---

[13] I was not looking for any grounds on which to suggest that teachers' own sex affected the ways in which they expressed their attitudes towards their pupils or towards gender issues. However, further work on this issue and on the question of teacher role-models in general could be very interesting.

- ... I have built up the number of boys playing clarinet, though only one plays flute – despite my persuading a popular male PE teacher to play in the Concert Band! ...

- I feel, as a male teacher, very conscious of the difficulty some (or all?) girls have in relating to music. There are a few able girls for whom this obstacle is overcome, but mostly I am aware that the girls would benefit from more contact with female musicians.

- ... I've always asked for male students [i.e. student-teachers] since the pupils only see a woman teaching the subject otherwise.

Some of the older pupils whom I interviewed also noted the importance of role-models for girls. For example:

Three Year 10 GCSE boys (age 14–15):
- Yeah they [girls] are into popular music a lot more than we are, but they don't play it and they usually play classical music.
- LG: Do you think there are any reasons for this that you can put your finger on?
- No one to look up to. There's not many women rock bands.
- And that's a shame really.
- And there's not many women jazz musicians.
- I think they should encourage women to make their own rock band because, I mean it'd be a nice change to see a woman, and after a couple of men, and a girls' rock band, when you hear the music, that'd be nice to hear one day. But I never heard a girls' band. I never heard of a girls' rock band.
- It's not something you can impose on them.
- I mean, I've seen them play, but two months later, oh well they're gone, sort of.

A growing body of empirical work supports the intuitive suppositions of the teachers and pupils above. In the USA Abeles and Porter (1979) (also Porter and Abeles (1978)) measured girls' and boys' choices of instrument, finding that girls in the top end of the junior school tended to opt for those instruments which were associated with femininity, the same instruments that we have seen are also associated with femininity in English schools today. Boys, on the other hand, opted for masculine-associated instruments.[14] Rosemary Bruce (Bruce and Kemp 1993) did some experimental research to find out whether such choices could be affected by the sex of a live role-model playing the instrument. She organised concert-demonstrations of woodwind, brass and stringed orchestral instruments, played by men and women to mixed groups of

[14] See Griswold and Chroback (1981) for an extension of the Abeles and Porter work; and Delzell and Leppla (1992), Fortney, Boyle and DeCarb (1993) for more recent studies.

primary school children. Each concert was given twice, to a different audience, switching round the sex of the players. At the end of each demonstration the children were asked to choose one instrument to look at. The researcher counted how many pupils of each sex moved towards which instrument. She found that the sex of the player appeared to have a striking effect on the sex of the children who went towards that instrument. 'For example, 23.5 per cent of girls looked at the trombone when it was demonstrated by a woman, but only 1.5 per cent did so when the player was male. A similar example can be found in the boys' choice of the flute' (1993, p. 125). Although the pupils' spontaneous choices may not reflect any enduring qualities in the face of the gendered meaning of music as it operates in their lives as a whole, this is clearly a provocative area in which further work could be beneficial.

There is evidence that many successful contemporary women composers have observed and regretted the lack of role-models provided in their own music education.[15] Although teachers did stress the role-model of the performer, this is to be contrasted with a relative lack of emphasis or an ambivalence apparently attached to the role-model figure of the composer. Only two teachers volunteered the unmitigated opinion that role-models are important in composition:

Which group is most successful at composing?
– Both equally. Again, creativity must express itself, but I have noticed that girls have only recently come forward as composers – (In the last four years or so). This is undoubtedly due to the influence of innovators like Kate Bush.
– Both equally. Given lots of scope to develop their performing skills both boys and girls respond extremely well to the composing element . . . Plus the opportunity to work with local composers has enhanced youngsters' work. I think also that the youngsters can relate this to the world of work and see a practical application because of use of Artists in Residence.

Only one teacher had a conscience about not using any female composers:

Which group prefers to engage in classical music(s)?
– Both equally. Both boys & girls respond well to the 'diet' they are given e.g. Bolero, Sorcerer's Apprentice, Greensleeves, Rite of Spring (perhaps I ought to consider some *female* composers!)

And one teacher was aware of the over-representation of male composers in the history books, but did not regard this as a problem:

[15] See Barkin's (1980), (1982) survey of contemporary, mainly North American, women composers; also Jill Halstead (1995).

Which group is most successful at composing?
- Both equally. Composing in the classroom is a relatively recent classroom activity (as compared with appreciation/performance opportunities) – presented on an equal opportunity basis – and as such does not suffer from the fact that historically 'known' composers are male dominated.

None of the pupils mentioned any lack of female role-models in composition, and even when I asked them whether there were any differences between boys' and girls' attitudes and aptitudes in composition, this obvious historical point never emerged. The normality and ubiquity, the invisibility and the unquestionability, of the masculine delineation of music are again proven by the fact that the lack of women composers remains barely remarked by teachers and thoroughly ignored by pupils. Most music teachers would readily agree with the teacher cited immediately above that composing as a general classroom activity is far newer than listening and even playing. Therefore there is not an entrenched way of presenting composing to pupils; new materials are being developed at a rapid rate; and there is space for intervention here before conventionally rooted habits become established.

Equality of access

No teachers in my survey mentioned any worries about providing access to music education for girls. This is hardly surprising since, as we have seen, girls are understood to take full advantage of what is on offer both in the general music curriculum and in the extended curriculum. When girls do not do so, this fact goes unremarked. Contrastingly, a few teachers did express concern that boys were not experiencing equality of access to music education, and several teachers suggested that boys are in need of remedial help. Here are three explicit expressions of this:

Further comments
- More girls than boys participate in Concerts and musical activities . . . It is a problem we have tried to address. In the end music is a voluntary activity and a teacher can only encourage boys to participate. I would be glad to hear any suggestions as to how to get more boys involved.
- . . . The important thing, I feel, is that all pupils enjoy music and that (boys in particular) feel comfortable and 'normal' doing music. (In my day boys who did music were considered very strange!) The opportunity is there for everyone to get something out of music at whatever level they are able to achieve . . .

Which group is the most successful at singing?
–　Girls. Very few boys make an attempt to sing . . . I feel that I don't have
　enough training to be able to overcome this. Persuasive measures or
　boosting confidence don't solve the problem.

Providing genuine opportunities and encouragement for pupils to cross
over into the gendered musical territory of the other would seem to be
an obvious step for any teacher committed to gender-equality in music.
Such opportunities are already increasingly being provided by the
content of the curriculum itself. For example, the growing number of
boys opting for music at age fourteen (GCSE) is clearly an indication of a
positive response to the changing content of the syllabus.[16] Boys'
increased interest, although sparked perhaps by the entrance of technology and popular music into the curriculum, may well expand, finding
ways in which to carry some of the masculine delineations from those
areas over into the realm of classical music. On the other hand, access to
popular music and jazz has vastly improved for girls in recent years.
Until now, these musical styles have reproduced themselves as male bastions, not only without the aid of any formal educational mechanism at
all but by virtue of their very exclusion from education, an exclusion
which has indeed been a definitive part of their anti-conformist delineations. These styles, or at any rate aspects of them somewhat denuded of
their masculine delineations by their institutionalisation, are now more
available to schoolgirls and women students than ever before.

　Curriculum content is certainly to this extent under the control of
teachers: but how can pupils be encouraged to take advantage of what is
provided? One possibility is to institute positive discrimination policies
in, for example, the allocation of instrumental tuition, instrument loan
or other resourcing. If equal numbers of boys and girls play the flute and
the drums, they then begin to provide positive role-models for each
other. Another possibility is to foster practical groups with crossed-over
roles, such as an all-boys' choir or a rock band in which the boys were
required to sing and the girls to play the instruments. Policies of this
nature are unlikely to do any harm. But at the same time no one should
be surprised if they are very difficult to implement, or if any benefits are
slow to manifest themselves. I have already suggested that offering girls
the chance to play the drums and compose with a synthesiser, or encouraging boys to join the choir and appreciate Schubert Lieder, will not

---

[16] Over the first four years of the GCSE the number of boys opting rose gradually from c. 10,500 to
　c. 13,500; whereas the number of girls rose from c. 19,500 to c. 21,500 in the first year then fell back
　to c. 20,000. Further details are available in Green (1993, p. 221).

necessarily match the 'whirlpool of desire' (Walkerdine 1990, cited above, p. 188) in which they are caught, as they invest their gender-identities in their musical practices and in the musical meanings that accompany those practices. It is again teachers' sensitivity to gender issues in music that must be the primary factor in effecting any enhancement of opportunity to engage in musical practices for girls and boys.

Single-sex and mixed-sex teaching

There has been some discussion about whether single-sex education as a whole is beneficial to either sex or both sexes.[17] Even within a mixed school, it is an issue whether students should work in single-sex groups. In many mixed schools, informal separatism occurs as a result of gender-identification in friendship groups, affecting class lessons particularly when small-group work is involved. Three teachers in my survey noted that girls' and boys' inclinations to work in single-sex groups were difficult to dislodge. We have also seen that the symbolic content of particular musical practices and particular music has its own way of segregating pupils, both in the classroom and in extra-curricular activities. In many schools, religious beliefs make separate musical practices a necessity. Two teachers commented upon this, one with reference to Orthodox Judaism, and the other with reference to Islam. For example:

Further comments
. . . Asian boys are allowed to do far more than girls anyway, pupils here are mainly from strict Muslim villages. I've just got 2 prs tabla, 2 dholaks, [?] bansery and harmonium. Particular interest from boys, but I have promised to teach single sex groups otherwise parents will not allow girls to participate . . .

Four teachers mentioned that they have successfully tried or are thinking of trying single-sex choral groups, in order to counter the disadvantage experienced by boys who are intimidated by what I have called the affirmative femininity of these activities. Only one teacher (the one cited immediately above) commented that she or he had purposely set up all-female groups, in order to give opportunities to girls.

Questions concerning the advantages and disadvantages of single-sex groupings are particularly pertinent with reference to those aspects of musical practice that involve students in working constructively together towards, for example, a performance, a group composition or an

---

[17] See e.g. Deem (1984). Findings suggest that single-sex education may enhance girls' achievement levels in some subjects.

improvisation. The gendered meaning of music is made poignant by the enactment of display when students are required to perform in front of each other. The following, not uncommon, scene occurred in a London comprehensive school I was visiting in 1991. I was talking to the (male) drum teacher (DT).

- LG: How many girls do you have doing drums?
- DT: Oh, quite a lot really.
- LG: I used to find girls were very keen to play the drums when I taught in [X school].
- DT: Yes, they're keen. Some of them are really good too. You get the coasters: the good ones won't come without their friend, so I give the friend something easy to do, like tap on the ride cymbal on two and four, or something like that, just to keep them coming.
- LG: Yes, I suppose it's not like other technology. Like the boys just now – did you see them – all swarming round the keyboards, playing; and the girls? Where were they? Gone!
- DT: Yes. But they won't play if a boy comes into the room. No way! They go [crouching] 'no! no!' They like drums because they get to do it on their own: no boys.

Some of the girls whom I interviewed also expressed a reticence to play certain instruments in front of boys. Bayton (1990) describes how the female popular instrumentalists with whom she did her research wanted to work in all-female bands because they perceived males to be judgemental and threatening. Sara Cohen's (1991) analysis of the intimidation of girls and women in Liverpool rock bands provides its own testimony. In several examples in Chapter 7 I have illustrated ways in which boys are openly critical of girls' music and of girls' musical practices in schools, where they are constructed as 'cissy'. Boys are also perceived to be 'naughty' and this non-conformity is associated with a higher level of musical creativity linked to the masculine delineation of music. Those aspects of musical meaning that are interruptive and threatening for femininity, I want to suggest, are strengthened by the physical presence of males as onlookers to the display of the female musical performer. For these reasons, all-girl groups present distinct advantages as learning environments in which the sexual risk of female display and the interruption and threat to femininity caused by masculine delineations can be reduced.

But all-girl groups are not necessarily beneficial in every respect. Bayton (1990) refers to one disadvantage experienced by members of the all-female bands she interviewed: many of the players said that criticism was missing, because the band-members were all too 'nice' to each other. This provocative situation once more illustrates the power of the masculine delineation of music. In the absence of real-life males, the delineation can enforce its office through the inhibition of a critical stance. The masculine delineation of music threatens to enter all-female bands and musical groups through the music itself. It cannot be ignored. Nor will the alternative musical perspectives of girls and boys benefit from having no communion. Within a co-educational school, a judicious mixture of single-sex groups, crossed-over roles and mixed groups might be the most educative set-up, although difficult in practice to achieve. Many single-sex schools already find it helpful to mount extra-curricular activities in combination with a neighbouring school attended by pupils of the opposite sex. This practice seems to benefit from the best of both worlds. Group work makes gendered musical meaning highly volatile, through inter-personal negotiation over symbolic values which are powerful and yet non-verbal, indeed which are the more powerful *because they are* non-verbal: ubiquitous yet concealed, vital yet hardly understood. Sensitive management of mixed as well as single-sex groups by teachers and lecturers can penetrate not merely the overt practices of pupils or students, but musical meaning itself.

THE CENTRALITY OF MUSICAL MEANING AND EXPERIENCE

The curriculum can provide a vital interventionary force in the reproduction of the gender politics of music. Some possible measures, such as those I have discussed above, include the gradual incorporation of information about women musicians in the curriculum; the recognition of gender issues represented in lyrics or libretti; the reconsideration of the role of the canon in the curriculum, combined with the use of pertinent music by women in teaching strategies; a re-examination of assessment procedures with reference to girls' and boys', or women's and men's, musical practices and values; further inspection of assessment in terms of our own assumptions about the musicality of our pupils and students according to gender; the provision of role-models that challenge accepted gendered musical practices; the encouragement of girls and boys or women and men to take up musical activities that cross over stereotypical expectations; the setting-up of a variety of choices between mixed and single-sex groupings in which pupils and students can work; and undoubtedly there are many other possibilities.

But any such strategies would remain only superficial if they were not to be accompanied by teachers' and lecturers' sensitivity to the symbolic power of music itself, as it is constructed in the society at large, as it is mediated within the educational institution, and as it manifests itself in the experience of ourselves, our pupils and students: its symbolic power, discussed throughout this book, to *produce* gender, to regulate the boundaries of femininity through affirmative, interruptive or threatening delineations, to posit masculinity as a relatively unproblematic and unquestioned norm, and to inveigle itself into the musical experiences of us all, wherein it participates in our constructions of our own gender-identities. If gender is partly constituted by music itself, then we cannot change gendered musical behaviour by simply changing the musical activities that are made available through education to members of the society. Any campaign concerned with intervening in the field of gender and music education must have as an integral part of its strategy a consideration of musical meaning.

I believe that the task of exploring music's production of gender through education must fundamentally involve students in a *fulfilling*, physically or mentally active interaction with musical *inherent meanings*. When music is not only heard or discussed as a fact, 'out there', but *created* through performance or composition, or *closely appraised* in a concentrated listening experience, and when at the same time its inherent meanings are fulfillingly assimilated, this experience forms one necessary step before there can emerge, under certain conditions, that chink of light to which I have occasionally referred in previous chapters. It is through the experience of inherent meanings that we countenance that virtual aspect of musical meaning which is in itself free of symbolic content, free therefore of gendered delineations. In that logical freedom, there is contained the possibility of exposing and exploding the ubiquitous influence of gendered delineations over our listening experiences. In order to explain what I mean here I wish to have recourse again to Figure 1 (see p. 251).

I have argued that pupils in classrooms will relate to music in ways that are, amongst other things, connected with their gender-identities in combination with the delineations which any particular piece or style of music carries for them. If pupils are to be wholly celebrated by music, this will require that the music's inherent meanings are familiar, readily understood and enjoyed whilst the delineations are inviting and easily absorbed. For a girl to be fulfilled by the inherent meanings of classical music is very possible. This is partly due to the ready willingness of girls to involve themselves in classical music in schools, a willingness which is

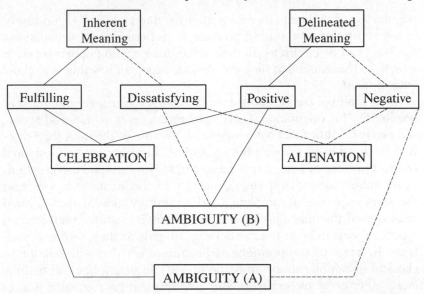

Figure 1. Adapted from Green 1988, p. 138 and cited above, p. 133

not only empirically manifested but also discursively constructed. Their involvement then affords fulfilment by inherent meanings, owing to the familiarity which comes through exposure to and control of the music. At the same time, girls are able to relate positively to the gendered performance delineations of classical music, owing to the affirmative femininity of such music in the classroom environment. Girls can thus be what I have termed relatively celebrated by the music. Contrastingly, boys will tend to be unfamiliar with the inherent meanings of such music. This unfamiliarity is again not only the result of the empirical lack of boys' involvement in classical music performance practices but is produced and even exaggerated by the discourse surrounding the music and by musical meaning itself: for boys are also negatively disposed towards the music's gendered performance delineations, which carry 'cissy' connotations within the school environment. They are relatively alienated from such music.

Regarding popular music in school, the situation is somewhat reversed. Girls, including those for whom classical music is not affirmative, tend to be thrown off popular music performance practices, because of the risqué femininity or the masculine delineations which the music transmits. Although they may be fulfilled by a familiarity with popular music's inherent meanings, they cannot relate entirely positively, in terms of their own musical practice, to its performance delineations. But boys can be celebrated in their relationships with popular music in school, to the extent that they are able to engage in it within the school environment.

In the realm of composition, a vital qualification arises regarding girls' possibilities for celebration. Girls' celebration, even by classical music, will rarely be quite full, I have suggested, because of the masculine cerebral delineation of classical music, and of all music, in compositional terms. Furthermore, the threat presented to conventional constructions of femininity arising from the delineation of the female composer and the stark exposure of problematised femininity against the assumed backdrop of the masculine delineation of music to some extent lend an aspect of negativity to the relationship of girls to their own compositions. In terms of compositional delineations, whether with relation to classical or popular music, only the highly competent boy can be fully celebrated: he whose expertise and commitment have enabled him to overcome the feminine connotations of classical music in school and who is a candidate for the award of that creative genius which is denied to girls.

Where the musical experience of pupils in classrooms is ambiguous, this provides a particularly promising opportunity for effective teaching. On one hand, pupils may be positive to delineations but dissatisfied by inherent meanings (referred to in the chart as ambiguity A). (For example, studying the life of Billie Holiday may incline a class of twelve- and thirteen-year-olds towards her music's delineations, even if, on first hearing, they find the inherent meanings strange.) In such a case, prior positive relationships to delineations can provide a helping hand into a more fulfilling involvement with the music's inherent meanings. Barriers to motivation and interest tend to be reduced, and pupils are more willing to become involved with the music not only as listeners but also as performers and composers. On the other hand, pupils may be negative to delineations but fulfilled by inherent meanings (ambiguity B). (For example, boys were likely to be negative towards the 'girlie' delineations of a female popular vocalist such as Kylie Minogue in the late 1980s, and yet would have been entirely familiar with the stylistic demands made by the inherent meanings of her music, which was composed and produced by the eighties British hit-factory Stock, Aitken and Waterman.) In this instance it is possible for teachers to build upon pupils' prior fulfilment by inherent meanings, in such a way as to lead to a change in pupils', and indeed in our own, conceptions of the femininity or masculinity of the music's delineations.

This is, to me, the most powerful interventionary point of music teaching concerning gender. When we experience inherent meanings in ways that lead to an alteration in our understanding of delineations, this experience comes to us with the appearance of being musical 'truth'. It is here that interventions have occurred throughout history, when women performers and composers have resisted damaging gendered delineations and presented their music in taboo circumstances, to be gradually accepted through the public's realisation that the music's inherent meanings were able to be judged in terms which *contradict* the normative, negative gendered delineations. This possibility is even further enhanced in classroom situations, I would like to suggest, when pupils and students are engaged in the peculiarly and wonderfully intimate practice of making music together or listening to each other's music. Here, we are dealing not only with gendered musical practices or only with gendered musical delineations, but with the very processes of musical inherent meanings themselves in the making. I wish to illustrate the interventionary possibilities to which I am referring by way of three examples.

First, we have seen that in the discourse surrounding music in schools, boys are characterised as boisterous players of loud instruments or as loud players of any instruments, whilst girls are perceived to play quieter instruments, or to play instruments more quietly and to be generally less extrovert. We have also seen that boys present themselves as composers or improvisers with the confidence derived from a positive identification with the world of 'other people' who make music, whereas girls are more reticent about putting themselves forward as composers. I have argued that such characteristics are discursive constructions which both result from the musical practices of boys and girls and feed back into those practices and into the meanings which are taken on by the music played or composed, finally influencing the musical experiences of both teachers and pupils. Teachers' sensitivity in the handling of such meanings in a group situation can provide a crucial counter to their perpetuation.

A task that I often set a group of [primary] children is for one to hold a steady pulse whilst the others take it in turns to improvise with it. In one such group John had the drum and offered to play the pulse. He played it steadily and at a consistent volume through each person's improvisation, despite the fact that the three girls in the group had chosen to play glockenspiels. After the piece had finished I asked if anyone had comments to make about the piece. 'Yes', said one of the boys. 'You couldn't hear the girls.' 'Why was that?' I asked. 'They were too soft', said John quickly. 'That is true', I said. 'What can we do about it?' 'They must play louder', he responded. I suggested that he might also play more softly when they were playing. A look of immense amazement fell across his face. It had simply not occurred to him as a possibility. The responsibility so far had rested totally on the girls. 'Next time', I suggested, 'perhaps the girls can play a little louder and can you, John, try to vary the volume of your beat to suit whoever is playing.' He proved to be an able and sensitive accompanist the next time round, varying the dynamics for each improvisation. In approximately ten minutes of group improvisation, both we as a group, and John in particular, learned a lot about how sexism operates, and more importantly, how to do something about it. (Boyce-Tillman, 1993, p. 160)

No one is trying to suggest that John was individually 'to blame' for being sexist. Rather, the whole situation was infused with a symbolic potency which, without always being articulated in words, surrounds the musical practices of boys and girls in schools, and acts back from those practices to symbolise their ideas and our ideas not only of music but also of femininity and masculinity themselves.[18]

Secondly, a group of girls at a community centre near Liverpool got together with a youth leader in the late 1980s to produce some rap, in which they played electric and percussion instruments, and in which they created both the lyrics and the music themselves (Allcock 1989). In this one activity, the girls were invoking and recreating many of the gendered musical meanings that I have been discussing throughout this book: the sexual innuendoes that arise from a female popular vocalist; the interruptive delineation of girls playing electric guitars and drum-kits; the delineated threat of girls' cerebral control of the compositional organisation of inherent meanings themselves. The girls and their music were at first aggressively ridiculed by boys, who referred to the girls as 'slags' and 'tarts' and to their music as 'rubbish', amongst other expressions. The girls persisted with their music-making, and one day, having finished a number, they relayed it at high volume outside to where a group of boys were standing. Now, the meaningful process, whereby the interruptive and threatening feminine delineations of the music caused the boys to denigrate both the girls and the inherent meanings, acted in reverse: the confrontational political situation combined with the stylistically familiar inherent meanings, causing the boys to listen again. They got past the problematic delineations and listened more closely to the

---

[18] Also see Ford (1995) who discusses the pedagogic potential of improvisation as an ethical strategy. See Askew and Ross (1988) for some constructive strategies to combat male competitiveness and the assertion of machismo in schools through the encouragement of discussion and self-awareness.

inherent meanings, they found them convincing, and they then also changed their minds both about the music's value and about the girls' 'femininity'. For the girls themselves, this experience, bound up as it was with direct musical practice, must have shed an even brighter light on new possibilities, even if only fleetingly.

Thirdly, I recall mention of Louise, the girl composer who was described by her classmates as 'superb', 'brilliant'; and I remember Lorraine, the girl composer whom I thought talented at a school where I used to teach (both discussed on pp. 222–3 above). Girls such as these must, like everyone else, operate within the symbolic bounds of convention without which we would have no meanings, no relationships, no society at all. But, even if their music were ultimately to be deemed 'safe', immature, or inferior in any number of ways, its production and transmission within the context of the school nonetheless also represent a challenge to convention, an expansion of horizons. When their fellow pupils and teachers listen with admiration to their music, it can afford a relationship of fulfilment by its inherent meanings: perhaps owing to a prior extensive involvement with its style, perhaps owing to that sheer musical inherent quality which it is virtually impossible to describe in words, perhaps also owing to that special sense of identification that we have on observing or listening to someone we know personally, who is engaged in a difficult task with which our own previous practical engagement allows us to empathise. In that virtual moment of such fulfilment by the inherent meanings of music composed by girls like Louise and Lorraine, we are able to touch upon a quality of musical experience which, precisely because of its logical freedom from delineation, at the same time exposes the inevitability of delineation: then the fact of delineated femininity surfaces, the assumption of the masculine delineation is made audible, the absurdity of the construction of femininity as lacking in creative energy presents itself. A host of new delineations, new conceptions both of music and of femininity, may then, at best, seem possible.

Such interventions can take place with reference to any style of music or level of musical expertise. They do not require specialist resources concerning women in music or theoretical knowledge about musical meaning on the part of teachers or lecturers so much as commitment and a high level of personal sensitivity to the complexity and pervasiveness of gendered musical meanings, not only in our educational structures but also in our musical experiences. Through challenging such experiences in musical interactions, the reproduction of patriarchal constructions of femininity is challenged far more forcefully that it ever could be by studying history from books or listening to professional recordings. It is not just in the overt content and organisation of the curriculum but in musical meanings and musical experience themselves that the gender politics of music are played out. The most fundamental interventionary possibilities therefore exist in the way we make available to pupils, to students and to ourselves the enactment of gender politics in interpersonal relationships through the construction and appraisal of musical inherent meanings, in a virtual moment whose logical freedom from delineation at the same time reveals delineation. Just as gendered meanings are carried by music itself, so it is necessary to challenge them through music itself. At its most powerful, such a challenging musical experience can cause shackles to fall, whilst no mention need be made of gender, no words need be spoken.

SUMMARY: THE GENDER POLITICS OF MUSIC: PRACTICE, MEANING AND EDUCATION

In Part I of this book I presented a theory of gendered musical meaning as it is manifested through women's historical musical practices and the discourses surrounding them. Singing, instrumental performance in certain areas, and women's roles as teachers and custodians of tradition allow for an affirmative feminine delineation in the music with which they are involved; other types of instrumental performance convey an interruptive feminine delineation which throws women off; and composition constructs a threat to femininity through its masculine cerebral associations and the hegemony of men in composition. These musical meanings are not merely representations conveyed by music; they enter into musical experience itself, affecting the relationship listeners have to the inherent meanings of the music, and to their own gender-identities. In Part II, I have attempted to trace the theories of gendered musical meaning that were put forward in Part I, in order to reveal their workings in the contemporary school. I have discussed some of the ways in which the gender politics of music continue to be reproduced in contemporary society, not in spite of, but partly *by way of* an education system which affords every opportunity to girls.

In schools we can discern a symbolic affirmation of femininity through girls' involvement in singing and in orchestral, plucked and keyboard instrumental performance mainly in what is called classical music, and in what are perceived to be girls' 'enabling attitudes' towards music.

Although schoolgirls do play musical instruments in great numbers, their involvement perpetuates the historical practices of girls' and women's restrictions to certain kinds of instruments only and, concomitantly, to certain musical styles and venues of performance. With this historically reproductive instrumental performance of classical music in the school, girls can join in the affirmative symbolisation of femininity which has been retrieved by so many women classical instrumentalists today; or they can escape to a more neutral territory afforded by the educational environment. Physicality plays a greater part in the performance of popular music, and the body frequently becomes an explicit part of popular music's delineations, which themselves take on a greater importance in the discourse surrounding the music. Singing in popular music begins to risk the sexual reputation of a girl, who can be seen to be putting her body on display and affirming this fact through the strength of the musical delineations. The technology of popular music, and many of its associated instruments, on the other hand, produce an interruption to patriarchal definitions of femininity, as the girl drummer, the girl electric bass player, is seen to challenge her inability to manipulate technology. In the culture of the school, and in pupils' discourse, 'popular' or 'fast' music contrasts with the conformist, feminine image of classical or 'slow' music, and appears more 'macho', up-to-date, vital. In this crevice, boys enter the school music scene, and the masculine delineation of music stakes its first claim. This claim is most fully realised through the delineations of masculinity that are associated with compositional and improvisational practices, in which girls are subject to the threat posed to femininity; boys meanwhile are able to harness this delineation to an experience of celebration in their musically constructed gender-identity.

In the present chapter I have reviewed a number of pragmatic steps which are available for teachers and lecturers who wish to combat the apparently unremitting perpetuation of the gender politics of music through education. But, most fundamentally, I believe in a non-pragmatic response: an *awareness* of gendered musical meaning and of its influential presence within our musical experiences, which must in and of itself be the first necessity and the last objective of any intervention. This would seem to be a classically idealist position, in that it refers only to what exists in the mind. But what exists in the mind never just stays there. Through the unpredictable and unspeakable machinations of human consciousness and action, just as practice affects ideas, so ideas translate into practice. It is in fact this very tendency with relation to gender and music which has been the central focus of this book: the influence of gendered musical practices on gendered musical meanings, the integration of these meanings within our experiences of music and our very constructions of ourselves, and their translation again into our musical practices.

Bibliography

Abbate, Carolyn (1991) *Unsung Voices: Opera and Musical Narrative in the Nineteenth Century*, Princeton, New Jersey: Princeton University Press.

(1993) 'Opera; or, the envoicing of women' in Solie (1993).

Abeles, Harold F. and Porter, Susan Yank (1979) 'So your daughter wants to be a drummer?', *Music Educators' Journal*, 65/5.

Adorno, T. W. (1986) *Prisms*, trans. S. Weber and S. Weber (first published by Neville Spearman, 1967; third printing of 1981 edition), Cambridge, Massachusetts: MIT Press.

(1976) *Introduction to the Sociology of Music*, trans. E. B. Ashton, New York: Seabury Press.

Allcock, Edwina (1989) Unpublished discussion presentation on 'Equal and unequal opportunities in popular music' panel, seminar on popular music and social policy, Liverpool University Institute of Popular Music, June.

Ammer, Christine (1980) *Unsung: A History of Women in American Music*, London, Connecticut: Greenwood Press.

Amos, Valerie and Parmar, Prathiba (1981) 'Resistances and responses: the experience of black girls in Britain' in McRobbie and McCabe (1981); also in Arnot and Weiner (1987).

Antelyes, Peter (1994) 'Red hot mamas: Bessie Smith, Sophie Tucker, and the ethnic maternal voice in American popular song' in Dunn and Jones (1994).

Arnot, Madeleine (1982) 'Male hegemony, social class and women's education', *Journal of Education*, 164/1.

(1984) 'A feminist perspective on the relationship between family life and school life', *Journal of Education*, 166/1.

(1986) (ed.) *Race and Gender: Equal Opportunities in Education*, Oxford: Pergamon Press.

Arnot, Madeleine and Weiner, Gaby (1987) (eds.) *Gender and the Politics of Schooling*, 2nd edition, London: Hutchinson.

Askew, Sue and Ross, Carol (1988) *Boys Don't Cry*, Milton Keynes: Open University Press.

Austern, Linda (1989) '"Sing Againe Syren": the female musician and sexual enchantment in Elizabethan life and literature', *Renaissance Quarterly*, 42/3 (Autumn), pp. 420–48.

(1994) 'Music and the English renaissance controversy over women' in Cook and Tsou (1994).

Baldauf-Berdes, Jane L. (1993) *The Women Musicians of Venice: Musical Foundations, 1525–1855*, Oxford University Press.

(1994) 'Anna Maria della pietà: the woman musician of Venice personified' in Cook and Tsou (1994).

Barkin, Elaine (1980) Questionnaire to women composers, *Perspectives of New Music*, 19.

(1981) Response from women composers, *Perspectives of New Music*, 20.

(1982) Response from women composers continued, *Perspectives of New Music*, 21.

Barrett, Michèle (1988a) 'Introduction to the 1988 edition' in Barrett (1988b)

(1988b) *Women's Oppression Today*, 2nd edition, London: Virago Press.

Barthes, Roland (1977) 'The grain of the voice' in *Image–Music–Text*, Glasgow: Fontana/Collins.

Battersby, Christine (1989) *Gender and Genius*, London: The Women's Press.

Bayton, Mavis (1990) 'How women become musicians' in Frith and Goodwin (1990).

(1993a) 'Feminist musical practice: problems and contradictions' in Tony Bennett, Simon Frith, Lawrence Grossberg, John Shepherd and Graeme Turner (eds.) *Rock and Popular Music: Politics, Policies, Institutions*, London and New York: Routledge.

(1993b) Review of Gillian Gaar, *She's a Rebel: The History of Women in Rock and Roll*, *Popular Music*, 12/3.

Beauvoir, Simone de (1988) *The Second Sex* (first published as *Le deuxième sexe*, 1949), London: Pan Books Ltd.

Berger, P. and Luckmann, T. (1967) *The Social Construction of Reality*, London: Doubleday.

Bernstein, Jane (1986) 'Shout, shout, up with your song! Dame Ethel Smyth and the changing role of the British woman composer' in Bowers and Tick (1986).

Berry, Venise T. (1994) 'Feminine or masculine: the conflicting nature of female images in rap music' in Cook and Tsou (1994).

Betrock, Alan (1982) *Girl Groups: The Story of a Sound*, New York: Delilah.

Block, Adrienne F. and Neuls-Bates, Carol (1979) *Women in American Music: A Bibliography of Music and Literature*, Connecticut: Greenwood Press.

Bogin, Meg (1980) *The Women Troubadours* (first published as *Les femmes troubadours*, 1978), New York: W. W. Norton.

Bohlman, Philip (1993) 'Musicology as a political act', *Journal of Musicology*, 11/4.

Born, Georgina (1992) Review article: 'Women, music, politics, difference: Susan McClary, *Feminine Endings*', *Women: A Cultural Review*, 3/1.

Bourdieu, Pierre (1973) 'Cultural reproduction and social reproduction' in R. Brown, *Knowledge, Education and Cultural Change*, London: Tavistock.

(1974) 'The school as a conservative force' in S. J. Egglestone, *Contemporary Research in the Sociology of Education*, London: Methuen.

Bourdieu, Pierre and Passeron, J. C. (1990) *Reproduction in Education, Society and Culture*, trans. R. Nice (first published as *La réproduction*, 1977), London and Beverly Hills: Sage.

Bowers, Jane (1986) 'The emergence of women composers in Italy 1566–1700' in Bowers and Tick (1986).

Bowers, Jane and Tick, Judith (1986) (eds.) *Women Making Music: The Western Art Tradition 1150–1950*, Urbana: University of Illinois Press.

Boyce-Tillman, June (1993) 'Women's ways of knowing', *British Journal of Music Education*, 10/3.

Boyd, Malcolm (1980) *Grace Williams*, Cardiff: University of Wales Press.

Brackett, David (1995) *Interpreting Popular Music*, Cambridge University Press.

Bradby, Barbara (1989) 'Essay review; God's gift to the suburbs?', *Popular Music*, 8/1.

   (1990) 'Do-talk and don't-talk: the division of the subject in girl-group music' in Frith and Goodwin (1990).

   (1992) 'Like a virgin-mother?: Materialism and maternalism in the songs of Madonna', *Cultural Studies*, 6/1.

   (1993a) 'Lesbians and popular music: does it matter who is singing?' in Gabrielle Griffin (ed.), *Outwrite: Lesbianism and Popular Culture*, London: Pluto Press.

   (1993b) 'Sampling sexuality: gender, technology and the body in dance music', *Popular Music*, 12/2.

Bradby, Barbara and Torode, Brian (1984) 'Pity Peggy Sue', *Popular Music*, Yearbook 4, pp. 183–205.

Brah, Avtar and Minhas, Rehana (1985) 'Structural racism or cultural difference: schooling for Asian girls' in Gaby Weiner (ed.), *Just a Bunch of Girls*, Milton Keynes: Open University Press.

Brett, Philip (1993) 'Britten's dream' in Solie (1993).

   (1994) 'Musicality, essentialism, and the closet' in Brett, Thomas and Wood (1994).

Brett, Philip, Thomas, Gary and Wood, Elizabeth (1994) (eds.) *Queering the Pitch*, New York and London: Routledge.

Brewer, Heather (1995) 'Sexism and stereotyping in the text of children's songbooks', *Primary Music Today* (April), pp. 20–2.

Briscoe, James (1987) (ed.) *Historical Anthology of Music by Women*, Bloomington: Indiana University Press.

British Journal of Music Education (1993) Special issue on gender, 10/3.

Brower, Edith (1894) 'Is the musical idea masculine?', *Atlantic Monthly*, March 1894, pp. 332–9.

Brown, Howard Mayer (1986) 'Women singers and women's songs in fifteenth-century Italy' in Bowers and Tick (1986).

Bruce, Rosemary and Kemp, Anthony (1993) 'Sex-stereotyping in children's preference for musical instruments', *British Journal of Music Education*, 10/3.

Bunting, Robert (1987) 'Composing music: case studies in the teaching and learning process I', *British Journal of Music Education*, 4/1.

(1988) 'Composing music: case studies in the teaching and learning process II', *British Journal of Music Education*, 5/3.

Burnett, Michael (1972) 'Coming to terms with pop', articles 1–9, *Music Teacher*, 51/2 (February) to 51/10 (October).

Butler, Judith (1990) *Gender Trouble: Feminism and the Subversion of Identity*, New York: Routledge.

Campion, Thomas (1889) *Observations in the Art of English Poesie*, ed. Bullen (originally published 1602), London: Chiswick Press.

Cant, Stephanie (1990a) 'Gender differentiation and music education in Britain', unpublished paper (private communication).

(1990b) 'Women composers and the music curriculum', *British Journal of Music Education*, 7/1.

Caputo, Virginia (1994) 'Add technology and stir: music, gender and technology in today's music classrooms', *Quarterly Journal of Music Teaching and Learning*, 4/4–5/1.

Carby, Hazel V. (1987) 'White women listen! Black feminism and the boundaries of sisterhood' in Arnot and Weiner (1987).

(1990) ' "It jus be's dat way sometime": the sexual politics of women's blues' in Ellen Dubois and Vicky Ruiz (eds.), *Unequal Sisters*, New York: Routledge.

Castiglione, Baldassare (1928) *The Book of the Courtier* (first published as *Il libro del cortegiano*, 1528), trans. Sir Thomas Hoby, London: J. M. Dent and Son.

Castle, Terry (1993) 'In praise of Brigitte Fassbaender (a musical emanation)' in *The Apparitional Lesbian: Female Homosexuality and Modern Culture*, New York: Columbia University Press.

Citron, Marcia J. (1986) 'Women and the Lied, 1775–1850' in Bowers and Tick (1986).

(1991) 'European composers and musicians, 1880–1918' in Pendle (1991a).

(1993) *Gender and the Musical Canon*, Cambridge University Press.

(1994) 'Feminist approaches to musicology' in Cook and Tsou (1994).

Cixous, Hélène (1990) 'Castration or decapitation?' in Russell Fergusson, Martha Gever, Trinh T. Min-ha and Cornel West, *Out There: Marginalisation and Contemporary Cultures*, Cambridge, Masachusetts and London: MIT Press.

Cixous, Hélene and Clément, Catherine (1985) *The Newly-Born Woman* (first published as *La jeune née*, 1975), trans. Betsy Wing; introduction by Sandra Gilbert, Boston: Beacon Press; Manchester: Manchester University Press.

Clarricoates, Katherine (1978) 'Dinosaurs in the classroom – a re-examination of some aspects of the "hidden curriculum" in primary schools', *Women's Studies International Quarterly* 1, pp. 353–64.

(1980) 'The importance of being Ernest . . . Emma . . . Tom . . . Jane: the perception and categorisation of gender conformity and gender deviation in primary schools' in Deem (1980).

Clément, Catherine (1988) *Opera, or The Undoing of Women* (first published as *Opéra, ou la défaite des femmes*, 1979), trans. Betsy Wing, Minneapolis: University of Minnesota Press; London: Virago.

Cogan, Robert (1991) 'Hildegard's fractional antiphon', paper read at University of London, King's College, Conference on Music and Gender, June.

Cohen, Aaron I. (1988) (ed.) *International Encyclopedia of Women Composers*, London: Books and Music Company.

Cohen, Sara (1991) *Rock Culture in Liverpool*, Oxford University Press.

Coldwell, Maria (1986) 'Jongleresses and Trobairitz: secular musicians in medieval France' in Bowers and Tick (1986).

Colley, Ann, Comber, Chris and Hargreaves, David J. (1993) 'Girls, boys and technology in music education', *British Journal of Music Education*, 10/2.

Cook, Nicholas (1994) 'Music and meaning in the commercials', *Popular Music*, 13/1.

Cook, Susan C. (1994) ' "Cursed was she": gender and power in American balladry' in Cook and Tsou (1994).

Cook, Susan C. and Tsou, Judy S. (1994) (eds.) *Cecilia Reclaimed: Feminist Perspectives on Gender and Music*, Urbana: University of Illinois Press.

Cooper, Lindsay (1977) 'Women, music, feminism – notes', *Musics*, 14, (October).

Cox, Renée (1991) 'Recovering jouissance: an introduction to feminist musical aesthetics' in Pendle (1991b).

Culler, Jonathan (1982) 'Reading as a Woman' in *On Deconstruction: Theory and Criticism After Structuralism*, Ithaca, New York: Cornell University Press.

Cusick, Suzanne G. (1993a) 'Thinking from women's lives: Francesca Caccini after 1627' in Marshall (1993b).

  (1993b) 'Of woman, music, and power: a model from *seicento* Florence' in Solie (1993).

Dahl, Linda (1984) *Stormy Weather: The Music and Lives of a Century of Jazz Women*, London and New York: Quartet Books.

Dame, Joke (1994) 'Unveiled voices: sexual difference and the castrato' in Brett, Thomas and Wood (1994).

Deem, Rosemary (1980) *Schooling for Women's Work*, London and Boston: Routledge and Kegan Paul.

  (1984) (ed.) *Co-education Reconsidered*, Milton Keynes: Open University Press.

Delamont, Sara (1990) *Sex Roles and the School*, 2nd edition, London: Routledge.

Delzell, Judith K. (1994) 'Variables affecting the gender-role stereotyping of high school band teaching positions', *Quarterly Journal of Music Teaching and Learning*, 4/4–5/1.

Delzell, Judith K. and Leppla, D. A. (1992) 'Gender association of musical instruments and preferences of fourth-grade students for selected instruments', *Journal of Research in Music Education*, 40/2.

Dennis, Brian (1970) *Experimental Music in Schools*, Oxford University Press.

Department of Education and Science (DES) (1986) *GCSE: The National Criteria*, DES.

  (1992) *Music in the National Curriculum (England)*, London: HMSO (April).

Department for Education (DFE) (1995) *Music in the National Curriculum (England)*, DFE.

Doubleday, Veronica (1991) 'Women musicians in Afghanistan: the modest and the brazen', paper read at University of London, King's College, Conference on Music and Gender, June.

Drinker, Sophie (1948) *Music and Women: The Story of Women in Relation to Music*, New York: Coward and McCann.

Dunn, Leslie C. and Jones, Nancy A. (1994) (eds.) *Embodied Voices: Representing Feminine Vocality in Western Culture*, Cambridge University Press.

Eaklor, Vicki L. (1994) 'The gendered origins of the American musician', *Quarterly Journal of Music Teaching and Learning*, 4/4–5/1.

Edwards, J. Michèle (1991) 'Women in music to ca. 1450' in Pendle (1991b).

Ehrlich, Cyril (1985) *The Music Profession in Britain Since the Eighteenth Century: A Social History*, Oxford: Clarendon Press.

Elliott, David (1989) 'Key concepts in multicultural music education', *International Journal of Music Education*, 13, pp. 11–18.

 (1990) 'Music as culture: toward a multicultural concept of arts education', *Journal of Aesthetic Education*, 24/1.

 (1995) *Music Matters: A New Philosophy of Music Education*, Oxford University Press.

Ellmann, Mary (1968) *Thinking About Women* (first published in the USA), London: Virago 1979.

Evans, Liz (1994) *Women, Sex and Rock'n'Roll in their own words*, London: Pandora.

Farmer, Paul (1976) 'Pop music in the secondary school: a justification', *Music in Education*, 40/381.

Fletcher, Peter (1987) *Education and Music*, Oxford University Press.

Floyd, Samuel A. Jun. (1995) *The Power of Black Music*, Oxford University Press.

Ford, Charles (1991) *Così? Sexual Politics in Mozart's Operas*, Manchester and New York: Manchester University Press.

 (1995) 'Free collective improvisation in Higher Education', *British Journal of Music Education*, 12/2.

Fortney, P. M., Boyle, J. D. and DeCarb, N. J. (1993) 'A study of middle school band students' instrument choices', *Journal of Research in Music Education*, 41, pp. 28–39.

Foucault, Michel (1981) *The History of Sexuality Volume One: An Introduction* (first published as *La volonté de savoir*, 1976), trans. R. Hurley, London: Allen Lane.

Frith, Simon (1983) *Sound Effects: Youth, Leisure and the Politics of Rock*, London: Constable.

 (1985) 'Afterthoughts', *New Statesman*, 23 August; also in Frith and Goodwin (1990).

Frith, Simon and Goodwin, Andrew (1990) (eds.) *On Record: Rock, Pop and the Written Word*, New York: Goodwin, Pantheon Books.

Frith, Simon and McRobbie, Angela (1978) 'Rock and Sexuality', *Screen Education*, 29; also in Frith and Goodwin (1990).

Fudger, Marion (1975) 'The quota system and black shiny handbags' (Conference report from Musicians' Union debate about women), *Spare Rib*, 36.

Fuller, Mary (1980) 'Black girls in a London comprehensive school' in Deem (1980).

(1983) 'Qualified criticism, critical qualifications' in Jane Purvis and Margaret Hales, *Achievement and Inequality in Education*, London: Routledge and Kegan Paul.

Fuller, Sophie (1992) 'Unearthing a world of music: Victorian and Edwardian women composers', *Women: A Cultural Review*, 3/1.

(1994a) *The Pandora Guide to Women Composers: Britain and the United States*, London: Pandora.

(1994b) 'News from the archive and resource centre project', London: *Women in Music Bulletin*, 1/5 (September–October), p. 2.

Gaar, Gillian G. (1993) *She's a Rebel: The History of Women in Rock and Roll*, London: Blandford.

Gammon, Vic (forthcoming) 'The new right and the making of the music National Curriculum', unpublished paper (private communication). (A version was delivered at the Place of Music Conference, University College London, September 1993.)

Garnett, Liz (1995) '"The frozen, firm embodiment of music": romantic aesthetics and the female form', paper read at the first UK Critical Musicology Conference, University of Salford, April.

Garratt, Sheryl (1990) 'Teenage dreams' in Frith and Goodwin (1990); originally published in Steward and Garratt (1984), entitled 'All of us'.

Gatens, Moira (1983) 'A critique of the sex/gender distinction' in J. Allen and P. Patton (eds.), *Beyond Marxism? Interventions After Marx*, Sydney: Interventions Publications Collective.

Gaume, Matilda (1986) 'Ruth Crawford Seeger' in Bowers and Tick (1986).

Gergis, Sonia (1993) 'The power of women musicians in the ancient and near East: the roots of prejudice', *British Journal of Music Education*, 10/3.

Giles, Jennifer and Shepherd, John (1990) 'Theorising music's affective power' in Robert Witmer (ed.), *Ethnomusicology in Canada*, Toronto: Institute for Canadian Music.

Gill, John (1994) *Queer Noises: Homosexuality in Twentieth Century Music*, London: Cassell.

Gipps, Caroline (1990) *Assessment: A Teacher's Guide to the Issues*, London: Hodder and Stoughton.

Gottlieb, Jane (1991) 'Women in music organisations: a preliminary checklist' in Zaimont, Gottlieb, Polk and Rogan (1991).

Gourse, Lesley (1995) *Madame Jazz: Contemporary Women Instrumentalists*, Oxford University Press.

Glover, Jo and Ward, Stephen (1993) *Teaching Music in the Primary School*, London: Cassell.

Green, Lucy (1984) 'The reproduction of musical ideology', unpublished doctoral thesis, University of Sussex.

(1988) *Music on Deaf Ears: Musical Meaning, Ideology and Education*, Manchester and New York: Manchester University Press.

(1990) 'The assessment of composition: style and experience', *British Journal of Music Education*, 7/3.

(1993) 'Music, gender and education: a report on some exploratory research', *British Journal of Music Education*, 10/3.

(1994a) 'Can music raise our awareness?', *Women: A Cultural Review*, 5/1.

(1994b) 'Gender, musical meaning and education', *Philosophy of Music Education Review*, 2/2; also in Spruce (1996).

(1996) 'The emergence of gender as an issue in music education' in Charles Plummeridge (ed.), *Music Education: Trends and Issues*, University of London Institute of Education.

(forthcoming) 'Practice, meaning and identity in the music classroom: the case of gender' in Jorgensen (forthcoming).

Grieg, Charlotte (1989) *Will You Still Love Me Tomorrow? Girl Groups from the 'Fifties On*, London: Virago.

Griffiths, Dai (1994) 'Sometimes it's hard to be a woman: fixities and flexibilities of gender in recent song', paper read at the conference of Music Analysis, University of Lancaster, summer.

Griswold, P. A. and Chroback, D. A. (1981) 'Sex-role associations of musical instruments and occupations by gender and major', *Journal of Research in Music Education*, 29, pp. 57–62.

Halstead, Jill (1995) 'The woman composer: a study of factors affecting creativity and the gendered politics of musical composition', unpublished doctoral thesis, University of Liverpool.

Halstead, J. Mark (1994) 'Muslim attitudes to music in schools', *British Journal of Music Education*, 11/2.

Hambleton, Elizabeth (1975) 'Discrimination in orchestras: women organise in the Musicians' Union', *Spare Rib*, 34 (April).

Hamessley, Lydia (1994) 'Henry Lawes's settings of Katherine Philips's friendship poetry in his *Second Book of Ayres and Dialogues*, 1655: a musical misreading?' in Brett, Thomas and Wood (1994).

Hand, Jenny (1983) 'Gender and music: some historical perspectives on the debate about female composers, 1880–1920', unpublished master's dissertation, University of Sussex.

Handy, D. Antoinette (1981) *Black Women in American Bands and Orchestras*, Metuchen, New Jersey and London: The Scarecrow Press.

Hargreaves, David, Colley, Anne and Comber, Chris (1995) 'Girls, boys and music technology', *Yamaha Education Supplement* (Spring).

Harper, J. (1986) 'Sex-role stereotyping in music' in David Sell (ed.), *Studies in Music Education*, no. 1, New Zealand: University of Canterbury.

Hassinger, Jane (1987) 'Close harmony: early jazz styles in the music of the New Orleans Boswell sisters' in Koskoff (1987c).

Haweis, Revd H. R. (1977) *Music and Morals* (first published in 1877), London: Daldy, Isbister and Company.

Hebdige, Dick (1981) *Sub-culture: The Meaning of Style*, London: Methuen.

Hegel, G. W. F. (1975) *Aesthetics*, Vol. 1 (originally published as *Aesthetik* in *Georg*

Wilhelm Friedrich Hegels Werke, 1832–45), trans. T. M. Knox, Oxford University Press.

(1977) *The Phenomenology of Spirit,* trans. A. V. Miller (originally published as *Phänomenologie des Geistes,* 1807), Oxford University Press.

Hekman, Susan (1986) *Hermeneutics and the Sociology of Knowledge,* Cambridge: Polity Press.

Her Majesty's Inspectorate (HMI) (1985) *Music 5–16,* London: HMSO.

(1991) *Aspects of Primary Education: The Teaching and Learning of Music,* London: HMSO.

Herndon, Marcia and Ziegler, Susanne (1990) (eds.) *Music, Gender and Culture,* International Institute for Traditional Music.

Hisama, Ellie (1993) 'Postcolonialism on the make: the music of John Mellencamp, David Bowie and John Zorn', *Popular Music,* 12/2.

Horn, David (1994) 'From Catfish Row to Granby Street: contesting meaning in *Porgy and Bess*', *Popular Music,* 13/2.

Howes, Frank (1966) *The English Musical Renaissance,* London: Secker and Warburg.

Hurley, Jennifer M. (1994) 'Debate: Music video and the construction of gendered subjectivity (or how being a music video junkie turned me into a feminist)', *Popular Music,* 13/3.

Jackson, Barbara Garvey (1991) 'Musical women of the seventeenth and eighteenth centuries' in Pendle (1991b).

Jackson, Travis (1993) 'Where's your girl: African-American women and the ritual of jazz performance', *Abstracts,* Conference of Feminist Theory and Music II: A Continuing Dialogue (dal segno), Rochester, New York, 19 June.

Jepsen, Barbara (1991) 'Women in the classical recording industry' in Zaimont, Gottlieb, Polk and Rogan (1991).

Jezic, Diane Peacock (1988) *Women Composers: The Lost Tradition Found,* New York: Feminist Press (with cassette tape).

Jezic, Diane and Binder, David (1987) 'A survey of college music text-books: benign neglect of women composers' in Zaimont, Overhauser and Gottlieb (1987).

Jones, Leroi (1963) *Blues People: Negro Music in White America,* New York: William Morrow.

Jorgensen, Estelle (forthcoming) (ed.) *Music Education and Society: Essays in the Sociology of Music,* publisher t. b. a.

Kallberg, Jeffrey (1992) 'The harmony of the tea-table: gender and ideology in the piano nocturne', *Representations,* 39, pp. 102–33.

Kaplan, E. Ann (1984) 'Is the gaze male?' in Ann Snitow, Christine Stansell and Sharon Thompson (eds.), *Desire: The Politics of Sexuality,* London: Virago.

(1987) *Rocking Around the Clock: Music Television, Postmodernism, and Consumer Culture,* London: Methuen.

(1993) 'Madonna politics: perversion, repression, or subversion? Or masks and/as master-y', in Schwichtenberg (1993).

Keil, Charles (n.d.) '*Paideia con salsa*: ancient Greek education for active citizenship and the role of Afro-Latin dance-music in our schools', *Muse*, 2, Musicians United for Superior Education Incorporated, Buffalo, Kenmore, New York.

Kelly, Joan (1984) *Women, History and Theory: The Essays of Joan Kelly*, University of Chicago Press.

Kemp, Anthony (1982) 'The personality structure of the musician III: the significance of sex differences', *Psychology of Music*, 10, pp. 48–58.

Kendrick, Robert (1993) 'Feminized devotion, musical nuns, and the "new-style" Lombard motet of the 1640s' in Marshall (1993b).

Kent, Greta (1983) *A View from the Bandstand*, London: Sheba Feminist Publishers.

Kerman, Joseph (1985) *Musicology*, London: Fontana Paperbacks and William Collins.

Kessler, S., Aschenden, R., Connell, R. and Dowsett, G. (1985) 'Gender relations in secondary schooling', *Sociology of Education*, 58/1.

Kilminster, Sally (1992) 'Aesthetics and music; the appropriation of the Other', *Women: A Cultural Review*, 3/1.

Koestenbaum, Wayne (1994a) *The Queen's Throat: Opera, Homosexuality and the Mystery of Desire*, New York: Vintage Books.

(1994b) 'Queering the pitch: a posy of definitions and impersonations' in Brett, Thomas and Wood (1994).

Koskoff, Ellen (1987a) 'An introduction to women, music and culture' in Koskoff (1987c).

(1987b) 'The sound of a woman's voice: gender and music in a New York Hasidic community' in Koskoff (1987c).

(1987c) (ed.) *Women and Music in Cross-cultural Perspective*, New York and London: Greenwood Press.

(1991) 'Gender, power and music' in Zaimont, Gottlieb, Polk and Rogan (1991).

(1993) 'Miriam sings her song: the self and the other in anthropological discourse' in Solie (1993).

Koza, Julia Eklund (1992) 'Picture this: sex equity in textbook illustrations', *Music Educators' Journal*, 78/7.

(1994a) 'Big boys don't cry (or sing): gender, misogyny, and homophobia in college choral methods texts', *Quarterly Journal of Music Teaching and Learning*, 4/4–5/1.

(1994b) 'Aesthetic music education revisited: discourses of exclusion and oppression', *Philosophy of Music Education Review*, 2/2.

Kwami, Robert (1996) 'Music education in and for a multi-cultural society', in Charles Plummeridge (ed.), *Music Education: Trends and Issues*, University of London Institute of Education.

Lacan, Jacques (1979) *The Four Fundamental Concepts of Psycho-analysis* (first published as 'Les quatre concepts fondamentaux de la psychanalyse', 1973), trans. Alan Sheridan, Great Britain: The Hogarth Press and the Institute of Psycho-Analysis, Penguin.

Laing, Dave (1985) *One-Chord Wonders: Power and Meaning in Punk Rock*, Milton Keynes: Open University Press.

Laing, Dave and Taylor, Jenny (1979) 'Disco–pleasure–discourse: on rock and sexuality', *Screen Education*, 31, pp. 43–8.

Lamb, Roberta (1987) 'Including women composers in music curricula: development of creative strategies for the general music classes, grades 5–8', unpublished doctoral dissertation, Teachers' College, Columbia University.

(1990) 'Are there gender issues in school music?', *Canadian Music Educator*, 31/6.

(1991a) 'Including women composers in school music curricula, Grades 5–8: a feminist perspective' in Zaimont, Gottlieb, Polk and Rogan (1991).

(1991b) 'Medusa's aria: feminist theory and music education' in J. Gaskell and A. McLaren (eds.), *Women and Education*, Calgary: Detselig.

(1993) 'The possibilities of/for feminist criticism in music education', *British Journal of Music Education*, 10/3.

(1994a) *'Aria senza accompagnamento*: a woman behind the theory', *Quarterly Journal of Music Teaching and Learning*, 4/4–5/1.

(1994b) 'Feminism as critique in philosophy of music education', *Philosophy of Music Education Review*, 2/2.

(1996) 'Discords: feminist pedagogy in music education, *Theory into Practice*, 36 (May).

Lamburn, Rosalie (1991) 'Critical issues in the advancement of professional women musicians of Istanbul', University of London, King's College, Music and Gender Conference, June.

Landon, H. C. Robbins and Jones, David Wyn (1988) *Haydn: His Life and Music*, London: Thames and Hudson.

Langer, Suzanne (1955) *Philosophy in a New Key* (copyright 1942), Mentor Books, New American Library: Harvard University Press.

Lather, Patti (1991) *Getting Smart: Feminist Research and Pedagogy With/In the Postmodern*, New York: Routledge.

Lauretis, Teresa de (1987) *Technologies of Gender: Essays on Theory, Film and Fiction*, Bloomington: Indiana University Press; also in 1989, London: Macmillan.

Lees, Sue (1986) *Losing Out: Sexuality and Adolescent Girls*, London: Hutchinson.

LeFanu, Nicola (1987) 'Master musician: an impregnable taboo?', *Contact* (Autumn).

LePage, Jane Weiner (1980) *Women Composers, Conductors, and Musicians of the Twentieth Century: Selected Biographies*, Metuchen, New Jersey and London: The Scarecrow Press.

Leppert, Richard (1987) 'Music, domestic life and cultural chauvinism: images of British subjects at home in India' in Leppert and McClary (1987).

Leppert, Richard and McClary, Susan (1987) (eds.) *Music and Society: The Politics of Composition, Performance and Reception*, Cambridge University Press.

Lewis, Lisa A. (1990) 'Consumer girl culture: how music video appeals to girls', in Mary Ellen Brown (ed.), *Television and Women's Culture: the Politics of the Popular*, London: Sage.

(1992) *Gender Politics and MTV*, Philadelphia: Temple University Press.

Lidov, David (1987) 'Mind and body in music', *Semiotica*, 66, pp. 69–97.

Loesser, Arthur (1954) *Men, Women and Pianos: A Social History*, New York, London: Victor Gollancz.

Lotman, Jurij (1979) 'The origin of plot in the light of typology', trans. Julian Graffy, *Poetics Today*, 1/1–2 (Autumn).

McClary, Susan (1987) 'The blasphemy of talking politics during Bach Year' in Leppert and McClary (1987).

(1991) *Feminine Endings: Music, Gender and Sexuality*, Minnesota, Oxford: University of Minnesota Press.

(1992) 'Structures of identity and difference in *Carmen*', *Women: A Cultural Review*, Vol. 3, no. 1.

(1993) 'Narrative agendas in "absolute" music: identity and difference in Brahms' third symphony' in Solie (1993).

(1994) 'Constructions of subjectivity in Schubert's music' in Brett, Thomas and Wood (1994).

McClary, Susan and Walser, Robert (1990) 'Start making sense: musicology wrestles with rock' in Frith and Goodwin (1990).

MacDonald, Madeleine (later Arnot) (1979–80) 'Cultural reproduction: the pedagogy of sexuality', *Screen Education*, 17–30.

(1980) 'Socio-cultural reproduction and women's education' in Deem (1980).

McRobbie, Angela (1981) 'Just like a *Jackie* story' in McRobbie and McCabe (1981).

(1991) *Feminism and Youth Culture: From Jackie to Just Seventeen*, London: Macmillan.

McRobbie, Angela and McCabe, Trisha (1981) (eds.) *Feminism for Girls*, London and Boston: Routledge and Kegan Paul.

McRobbie, Angela and Nava, Mica (1984) *Gender and Generation*, London: Macmillan.

Magee, Bryan (1989) 'Women's rights and wrongs', *The Weekend Guardian*, 11 November.

Marshall, Kimberley (1993a) 'Symbols, performers and sponsers: female musical creators in the late Middle Ages' in Marshall (1993b).

(1993b) (ed.) *Rediscovering the Muses: Women's Musical Traditions*, Boston: Northeastern University Press.

Martin, Peter (1995) *Sounds and Society: Themes in the Sociology of Music*, Manchester and New York: Manchester University Press.

Marx, Karl (1977) *Economic and Philosophic Manuscripts* in *Early Writings*, trans. from the German by R. Livingstone and G. Benton, London: Penguin.

Maultsby, Portia I. (1990) 'Africanisms in African-American music' in Joseph E. Holloway (ed.), *Africanisms in American Culture*, Bloomington: Indiana University Press.

Measor, Lynda and Sikes, Pat (1992) *Gender and Schools*, London: Cassell.

Mellers, Wilfrid (1986) *Angels of the Night: Popular Female Singers of our Time*, Manchester and New York: Manchester University Press.

Meyer, Leonard B. (1956) *Emotion and Meaning in Music*, Chicago and London: University of Chicago Press.

 (1973) *Explaining Music*, Berkeley, Los Angeles and London: University of California Press.

Meyers, Carol (1993) 'The drum–dance–song ensemble: women's performance in Biblical Israel' in Marshall (1993b).

Michelini, Ann N. (1991) 'Women and music in Greece and Rome' in Pendle (1991a).

Middleton, Richard (1990) *Studying Popular Music*, Milton Keynes: Open University Press.

Miller, Simon (1993) (ed.) *The Last Post: Music After Modernism*, Manchester and New York: Manchester University Press.

Mills, Janet (1991) *Music in the Primary School*, Cambridge University Press.

Mockus, Martha (1994) 'Queer thoughts on country music and k. d. lang' in Brett, Thomas and Wood (1994).

Moi, Toril (1990) *Sexual/Textual Politics: Feminist Literary Theory* (first published by Methuen, 1985, reprinted 1986, 1987), London: Routledge (first printed 1988, 1989).

Moore, Allan (1993) *Rock: The Primary Text*, Buckingham: Open University Press.

Morris, David (1995) 'Jane Siberry's "Mimi on the beach": a consideration of textual and musical ambiguities', paper read at the first UK Critical Musicology conference, University of Salford, April; distributed in Dai Griffiths (ed.), *Critical Musicology Newsletter*, 3, Oxford Brookes University.

Morris, Mitchell (1993) 'Reading as an opera queen' in Solie (1993).

Mulvey, Laura (1975) 'Visual pleasure and narrative cinema', *Screen*, 16/3.

 (1989) *Visual and Other Pleasures*, London: Macmillan.

Murphy, Christopher (1993) 'Muslim attitudes to music in the National Curriculum: a case study', unpublished master's dissertation, University of London Institute of Education.

Music Advisers' National Association (MANA) (1986) *Assessment and Progression in Music Education*, GB: MANA.

Music Educators' Journal (1992) 78/7, special issue on gender.

National Association For Education in the Arts (NAEA) (1988a) *Assessment in the Arts 1*, Take-up Series no. 7, GB: NAEA.

 (1988b) *Assessment in the Arts 2*, Take-up Series no. 8, GB: NAEA.

Neuls-Bates, Carol (1982) (ed.) *Women in Music: An Anthology of Source-Readings from the Middle Ages to the Present*, New York: Harper and Row.

 (1986) 'Women's orchestras in the United States, 1925–45' in Bowers and Tick (1986).

Newcomb, Anthony (1986) 'Courtesans, muses or musicians? Professional women musicians in sixteenth-century Italy' in Bowers and Tick (1986).

O'Brien, Karen (1995) *Hymn to Her: Women Musicians Talk*, London: Virago.

O'Brien, Lucy (1994) *She Bop: The Definitive History of Women in Rock, Pop and Soul*, London: Penguin.

Olson, Judith (1986) 'Luise Adolpha Le Beau: Composer in late nineteenth-century Germany' in Bowers and Tick (1986).

Ortner, Sherry B. (1974) 'Is female to male as nature is to culture?' in Michelle Zimbalist Rosaldo and Louise Lamphere (eds.), *Woman, Culture and Society*, Stanford, California: Stanford University Press.

Parker, Rozsika and Pollock, Griselda (1981) *Old Mistresses*, London: Routledge.

(1987) *Framing Feminism: Art and the Women's Movement 1970–85*, London: Pandora.

Payne, Helen (1993) 'The presence of the possessed: a parameter in the performance practice of the music of Australian Aboriginal women' in Marshall (1993b).

Paynter, John (1982) *Music in the Secondary School Curriculum*, Cambridge University Press.

(1992) *Sound and Structure*, Cambridge University Press.

Paynter, John and Aston, Peter (1970) *Sound and Silence: Classroom Projects in Creative Music*, Cambridge University Press.

Pegley, Karen (1994) 'Gender, voice and place: issues of negotiation in a technology music programme', unpublished paper (private communication). (A previous verson was presented at the conference, Feminist Theory and Music II, Eastman School of Music, June 1993.)

Pegley, Karen and Caputo, Virginia (1993) 'Growing up female(s): retrospective thoughts on musical preferences and meanings' in Brett, Thomas and Wood (1993).

Pendle, Karin (1991a) 'Women in music, ca. 1450–1600' in Pendle (1991)(b).

(1991b) (ed.) *Women and Music: A History*, Bloomington and Indianapolis: Indiana University Press.

Petersen, Karen E. (1987) 'An investigation into women-identified music in the United States' in Koskoff (1987c).

Philosophy of Music Education Review (1994), 2/2, special issue on gender.

Placksin, Sally (1985) *Jazz Women: 1900 to the Present: Their Words, Lives and Music*, London: Pluto Press (first published as *American Women in Jazz: 1900 to the Present*, Wideview Books, 1982).

Plummeridge, Charles (1991) *Music Education in Theory and Practice*, London, New York, Philadelphia: Falmer Press.

Polk, Joanne (1991) 'Distaff dynasties' in Zaimont, Gottlieb, Polk and Rogan (1991).

Pollock, Griselda (1988) *Vision and Difference: Femininity, Feminism and the Histories of Art*, London and New York: Routledge.

Pope, Rebecca A. (1994) 'The diva doesn't die: George Eliot's *Armgart*' in Dunn and Jones (1994).

Porter, Susan Yank and Abeles, Harold F. (1978) 'The sex stereotyping of instruments', *Journal of Research in Music Education*, 26/2.

Post, Jennifer (1994) 'Erasing the boundaries between public and private in women's performance traditions' in Cook and Tsou (1994).

Potter, John (1994) 'The singer, not the song: women singers as composer-poets', *Popular Music*, 13/2.

Propp, Vladimir (1968) *Morphology of the Folk Tale*, Austin: University of Texas Press.

Pucciani, Donna (1983) 'Sexism in music education: survey of the literature, 1972–1982', *Music Educators' Journal*, 70/1.

Pugh, Aelwyn (1992) *Women in Music*, Cambridge University Press.

Quarterly Journal of Music Teaching and Learning, 4/4–5/1, special issue on gender.

Rainbow, Bernarr (1989) *Music in Educational Thought and Practice*, Aberystwyth: Boethius Press.

Raitt, Suzanne (1992) 'The singers of Sargent: Mabel Batten, Elsie Swinton, Ethel Smyth', *Women: A Cultural Review*, 3/1.

Raphael, Amy (1995) *Never Mind the Bollocks: Women Re-write Rock*, London: Virago.

Reich, Nancy B. (1986) 'Clara Schumann' in Bowers and Tick (1986).

  (1989) *Clara Schumann: The Artist and the Woman*, Oxford University Press.

  (1991) 'European composers and musicians, ca. 1800–1900' in Pendle (1991b).

  (1993) 'Women as musicians: a question of class' in Solie (1993).

Reynolds, Simon and Press, Joy (1995) *The Sex Revolts: Gender, Rebellion and Rock'n'Roll*, London: Serpent's Tail.

Richards, Christopher (1997) *Youth, Identity and Difference in Media Education*, London: Taylor and Francis.

Rieger, Eva (1985) ' "*Dolce semplice*"? On the changing role of women in music' in Gisella Ecker (ed.), *Feminist Aesthetics*, trans. from the German by H. Anderson, London: the Women's Press.

Robertson, Carol E. (1987) 'Power and gender in the musical experiences of women' in Koskoff (1987c).

  (1993) 'The ethnomusicologist as midwife' in Solie (1993).

Rosand, Ellen (1986) 'The voice of Barbara Strozzi' in Bowers and Tick (1986).

Rose, Tricia (1994) *Black Noise: Rap Music and Black Culture in Contemporary America*, Hanover, New Hampshire and London: Wesleyan University Press.

Russell, David (1987) *Popular Music in England, 1840–1914: A Social History*, Manchester and New York: Manchester University Press.

Rycenga, Jennifer (1994) 'Lesbian compositional process: one lover-composer's perspective' in Brett, Thomas and Wood (1994).

Sadie, Julie Anne (1986) 'Musiciennes of the ancien régime' in Bowers and Tick (1986).

Sadie, Julie Anne and Samuel, Rhian (1994) (eds.) *New Grove Dictionary of Women Composers*, London: Macmillan.

Said, Edward (1978) *Orientalism*, Penguin.

Samuel, Rhian (1995) 'Women who call the tunes', *The Guardian* (Part 2), Friday 26 May, p. 11.

Schafer, R. Murray (1967) *Ear Cleaning: Notes for an Experimental Music Course*, New York: Associated Music Publishers Incorporated.

School Curriculum and Assessment Authority (SCAA) (1995) GCSE Regulations and Criteria, SCAA Ref. KS4/95/269.

Schuller, Gunther (1968) *The History of Jazz Volume V: Early Jazz: Its Roots and Musical Development*, New York and Oxford: Oxford University Press.

Schumann, Robert (1964) *On Music and Musicians* (from *Gesammelte Schriften über Musik und Musiker*, first collected and published 1914), trans. P. Rosenfeld, New York: McGraw Hill.

Schweickart, Patrocinio (1986) 'Reading ourselves: toward a feminist theory of reading' in Elizabeth A. Flynn and Patrocinio Schweickart (eds.), *Gender and Reading: Essays on Readers, Texts and Contexts*, Baltimore: Johns Hopkins University Press.

Schwichtenberg, Cathy (1993) (ed.) *The Madonna Connection: Representational Politics, Subcultural Identities, and Cultural Theory*, Boulder, Colorado: Westview Press.

Scott, Derek (1993) 'Sexuality and musical style from Monteverdi to Mae West', in Miller (1993).

Self, George (1967) *New Sounds in Class*, London: Universal Edition.

Shepherd, John (1987) 'Music and male hegemony' in Leppert and McClary (1987).

Shepherd, John and Vulliamy, Graham (1994) 'The struggle for culture: a sociological case study of the development of a national music curriculum' *British Journal of the Sociology of Education*, 15/1.

Silverman, Kaja (1988) *The Acoustic Mirror: The Feminine Voice in Psychoanalysis and Cinema*, Bloomington: Indiana University Press.

Singh, Basil R. (1994) (ed.) *Improving Gender and Ethnic Relations: Strategies for Schools and Further Education*, London: Cassell.

Small, Christopher (1977) *Music – Society – Education*, London: John Calder.

Smith, Catherine Parsons (1994) '"A distinguishing virility": feminism and modernism in American art music' in Cook and Tsou (1994).

Smith, Fanny Morris (1901) 'The record of women in music', *Etude*, 19/9 (September).

Smyth, Ethel (1919) *Impressions That Remained* (two volumes), London: Longmans, Green and Company.

(1921) *Streaks of Life*, London: Longmans, Green and Company.

(1928) *A Final Burning of Boats*, London: Longmans, Green and Company.

(1933) *Female Pipings in Eden*, London: Peter Davies.

Solie, Ruth (1991) 'What do feminists want? A reply to Pieter van den Toorn', *Journal of Musicology*, 9/4.

(1993) (ed.) *Musicology and Difference*, Berkeley: University of California Press.

South, Frances (1991) 'All things being equal', *Classical Music* (June).

Spruce, Gary (1996) (ed.) *Teaching Music*, London: Routledge, in association with the Open University.

Steward, Sue and Garratt, Sheryl (1984) *Signed, Sealed and Delivered: True Life Stories of Women in Pop*, London and Sydney: Pluto Press.

Stockbridge, Sally (1990) 'Rock video: pleasure and resistance' in Mary Ellen Brown (ed.), *Television and Women's Culture: the Politics of the Popular*, London: Sage.

Stone, Lynda (1994) (ed.) *The Education Feminism Reader*, New York, London: Routledge.

Swanwick, Keith (1968) *Popular Music and the Teacher*, Oxford: Pergamon Press.

(1979) *A Basis for Music Education*, NFER Publishing Company.

(1988) *Music, Mind and Education*, London: Routledge.

(1990) (ed.) *The Arts and Education*, National Association for the Arts in Education GB: NAEA.

(1992) *Music Education and the National Curriculum*, The London File: Papers from the Institute of Education, London: The Tufnell Press.

(1994) *Musical Knowledge: Intuition, Analysis and Music Education*, London: Routledge.

Swanwick, Keith and Tillman, June (1986) 'The sequence of musical development', *British Journal of Music Education*, 3/3.

Swanwick, K., Plummeridge, C., Taylor, D., Winter, J. and Whitehead, D. (1987) 'Music in schools: a study of content and curriculum practice', University of London Institute of Education, Research Report.

Tagg, Philip (1989) 'Open letter: Black music, Afro-American music and European music', *Popular Music*, 8/3.

(1990) 'An anthropology of stereotypes in TV music?', *Svensk tidskrift för musikforskning*, pp. 19–42 [*Swedish Journal for Music Research*, Gothenburg].

(1994) 'Debate: From refrain to rave: the decline of figure and the rise of ground', *Popular Music*, 13/2.

Teeter, Emily (1993) 'Female musicans in pharaonic Egypt' in Marshall (1993b).

Thomas, Gary (1994) '"Was George Frederick Handel gay?" On closet questions and cultural politics' in Brett, Thomas and Wood (1994).

Thorne, Barrie (1993) *Gender Play: Girls and Boys in School*, New Brunswick, New Jersey: Rutgers University Press.

Tick, Judith (1986) '"Passed away is the piano girl": Changes in American musical life, 1870–1900' in Bowers and Tick (1986).

(1991) '"Spirit of me . . . Dear rollicking far-gazing straddler of two worlds': the "autobiography" of Ruth Crawford Seeger (1901–1953)', paper read at University of London, King's College, conference on Music and Gender, June.

(1993) 'Charles Ives and gender ideology' in Solie (1993).

Tolbert, Elizabeth (1994) 'The voice of lament: female vocality and performative efficacy in the Finnish-Karelian *itkuvirsi*' in Dunn and Jones (1994).

Toorn, Pieter Van Den (1991) 'Politics, feminism and contemporary music theory', *Journal of Musicology*, 9/3.

Touliatos, Diane (1993b) 'The traditional role of Greek women in music from antiquity to the end of the Byzantine empire' in Marshall (1993b).

Treitler, Leo (1993) 'Gender and other dualities of music history' in Solie (1993).

Trollinger, Laree M. (1994) 'Sex/gender research in music education: a review', *Quarterly Journal of Music Teaching and Learning*, 4/4–5/1.

United Kingdom Council for Music Education and Training (UKCMET) (1993) 'Guidelines on music in the National Curriculum (England)', UKCMET (now disbanded/united with the Music Education Council (MEC)).

Upton, George (1880) *Woman in Music*, Chicago; also London: Stanley and Company, 1909.

Vulliamy, Graham (1976) 'Definitions of serious music' in Vulliamy and Lee (1976).

    (1977a) 'Music and the mass culture debate' in John Shepherd, Paul Virden, Trevor Wishart and Graham Vulliamy (1977), *Whose Music? A Sociology of Musical Language*, London: Latimer New Dimensions.

    (1977b) 'Music as a case study in the "new sociology of education" ' in ibid.

Vulliamy, Graham and Lee, Edward (1976) (eds.) *Pop Music in School*, Cambridge University Press (2nd edition, 1980).

    (1982) *Pop, Rock and Ethnic Music in School*, Cambridge University Press.

Walden, Rosie and Walkerdine, Valerie (1983) *Girls and Mathematics: From Primary to Secondary Schooling*, London: Heinemann.

Walkerdine, Valerie (1990) *Schoolgirl Fictions*, London, New York: Verso.

Walser, Robert (1993) *'Running With the Devil': Power, Gender and Madness in Heavy Metal Music*, Hanover, New Hampshire: Wesleyan University Press.

Weaver, Molly A. (1994) 'A survey of Big Ten institutions: gender distinctions regarding faculty ranks and salaries in schools, divisions and departments of music', *Quarterly Journal of Music Teaching and Learning*, 4/4–5/1.

Weber, William (1975) *Music and the Middle Class*, London: Croom Helm.

Weiler, Kathleen (1988) *Women Teaching for Change*, New York: Bergin and Garvey.

Weiner, Gaby (1994) *Feminisms in Education*, Buckingham and Philadelphia: Open University Press.

Weiner, Gaby and Arnot, Madeleine (1987) *Gender Under Scrutiny*, Open University, London: Unwin Hyman.

Weiss, Sarah (1993) 'Gender and *gender*: gender ideology and the female *gender* player in central Java' in Marshall (1993b).

Wexler, Philip (1987) *Social Analysis of Education: After the New Sociology*, London and New York: Routledge.

Wheelock, Gretchen A. (1993) *'Schwarze Gredel* and the engendered minor mode in Mozart's operas' in Solie (1993).

Whitesitt, Linda (1991) ' "The most potent force" in American music: the role of women's music clubs in American concert life' in Zaimont, Gottlieb, Polk and Rogan (1991).

Whitty, Geoff (1985) *Sociology and School Knowledge: Curriculum Theory, Research and Politics*, London: Methuen.

Wilkins, Margaret Lucy and Askew, Caroline (1993) 'The University of Huddersfield Department of Music project: women composers, 12th–20th centuries', *British Journal of Music Education*, 10/3.

Willis, Paul (1977) *Learning to Labour: How Working-Class Kids Get Working-Class Jobs*, Farnborough, Hants: Saxon House.

Wise, Sue (1990) 'Sexing Elvis' in Frith and Goodwin (1990).

Wolff, Janet (1981) *The Social Production of Art*, London: Macmillan.

(1990) *Feminine Sentences: Essays on Women and Culture*, London: Polity Press.

Wolpe, AnnMarie (1978) 'Education and the sexual division of labour' in Annette Kuhn and AnnMarie Wolpe (eds.), *Feminism and Materialism*, Boston and London: Routledge and Kegan Paul.

(1988) *Within School Walls: The Role of Discipline, Sexuality and the Curriculum*, London and New York: Routledge.

Women in Music (WIM) (n.d.) 'Towards delivering a balanced curriculum', pilot pack, c. 1993–4, London (WIM can be contacted at tel.: 0171-978-4823).

Wood, Elizabeth (1993) 'Lesbian fugue: Ethel Smyth's Contrapuntal Arts' in Solie (1993).

(1994) 'Sapphonics' in Brett, Thomas and Wood (1994).

Woods, Peter and Hammersley, Martin (1993) (eds.) *Gender and Ethnicity in Schools: Ethnographic Accounts*, New York, London: Routledge, in association with the Open University.

Yardley, Anne Bagnall (1986) '"Ful weel she soong the service dyvyne": the cloistered musician in the Middle Ages' in Bowers and Tick (1986).

Young, Michael F. D. (1980) *Knowledge and Control*, London: Collier-MacMillan.

Zaimont, Judith Lang, Overhauser, Catherine and Gottlieb, Jane (1984) (eds.) *The Musical Woman: An International Perspective*, Vol. *I*, Connecticut: Greenwood Press.

(1987) (eds.)*The Musical Woman: An International Perspective*, Vol. *II*, 1984–5, Connecticut: Greenwood Press.

Zaimont, Judith Lang, Gottlieb, Jane, Polk, Joanne and Rogan, Michael J. (1991) (eds.)*The Musical Woman: An International Perspective*, Vol. *III*, 1986–1990, Connecticut: Greenwood Press.

Index